Loving's the Strange Thing

Hispanic Studies: Culture and Ideas

Volume 77

Edited by
Claudio Canaparo

PETER LANG
Oxford · Bern · Berlin · Bruxelles · Frankfurt am Main · New York · Wien

Anne-Marie Storrs

Loving's the Strange Thing

Jungian Individuation in the Fairy Tales of Carmen Martín Gaite

PETER LANG
Oxford · Bern · Berlin · Bruxelles · Frankfurt am Main · New York · Wien

Bibliographic information published by Die Deutsche Nationalbibliothek.
Die Deutsche Nationalbibliothek lists this publication in the Deutsche Nationalbibliografie; detailed bibliographic data is available on the Internet at http://dnb.d-nb.de.

A catalogue record for this book is available from the British Library.

Library of Congress Control Number: 2017953992

Cover illustration: *Norham Castle, Sunrise* by Joseph Mallord William Turner. © Tate, London 2017.

Cover design by Peter Lang Ltd.

ISSN 1661-4720
ISBN 978-1-78707-844-4 (print) • ISBN 978-1-78707-845-1 (ePDF)
ISBN 978-1-78707-846-8 (ePub) • ISBN 978-1-78707-847-5 (mobi)

Published by Peter Lang Ltd, International Academic Publishers,
52 St Giles, Oxford, OX1 3LU, United Kingdom
oxford@peterlang.com, www.peterlang.com

This publication has been peer reviewed.

Printed in Germany

Contents

Acknowledgements

I would like to thank all those who have helped, supported, and encouraged me on the road to completing this book. First of all, Professor Alexis Grohmann, who supervised the PhD on which this book is based, for his wise and timely advice and encouragement. The interest and good advice of Dr José Saval, Dr Catherine O'Leary, and Dr Huw Lewis have been much appreciated. I would like to give thanks to Professor Jo Labanyi for her enthusiasm for my earliest work on Carmen Martín Gaite, which has sustained me along the way. Thanks for their support also go to Marion Spöring of the University of Dundee, Dr Robert Oakley of the University of Birmingham, Dr Mercedes Carbayo-Abengozar, Dr Susana Bayó Belenguer, Professor Maria Vittoria Calvi, and Dr Jessamy Harvey. I am grateful to the staff of the library at the University of Edinburgh, who have been unfailingly helpful, and also to the staff of the Biblioteca Nacional in Madrid, and of the libraries of the Universities of Dundee and St Andrews.

The values with which my parents, Margaret and Gerard Gartland, nurtured their children permeate this book and for this I am especially grateful to them. And thanks go to all my family for their support and encouragement, shown in so many different ways over the years.

My final thanks go to my husband, Chris – my ideal scholar – whose breadth and depth of learning and culture never cease to amaze me. I am grateful for the wonderful humour which has lightened the way and made it easier to retain a clear perspective, and for a rare and precious quality which he shares with Carmen Martín Gaite, namely the ability – so easily uttered and so difficult to achieve – to be completely oneself.

Abbreviations

Balneario	*El balneario*
Caperucita	*Caperucita en Manhattan*
Castillo	*El castillo de las tres murallas*
Cuadernos	*Cuadernos de todo*
Cuarto	*El cuarto de atrás*
Cuento	*El cuento de nunca acabar*
Fragmentos	*Fragmentos de interior*
Irse	*Irse de casa*
Nubosidad	*Nubosidad variable*
Parentescos	*Los parentescos*
Pastel	*El pastel del diablo*
Raro	*Lo raro es vivir*
Reina	*La reina de las nieves*

CHAPTER 1

A Natural Process: Individuation and the Impulse to Wholeness and Community

Introduction

Carmen Martín Gaite related her favourite joke in an interview published in 1995. It concerned a man

> que se iba a atar un zapato en un *derby* y se le subió encima un hombre, creyendo que estaba montando un caballo. Cuando lo contaba, alguien le preguntó: '¿Y tú qué hiciste?' La respuesta fue: 'Hice lo que pude, llegué el cuarto.' (Cantavella 1995: 41)
>
> [who went to tie his shoelace at a horserace and a man climbed on his back, thinking he was mounting a horse. When he told the story, someone asked him: 'And what did you do?' The answer was: 'I did what I could, I came fourth.']

The response of the man in the story seems incredible – he finds himself in an unfortunate situation because of the absurd misunderstanding of a stranger and, far from attacking, resisting, or rejecting, he responds *creatively* to the situation. A more typical reaction might have been to stand up, throw off the person who had climbed onto his back, remonstrate at such behaviour and become quite angry. Fear could provoke an even stronger, more violent reaction, whether verbally or physically. Or, if the person were clinging very tightly and refused to let go, it could prove very difficult to throw him off, leading to a struggle with a doubtful outcome. No wonder Martín Gaite called it *maravilloso* [wonderful], *divertido* [funny] and *aleccionador* [instructive], describing the sequence of reactions in the listener.

The context of Martín Gaite's story suggests that the last of these situations is what she had in mind – where it was impossible to shake off the stranger – as she refers in the interview to the importance of distinguishing between 'lo que tiene remedio' [what can be remedied] and 'lo que no lo tiene' [what cannot] (Ibid. 40). Instead of '[empeñarse] en dar cabezas contra el muro' [[insisting] on hitting your head against a [brick] wall], Martín Gaite counsels that 'lo más importante es saber aceptar las cosas que no tienen remedio' [the most important thing is knowing how to accept things that have no other way out] (Ibid. 40). It is an attitude of humility and also of responsiveness and, therefore, a feminine attitude, regardless of who adopts it, because it is concerned with responding and relating. As is clear from the *chiste* [joke], responsiveness is an attitude which, far from being passive and retiring, requires the alertness and attentiveness which are the mark of Martín Gaite's philosophy. It is a creative response in which ego plays its part, but does not dominate: 'Hago lo que puedo, que llego el cuarto, el segundo o no llego, pero no paro, sino que echo a correr' [I do what I can, I might come fourth, second or not get there, but I don't stop, I just start running] (Ibid. 41). It is the wholeness in the storyteller which enables him to respond as he does.

Accepting what you cannot change, not insisting on the dominance of the ego, implies acceptance of another reality. This was something addressed by Martín Gaite in an interview in 1989 when she told Maria Vittoria Calvi:

> Yo tengo mucho ese sentimiento religioso en el sentido de 'religare', volver a atar: dentro de mí, todo me va ocurriendo siempre de una manera muy significativa, no me parece que nada ocurra por casualidad, sino todas las cosas se van entendiendo con el tiempo. (Calvi 1990: 171)
>
> [I have a lot of that religious feeling in the sense of 're + ligare', to bind again: inside me, everything always happens in a very meaningful way, I don't think that anything happens by chance, rather that you end up understanding everything eventually.] [1]

1 In addition to this sense of wholeness and the meaning it brings, there are also examples in her notebooks of Martín Gaite's attitude towards more traditional religious – Catholic – practice. For example, she demonstrates a particular devotion to a saint – St Joseph. When referring to a forthcoming surgical intervention on a friend's mother, she writes, 'San José, danos buena suerte' [St Joseph, grant us good fortune] (2002a: 489). That same year, on the feast of San José, 19 March 1980, to which she makes reference in her notebook, Martín Gaite records that – 'le hice a san José solemne promesa de no volver a fumar' [I made a solemn promise to St

One of the most immediately striking aspects of this statement is that it was made about four years after the tragic death of Martín Gaite's only

---

Joseph not to smoke again] (2002a: 491). She also explains a reason for her dedication to this particular saint: 'Pensar que lo que más me corroe es la idea tánatos y que san José la puede conjurar mediante una alianza que se inició cuando metí su efigie dentro de la chaqueta de mamá muerta' [To think that what most eats away at me is the notion of death and that St Joseph can cast it out through an alliance that began when I put his image inside the jacket of my dead mother] (2002a: 491). St Joseph is associated with death, particularly with a peaceful death, on the grounds that he died surrounded by his family, Mary and the child Jesus. Martín Gaite's prayer to san José and the effect she anticipates is reminiscent of Sorpresa banishing the evil effects of *la bruja Balbina* in *Pastel*, although in the *cuento* Sorpresa buries a piece of amber in the ground which has been given to her by a man dressed as the devil in order to despatch the imaginary witch, whereas Martín Gaite, by placing a small image of the saint in the pocket of her dead mother, finds she has created a transcendental link between all three.

In 1983 she wrote: 'Entré en St. Patrick [la cathedral católica de Nueva York] a rezar. [...] Tomé agua bendita y pensé en Borau' [I went into St Patrick's [Roman Catholic cathedral of New York] to pray. [...] I took holy water and thought about Borau] (2002a: 575). The celebrated film director, Jose Luis Borau, himself recalls how he never spoke about religion with *la Gaitera* 'al considerarlo uno de esos temas íntimos que menos cabe tratar cuanto mayor es la confianza con una persona' [because I saw it as one of those personal matters that the closer you are to someone the less you can discuss it] (2007: 259). However, he suggests what New York's Roman Catholic cathedral might have offered the writer: 'Entraríamos alguna vez en la catedral de San Patricio, cuya silenciosa oquedad parecía ofrecer cierto amparo a mi amiga [...]; pero nada más' [We would sometimes go into Saint Patrick's cathedral, whose quiet emptiness seemed to afford a certain refuge to my friend [...], but no more than that] (2007: 259). Therefore, as he recalls, Martín Gaite's spontaneous imitation of Catholic ritual on one occasion was unexpected when, still singing the Beatles' song *Let it Be* 'ella se agachó para mojar dos dedos de la mano derecha en un charco del asfalto, hacer luego en su frente la señal de la cruz, y repetirlo a continuación sobre la mía' [she bent down to wet two fingers of her right hand in a puddle on the tarmac, made the sign of the cross on her forehead, and then did it again on mine] (2007: 259). This is a transfer of the Catholic practice – of dipping fingertips in a font of *agua bendita* [holy water] and making the sign of the cross – from the church to the street, from holy water to rainwater or any water.

daughter (and only living child), Marta, and leaves the reader both moved and impressed at the humility and at the profound spirit it reveals.

Also in her notebooks she records her reaction to the horrific murder of his five children by a tailor in Madrid in the early 1960s. Criticising the attitude of those who deemed it only a family tragedy, Martín Gaite argues that it is instead a message from God and that the tailor is 'un instrumento de Dios' [God's instrument] (2002a: 62). In contrast to those who argue that if there really was a God he would not allow such things to happen she counters that 'si hay algo sobrenatural son estas llamadas al espanto' [if there's anything supernatural it's these calls to be frightened] (Ibid. 62). She regards the tailor's act to be purposeful and demanding careful reflection precisely because of her perception of the inter-connectedness of all things, of the bond between the supernatural and the natural worlds. Her response to the murder confirms the 'sentido religioso' [religious feeling] she referred to as it enables her to see the meaningfulness of everything and the inter-connectedness of all human beings, both of which she has in common with Jung.

Martín Gaite's religious feeling as described to Maria Vittoria Calvi is, in fact, what is demonstrated by the man in the joke – an awareness of a broader reality than that perceptible by ego-consciousness alone, and to which the only possible response is a creative one. It also corresponds to the individuation process discovered by Jung, the aim of which is the relationship with the Self. A close colleague of Jung, Marie-Louise von Franz, describes the Self as 'the source of all creativity' (1997a: 250), and counsels that living consciously the individuation process requires that 'I ought not to think about what I should do or about what is generally considered the right thing to do, or about what usually tends to happen, but rather I should pay heed to what the inner wholeness, the Self, wants from me now in *this* situation or what it wants to bring about through me' (Ibid. 297). Von Franz gives an example using the image of a tree:

> It is as though, in the process of its growth, [the tree] came against a stone, and instead of feeling irritated or making plans for how to overcome the obstacle, it just tried to feel whether it should now move more to the left or to the right, and as if it then yielded to the slightest yet strongest signal [...]. The guiding impulses do not come from the ego, but rather from the psychic wholeness, the Self. (1997a: 297–8)

Such an attitude may be difficult in a society used to privileging the ego and championing the principle of getting whatever we want whenever we want it on the grounds that we always know what is best for us. Martín Gaite is saying something quite different to this prevailing view, namely that everything has meaning, that this meaning may only become clear over time, and that being able to understand it requires a religious attitude, that is, one which recognises the existence of another reality beyond the day-to-day world. It requires an attitude of trust and humility and a readiness to respond and participate such as that displayed by the man at the racecourse, and is not unlike that of Cinderella towards the fairy godmother in the traditional tale. In relation to Martín Gaite's fairy tales, it is the attitude of Serena in *Castillo* in her faithful response to the message in a dream; of Sara in *Caperucita* when she rejects the outer world of Manhattan in favour of the inner world; of Leonardo at the end of *Reina* when he decides to stop rehearsing and preparing in favour of an attentiveness which is open to the appearance of the miraculous; and it is the attitude which results in such a creative response from Sorpresa in *Pastel* to the negative collective projection of the adults around her.

Carl Gustav Jung and Carmen Martín Gaite

Jung does not conform to the critical image of psychiatrists presented in both Martín Gaite's notebooks and in the attitude of Mariana León, the psychiatrist protagonist of *Nubosidad*: 'Martín Gaite's disrespect for psychoanalysis is clear in her depiction of it through Mariana, a practising analyst, as a sterile and fruitless pursuit' (O'Leary & Ribeiro de Menezes 2008: 131). The Spanish writer has described psychiatrists as 'interlocutores pagados, mediadores de oficio' [paid interlocutors, professional mediators] and complained about their 'inautenticidad, su falta de interés real por el cuento que nos instan a contarles' [lack of authenticity, their lack of real interest in the story which they urge us to tell them] (2002a: 397). Catherine O'Leary and Alison Ribeiro de Menezes explore her hostility in their discussion of the *interlocutor ideal* [ideal interlocutor]:

> Martín Gaite seems to be suggesting that the ideal interlocutor cannot be a psychiatrist, but rather must be someone with whom one shares certain ties and perspectives; someone who will reflect without judgement; someone who will be there when needed and because they want to be there; someone who implicates himself or herself more than a professional. Parity of esteem, equality and respect must be present between the conversational partners, something that she suggests is absent from the unequal power dynamic of the psychiatrist-patient scenario. (2008: 85–6)

Marcia Welles, discussing Martín Gaite's criticisms in the context of *Ritmo lento*, refers specifically to Freud:

> In *Ritmo lento* the rejection of psychoanalytic discourse is unequivocal. In spite of Freud's designation of his practice as 'the talking cure,' the lack of mutuality, the time constrictions, the requirement of payment, perhaps its very attempt to establish itself as a science purporting to see cause and effect, all combine to make it, in Martín Gaite's world, false and inauthentic. (1992: 155)

This apparent determination of psychiatrists to cure their patients at all costs is another of Martín Gaite's targets: 'Ese hombre está loco, hay que curarlo' [that man is mad, he must be cured] (2002a: 391). However, Jung did not take this approach to his patients, as is shown in the following story about a seriously disturbed patient, related by Marie-Louise von Franz:

> I tried desperately with all the forces at my command to prevent her from slipping into a psychotic episode. [...] [Jung] listened to the whole story and then said very seriously, 'What makes you so sure that the analysand doesn't have to go through an episode? [...] Perhaps you are hindering the very thing that according to God's will should happen.' I was flabbergasted, and then I saw for the first time that my urge to produce an improvement was a power play. When I let go of my misguided pushing, the analysand got better rather than slipping into an episode. (1993b: 243)

While the professional nature of the relationship has to be recognised, von Franz's experience indicates that Jung aimed to create the kind of setting for analyst and patient which recognised the potential obstacles to communication, particularly 'the unequal power dynamic' referred to by O'Leary and Ribeiro de Menezes.

In *Nubosidad* Mariana's attitude is revealed when she writes to her friend, Sofía Montalvo that, when listening to her patients' stories, she would 'revolver con la mano derecha esa basura ajena, mientras [se] tapaba las narices con la otra' [stir that alien rubbish with her right hand while holding her nose with the other] (1992b: 184). Furthermore, Mariana stirs the stinking rubbish 'sin manchar[se] las manos' [without getting her hands dirty] (1992b: 184), further illustrating her lack of interest in her patients and the absence of any feeling of solidarity with them. This is, however, very different from the approach taken by Jung and his colleagues, illustrated in another story from Marie-Louise von Franz. Using an even stronger metaphor than Mariana's reference to stinking *basura* to describe her patients' stories, von Franz acknowledges that 'it is true that what an analyst has to sit in his office and listen to all day is not purely edifying. [...] It is horrible shit that the patients and all of us are stuck in' (1993b: 12). However, her response is characterised by a humility and respect absent from the professional figures criticised by Martín Gaite: 'But when one takes a closer look, one can see the hand of God in it!' (Ibid. 12). Von Franz's attitude is typical of Jung's own approach to his patients. In his memoir, *Memories, Dreams, Reflections*, for example, Jung refers to 'the richness and importance of [the] inner experience' of the mentally ill (1983: 152). Another Jungian analyst, Molly Tuby, takes a similar view of the experience, comparing it to a discarded cornerstone – 'it is usually the despised element which proves the most vitally important' (1977: 18). The image of the cornerstone refers to the words of Psalm 118 which were also quoted by Christ in relation to himself: '*The stone which the builders rejected / has become the cornerstone*' (Matthew 21: 42).

When one thinks of taking a psychological approach to a literary work, first thoughts tend to turn to Freud. However, there is another important difference between Freud on the one hand and Martín Gaite and Jung on the other. This is the one-sided, exaggerated emphasis Freud placed on sexuality as the reason for all psychological disturbances and which was one of the principal reasons for the ending of the collaboration between Jung and Freud:

> Sexuality evidently meant more to Freud than to other people. For him it was something to be religiously observed. [...]. Freud, who had always made much of his irreligiosity, had now constructed a dogma; or rather, in the place of a jealous God whom he had lost [Yahweh], he had substituted another compelling image, that of sexuality. It was no less insistent, exacting, domineering, threatening, and morally

> ambivalent than the original one. [...], the 'sexual libido' took over the role of [...] a hidden or concealed god. The advantage of this transformation for Freud was, apparently, that he was able to regard the new numinous principle as scientifically irreproachable and free from all religious taint. (Jung 1983: 174)

Jung himself took a quite different approach in his writings where for example, as James Jarrett points out, there is 'no mention of Eros as erotic in the usual sense' (1995: 4). Jarrett argues that 'this is typical of Jung [...]. He seems, early along, to have decided as a psychologist to leave the sexual realm to the Freudians. [...]. There is little doubt that, generally, he was more interested in spiritual development' (Ibid. 5).

Marcia Welles also refers specifically to 'the Freudian psychoanalytic focus on the sexual life of individuals' which 'also differentiates it from the narrative world of Martín Gaite, where, with the exception of *El balneario* [in which the protagonist, Matilde, arrives at the spa with a man who may be her lover], this is a subject conspicuous by its absence' (1992: 155). Welles was writing before the publication of Martín Gaite's later novels but, taking account of these, José Mª Pozuelo Yvancos comments that sexuality is only referred to obliquely (2009: 47).

A final similarity between Jung and Martín Gaite lies in her well-documented dislike of labels and definitions: 'La definición, para mí, es algo que he odiado siempre. Es decir, yo no puedo definirme a mí misma como nada' [For me, definitions are something I've always hated. I mean, I can't define myself as anything] (Ramos 1980: 117). Jung, too, looking back on his life, declared 'I have no judgement about myself and my life. There is nothing I am quite sure about' (1983: 391). One has only to think of the definitions which Freud used to pin down various phases of life – such as 'oral fixation', 'pleasure principle', 'Oedipal phase' – to realise that this is the antithesis of Martín Gaite's way of seeing life. In contrast, Jung challenged a system in which 'patients were labelled, rubber-stamped with a diagnosis' (1983: 135): 'No one concerned himself with the meaning of fantasies, or thought to ask why this patient had one kind of fantasy, another an altogether different one. [...] The fantasies were simply lumped together under some generic name as, for instance, "ideas of persecution"' (Ibid. 149). Although Jung coined a number of widely used terms, including extrovert and introvert, this was an attempt to clarify rather than pinning down and labelling. He constantly emphasised the uniqueness of every human being and that each one developed in a different way. When trainee analysts 'complained that there were [...] too few [courses] on case material', Jung responded that 'case material [...] differs in every case, and they would usually only do harm by applying what they had learned about one case to another' (Hannah 1977: 299). This focus by Jung on the person as a unique individual is confirmed in his emphasis on the fact that the individuation process is different for everyone – 'it always has a unique form' (von Franz 1990: 215). Martín Gaite's emphatic rejection of labels and her promotion of an attitude which is open and accepting has much to do with projection and its withdrawal, which are key features of the individuation process.

Projection

The purpose of projection 'is not only to keep painful insights at a distance, while their contents are ascribed to others, but also to serve the opposite purpose of making things consciously perceptible and distinguishable, for they confront the ego with the non-ego' (Jung & von Franz 1971: 50). Where any human being is destroyed or harmed or despised by another, where there is obsession, fascination, or idolising, one finds projection. In projection, other persons or groups of people act as hooks for unconscious contents which are projected onto them 'as one hangs a coat on a coat hook' (von Franz 1980: 3). This image illustrates the way in which the projection all but hides the reality of the other just as the coat hides the hook, and also reflects the relative proportions of the projection and the aspect glimpsed in the other which has acted as the hook.

To recognise that so much of what we think we see in others really belongs to us requires much humility and insight and honesty, qualities which are essential if we are to really relate to others: 'Only when projections are taken back does relationship – as opposed to archaic identity – become possible' (von Franz 1997a: 52). This outcome is confirmed by a contemporary Jungian psychologist, Murray Stein:

> Differentiating one's consciousness from the images offered by the syzygy (anima/animus) [inner figures encountered in the process of individuation] on the one hand and from the social persona identity on the other creates a mirror that can more accurately reflect whatever passes before it. As a consequence, there will be much less projection and distortion in consciousness, and objects will be seen more clearly and related to for what they truly are. Genuine intimate relationships, I to Thou, now become possible. (Stein 2006: 19)

The need to withdraw projections in order to really see ourselves and others lies at the heart of Christ's question 'Why do you observe the splinter in your brother's eye and never notice the great log in your own?' (Matthew 7: 3). The relative proportions of splinter and log recall Jung's image of the hook, described by Marie-Louise von Franz above.

Martín Gaite's definition of 'bad mirrors' seems an appropriate description of projection. She talks about those who 'se asoman desde lo más fuera posible, justamente desde la rendija que basta para poder meter un poco las narices' [lean out from as far away as possible, from exactly the gap which just allows them to poke a nose through] – for such people are not interested in using their eyes and really seeing. From that distance they are thus able to 'pegar una nueva etiqueta expeditiva, "ya está, a ése ya lo he entendido, ya puedo hablar de él"' [stick on a new easy label, 'that's it, now I've got the measure of him, now I can talk about him'] (1982: 19). This labelling is not based on real perception of the other in his/her uniqueness, but on a superficial perception of aspects which really belong to the one looking. However, when 'we awaken to the insight that certain presumptions and judgements of ours about other people do not apply to them but rather to ourselves' (von Franz 1997a: 52), the reality of both self and other is revealed and the projections can be withdrawn. This perception of reality is present in Martín Gaite's good mirror 'donde no se reflejaran más imágenes que las que se fueran produciendo al ponernos nosotros frente a él, por fragmentarias, incoherentes o indescifrables que fueran' [where the only images reflected are those which are created as we stand in front of it, however fragmentary, incoherent or indecipherable they might be] (1982: 17). The good mirror accepts us exactly as we are without the intervention of projection, including projections of more positive images from other times.

Martín Gaite's characters who become good mirrors do so by relating first to themselves, including Sofía and Mariana in *Nubosidad* and Leonardo in *Reina*. The importance of relating to oneself as a prerequisite for relating to others also finds a parallel in both Christianity – 'love your neighbour *as yourself*' [my italics] – and in the Jungian process of individuation. As Mario Jacoby reminds us, this religion of love has turned into 'one of terrific belligerence' (1975: 11). He argues that the reason for this is the projection of our shadow onto others and the consequent 'cruel attempts to destroy the devil outside' (Ibid. 11).

Projection is damaging, to oneself and to others. The wealthy landowner Lucandro in Carmen Martín Gaite's fairy tale *Castillo* projects his own greed onto his tenants and, unable and unwilling to recognise his own reality, suffers the loss of his humanity. The collective, negative projection of a group onto an individual is depicted in Martín Gaite's second fairy tale, *Pastel*, where the villagers, including the priest and Sorpresa's parents, label the little girl as 'mala' [bad]. The force of the projection is such that it threatens to bring about the projected reality, that is, turn the little girl, who is only lively and spirited, really bad. Only by holding fast to her own truth and remaining aware is she able to turn the destructiveness into creativity.

The group projecting onto the individual or another group can also be damaged and consciousness is essential if destructiveness is to be avoided. At a collective level, whole nations can be taken over by unconscious contents resulting in the projection of a collective shadow. The collective aspect of projections can be seen in, for example, the mutual cold-war attitudes of the Soviet Union and the United States of America, or the Hitler regime's attitude towards the Jewish people. The Jungian view is that the powerful grip which projections have on the individual and the group – at times resembling a possession – can (and should) be diluted through individual awareness. Barbara Hannah records Jung's view of the dangers facing Germany in the 1930s: 'He spoke again [...] of the panic that was gripping the German people and of his fear that nothing could stop a disaster. At least, the only thing that could possibly stop it, he said, would be for enough individuals to become *conscious* of the possessed state they were all in' (1977: 211). The impact of each individual growing in awareness would be to dilute the effects of collective possession. Aniela Jaffé, another contemporary of Jung, argues that this is part of the meaning behind the individuation process: 'The conscious personality, obeying its individual destiny, is the only bulwark against the mass movements of modern society. Herein lies the social meaning of individuation' (1986: 94).

Individuation

Individuation is 'an almost irresistible urge to become what one is, not what one would like to be, but what one is really' (Tuby 1977: 12). Stein identifies three 'great exemplars of individuation' as 'Buddha and Jesus and St Francis' (2006: 209, note 3). These examples of great spiritual leadership also emphasise that the process requires one to follow one's own path and turn away from the collective. Writers who describe individuation insist on the loneliness of the process. Von Franz describes having to give up 'the cozy "stall warmth" in which we can let ourselves go' (1993b: 265). Martín Gaite was aware of the demands entailed by following her unique path and sums it up succinctly as 'por una parte conciencia de excepcionalidad asumida como destino, por otra *regret* de la vida dulce, amable, burguesa a la que irremediablemente se renunciaba' [on the one hand an awareness of being exceptional accepted as fate, on the other *regret* for the gentle, kind, middle-class life which is inevitably given up] (2002a: 203). The struggles of her characters between these two poles are depicted in her novels and short stories, with some making progress and others unwilling to give up the 'cozy "stall warmth"'. Characters whose behaviour differs from the collective, who go their own way, like her *chicas raras* [strange girls], can be described as being on the path of individuation. Others who appear to reject the path of individuation out of fear or loneliness, are left empty, bored and dissatisfied like Matilde in *Balneario* or, when their life is left without meaning, they die, as happens to Manuela Roca in *Irse*. Many of Martín Gaite's protagonists, including all those in the fairy tales, are examples of *chicas or chicos raros*, taking the path which is uniquely theirs and, therefore, like Stein's exemplars, 'su comportamiento está presidido por el inconformismo' [their behaviour is dominated by non-conformism] (Martín Gaite 1987a: 100).

Individuation is an archetypal process. Some critics of Jungian psychology use the terms archetype and stereotype interchangeably and, therefore, erroneously. A stereotype is 'a standardized image or conception shared by all members of a social group' (Collins 1979: 1426) and is a reductive concept. In contrast, an archetype is simply the basic form which determines the general, but not the specific, pattern of development. There is general agreement, for example, that a snowflake has a basic form and at the same time it is accepted that every snowflake is unique. The basic form of a snowflake would correspond to the archetype, which does not hamper the unique development of each one. Similarly, there is an essential pattern of a human being, but each one is unique. The development of the unique human being is the aim and purpose of individuation as discovered and described by Jung. 'Discovered' because individuation is 'a natural process, which can be carried to a fruitful conclusion by every individual who works on himself or herself with honesty and perseverance' (von Franz 1997a: 261).

Jung has been described as '*the* great writer on individuation' (Samuels 2008: 6). However, some Jungian analysts today consider that individuation consists of three stages – 'first, the containment/nurturance [...] second, the adapting/adjusting [...] and third, the centring/integrating [...]' (Stein 2006: 199). Only the final stage corresponds to the process originally expounded by Jung and his contemporaries:

> The most significant and interesting contribution of Jungian psychology to the idea of psychological development is what it says about the part of life that follows the second stage of individuation. This is where most other psychoanalytic theories stop. [...] This is the phase of psychological development described classically by Jung in such works as 'A study in the process of individuation' [...] when [...] the religious function and the search for individual meaning become important. (Stein 2006: 209)[2]

2 O'Leary and Ribeiro de Menezes use the term 'individuation' in their assessment of *Raro* (2008: 165 & 166). However, the term appears to refer to the development of an individual identity vis-a-vis another, to become independent, for example, of parents: 'Águeda suggests that growing up involves a process of separation and individuation from the mother' (165); and 'she shifts from biological motherhood to mothering, or

While Jung outlined the main aspects of the individuation process and wrote extensively on it, it was his belief that, despite the common elements of experience of the unconscious, no two people experienced the process in the same way. However, 'in spite of being a unique event in a unique human being, it has certain typical recurring features which repeat themselves and are similar in every process of individuation' (von Franz 1990: 215). It involves encounters with inner figures, representing aspects of both personal and collective unconscious.

The main stages of the process are the encounters with the shadow, the animus and anima, and – the aim of the process – with the Self. However, as von Franz confirms, 'it would be a great mistake, as Jung himself often emphasized, to suppose that the shadow, the anima (or animus) and the Self appear separately in a person's unconscious, neatly timed and in definable order' (1995b: 144). Instead, these terms are meant as an aid to understanding the experience rather than a norm to be met or missed.

In dreams the shadow is generally personified by aspects of the same sex as the dreamer. The personal shadow is meant to be integrated as far as possible into the conscious personality, while in respect of the collective shadow what matters is that we should be aware. Both can be perceived in projection onto others, particularly where there are strong emotions such as love, hate or jealousy: 'The usual bond of feeling always contains projections that have to be withdrawn if one is to attain to oneself and to objectivity' (Jung in von Franz 1980: 177). The shadow has also been described as 'the mirror of the opposite within you' (Luke 1995: x). It can be both positive and negative, its essentially quality is that it is unknown to us.

Jung used the terms 'anima' and 'animus' to represent inner aspects of men and women respectively, which would also be encountered in the individuation process. More recent scholarship asserts that 'both can be constellated in men as well as women, and they often appear in tandem, as couples' (Kast 2006: 127). The writer and analyst, Mario Jacoby, reflecting on the more negative aspects of one of these figures, wondered 'whether

---

child-rearing, as a process of individuation for mother and child' (166). This use of the term seems more in keeping with the two earlier phases of individuation used by some contemporary Jungian analysts which precede the process identified by Jung.

only women have really an animus. Where do the ready-made defensive prejudices of men come from?' (1975: 14). A positive animus acts as a bridge, ensuring that a woman's inner life is expressed in the outer world: 'Without him the play is created in one's imagination, but never written down and never performed' (Estés 1998: 310).

There are a number of examples of these figures, both positive and negative, in Martín Gaite's work, with one of the most striking examples of an animus figure being the man in black in *Cuarto*. Several critics have identified this character in Jungian terms. Joe Rodríguez claims he is 'the projection of the narrator's unconscious, [...], the narrator's threatening dark other. He is, in Jungian terms, her "shadow psyche" and this fits in with his identification with the devil' (2006: 40). It is argued in Jungian psychology that the whole unconscious appears as undifferentiated shadow initially – 'at the beginning stage we can say that the shadow is all that is within you which you do not know about' (von Franz, 1995b: 4) – and, therefore, some work on the shadow would be necessary in order for the different aspects of the unconscious to become clearer. However, the man in black is quite a developed figure and is the opposite gender to the narrator of the novel with whom he converses. Despite the ambiguity with which he is rightly regarded by critics, he resembles a creative spirit as the dialogue, or interview, results in the creation of the novel itself. As Rodríguez confirms, he possesses qualities which make him an ideal interlocutor: 'His capacity to listen with interest, his choice of questions and stimulating manner of putting them, as well as his refreshing lack of preoccupation with conventional expectations' (2006: 48). Julian Palley, in a much earlier article, posits that the man in black is 'the alter ego, the positive animus, the strong and protective ideal masculine image which every woman (according to Jung) bears in her unconscious' (1983: 112). Although the man in black has a positive effect on C., the protagonist of *Cuarto*, the Jungian animus can be negative as well as positive. Ruth El Saffar also refers to the man in black, the stranger, as representing 'the psychopomp – the opposite-sex figure from the unconscious who, if accepted, if awaited, if called upon, will bring riches of lasting value' (1983: 194), which is what happens in this case.

In her *Cuadernos* Martín Gaite set out how the situation led her to 'imaginar en principio a un visitante pasivo e inocuo que se limitara a escuchar lo que aquella noche yo tenía necesidad de contarle a alguien' [imagine at first a passive and harmless visitor who would just be quiet and listen to what I needed to tell someone that night] (2002a: 324). However, the character turned out very differently, as the writer relates in a notebook entry from the early 1980s:

> Si hubiera rechazado la autonomía que este personaje tomó casi inmediatamente, rebelándose e imponiéndose a mi imaginación [...] como algo más que un oyente sumiso y abstracto, creo que el libro no hubiera tomado esos rumbos que lo caracterizan y que quebraron el molde mucho más pobre y menos imaginativo del proyecto inicial. Es el libro que más se me ha ido de las manos y, por eso mismo, del que he aprendido más cosas. (2002a: 324)

> [If I had rejected the autonomy which this character took on almost immediately, by rebelling and imposing himself on my imagination [...] as something more than a passive and abstract listener, I believe the book would not have taken the course which distinguishes it and which broke the much more impoverished and less imaginative mould of the initial plan. It is the book over which I have had least control and, for that very reason, the one from which I have learnt most.]

Such autonomy is characteristic of the archetypal figures identified by Jung and is a further aspect supporting the man in black as a positive animus figure. In an interview Martín Gaite claimed that 'en *El cuarto de atrás* se va viendo mi concepto del amor' [in *The Back Room* you gradually see my concept of love] (Lacruz Pardo 1978: 16). Clarissa Pinkola Estés, a contemporary Jungian analyst and writer, agrees, claiming that 'when this opposite-gender nature is healthy [...] it loves the woman it inhabits' (1998: 58). Love is an important part of the individuation process.

The final stage of the process described by Jung is the encounter and relationship with the Self, which is regarded as the totality of the personality in which opposites are reconciled: 'Coming into contact with the Self is without a doubt the supreme goal of the individuation process' (von Franz 1997a: 250). Individuation is a lifelong process and Jung goes so far as to assert that the realisation of the Self is the meaning of life: 'All life is bound to individual carriers who realise it ... But every carrier is charged with an individual destiny and destination [the self], and the realisation of these alone makes sense of life' (in Jaffé 1986: 79).

The connection between Christ and the Self, which Jung made – 'psychologically, Christ must be understood as a symbol of the self' (1958: 194) – also links Christianity to individuation, as does the shift from a focus on behaviour and externals towards relatedness with the inner reality and an emphasis on the spiritual outlook. This shift is exemplified in the teachings of Christ, for example, from an emphasis on behaviour in the Old Testament – you shall not steal, kill, commit adultery – to an inner level in the New, for example: 'you have heard how it was said, *You shall not commit adultery*. But I say this to you, if a man looks at a woman lustfully, he has already committed adultery with her in his heart' (Matthew 5. 27–8). Jung, discussing meaning in a series of dreams, asserted that the process of individuation 'has constantly been held up to Western man in the dogmatic and religious pattern of the life of Christ' (1953: 176).

Jung went on to say that 'the descent of the Holy Ghost [must be understood] as the self's actualization in man' (1958: 194). The third person of the Christian Trinity is symbolised by a dove, as seen, for example, in depictions of the Annunciation. For Jung, 'it is not without reason that the dove of Aphrodite is the symbol of the Holy Ghost' (1956: 138), thus identifying the Holy Ghost (or Holy Spirit) and the aim of the individuation process with love.

Individuation and Love

Jung suggested that the aim of the individuation process seems to be 'objective cognition': 'This kind of relationship, by way of the Self, has something strictly objective, strangely transpersonal about it. [...] "Objective cognition lies hidden behind the attraction of the emotional relationship; it seems to be the central secret"' (von Franz 1980: 177). This rather cerebral description seems to correspond very well with the philosopher John Macmurray's definition of love:

> Love, which is the fundamental positive emotion characteristic of human beings, can be either subjective and irrational, or objective and rational. In feeling love for

> another person, I can either experience a pleasurable emotion which he stimulates in me, or I can love *him*. [...] The difference between these two kinds of love is the ultimate difference between organic and personal life. (1992: 15)

An example of objective cognition, or objective, rational love in Macmurray's description, can be seen in a story by the Persian poet and mystic, Rumi, which was a favourite of the writer and Jungian counsellor, Helen Luke (1995: xv-xvi).

The story concerns a group of nomadic people in a desert who stop at a place where they believe they can get water. However, when they let down a bucket, not only is there no water when they pull up the rope, there is no bucket either. After several more attempts, one of the young men offers to go down and see what has happened. As with the bucket, the rope is pulled up without the young man and, after losing several others in the same way, an elderly man proposes that he should go down, to avoid any further loss of those who will be the future of the tribe.

The old man feels fear but promises himself that he will remain aware, whatever happens. When he reaches the bottom of the well he finds himself face to face with a horrible monster. The monster says it will ask the old man a question and his fate will depend on the answer. The monster's question is 'where is the best place to be?' The old man looks at the monster in front of him and is reluctant to hurt its feelings by giving an answer that would not be meaningful to one who lives deep under the earth in a place that is dark and dank. So he replies that the best place to be is wherever you feel at home, even if it's in a hole in the ground. Delighted with the answer, the monster praises the wisdom of the old man and releases in addition the young men and the water.

The old man's response is not borne of fear. Fear might have led him to say that the best place to be was at the bottom of a well, anything to please the monster and get out quickly. Or he could have answered from his own perspective, describing his idea of the best place to be as above ground where there is sunlight and warmth, which seems likely to be how the young men responded, rejecting outright the possibility of an alternative view. Instead, the old man chooses an answer that embraces all realities – his own, the monster's and others. He sees the monster in itself, with its differences, and does not reject them but takes towards it an attitude of respect and kindness. It is an objective, rational attitude but which has nothing of the coldness or impersonality which we often mistakenly associate with both reason and objectivity.

The old man's response also recognises the importance of feeling rather than physical reality. Kathrin Asper, a Jungian analyst who has written about and lectured on the importance of regaining a sense of self-worth, considers that 'it is where our heart is that we feel at home' (1994: 22). This represents a shift from the physical to the emotional plane, to feeling and love, and it is also implicit in the old man's reply to the monster. The atmosphere created in *Caperucita* the day Sara's grandmother wins at bingo and shares her winnings with her granddaughter, is an example of the way in which the heart leads the way in defining the home. On that day even Sara's mother's weekly strawberry tart, which the grandmother usually gives away, tastes delicious, confirming that what matters is the feeling, the relatedness between the two. Marie-Louise von Franz, describing the experience of the highest level of the feminine process of individuation, argues that what is attained is a degree of feeling which enables one to '[find] the attitude which suits the situation, [know] instinctively what is right *in this special case*, [know] how to act in each individual case' (1993a: 213). Von Franz also clarifies what is meant by feeling: 'Generally we identify feeling with affect and emotion, but that is only inferior feeling' (in Boa 1994: 198), and she cites as an example the strong emotions expressed by young people in large gatherings such as concerts where 'their feelings spill all over the place. They are not individually pointed' (Ibid. 198). What she calls 'differentiated feeling' is something quite different, much closer to Macmurray and Jung. It means 'to love that unique person for his or her uniqueness. [...] [which] presupposes that you are capable of seeing the uniqueness of the other person, of getting rid of all schematic psychological judgements' (Ibid. 198). In other words, if you are no longer projecting parts of yourself onto the other person, if you are a good mirror.

Thus the impact of the individuation process is not only on the individual: 'There exists no individuation process in any one individual that does not at the same time produce this relatedness to one's fellowmen' (von Franz 1980: 177). It is easier to see more clearly: 'The more one becomes a unique individual oneself, the more one individuates in the Jungian sense of the word, the more one becomes able to see the other person as a unique person and not have some cliché judgment about him or her' (in Boa 1994: 198–9). Having argued that there were several levels or stages of eros ranging from 'relations based merely on projection [and] characterized by fascination and magical dependence' (in von Franz 1980: 177), to conscious relatedness, person to person, Jung described the highest level as 'a kind of return to the first stage, but on a higher, more conscious level. It is a relationship with the Self in the other person, with his or her wholeness [...]. Only love, not intellect, can apprehend another person in this way' (von Franz 1997a: 53). The outcome of progress in the individuation progress is, therefore, for Jung, not only greater awareness and completeness and a new inner relatedness, but also a new relatedness to others. This has implications for the development of community.

Individuation and the Development of Christianity

For John Macmurray, the development of community is related to the essence of Christianity and the outcome of the process of individuation seems to represent just such a development. Barbara Hannah, in her memoir of Jung, claims that 'the process of individuation is the central theme of original Christianity' (1977: 335), citing Jung's challenging question 'Are not Jesus and Paul prototypes of those who, trusting their inner experience, have gone their individual way in defiance of the world?' (1977: 335).

The outcome of individuation has also been linked to a new phase of religious development – the Age of the Holy Spirit. In *Memories, Dreams, Reflections* Jung suggests a possible development of Christianity: 'A further development of the myth [of Christianity] might well begin with the outpouring of the Holy Spirit upon the apostles, by which they were made into sons of God, and not only they, but all others who through them and after them received the *filiatio* – sonship of God' (1983: 365). Particularly during the twelfth and thirteenth centuries, movements emerged which anticipated a third period following those of the Father/the Old Testament and the Son/Christ/the New Testament, which would be characterised by the Holy Spirit: 'This third phase, the Age of the Holy Spirit, corresponds on the human level to an attitude that, through recognition of the guiding and enlightening function of the unconscious, strives to move beyond the state of being suspended in conflict (associated with the Piscean age and the two fishes representing Christ and Satan or anti-Christ)' (Jung & von Franz 1971: 322). Aniela Jaffé, a Jungian analyst who worked with Jung on *Memories, Dreams, Reflections*, explains how this third phase corresponds to the realisation of the self in individuation: 'Jung recognised that the self which is constellated and being brought into reality in the psyche of modern man corresponds to the God-image of the Holy Ghost, the final efflorescence of the Christian conception of God' (1986: 113). According to the New Testament, the Holy Spirit was only able to appear after Christ had left the earth – 'unless I go, the Paraclete will not come to you' (John 16. 7)[3] – which seems to confirm a shift in emphasis from the outer or physical to the inner or spiritual plane. In an expression of exasperation at the failure of so many to interpret events in a meaningful way, Martín Gaite exclaimed in a notebook entry from the early 1960s relating to the murder by the tailor discussed earlier, that its purpose was 'para ver si al fin se conmueven las piedras y los sordos oyen y los ciegos ven' [to see if at last the stones are shaken and the deaf hear and the blind see] (2002a: 62). This is not the desire for the kind of miracles of physical healing so frequently recorded in the New Testament, but represents that same shift from the physical to the spiritual plane. Being cured of such blindness or deafness would mean that, instead of the prevailing complacency and unconsciousness, there was a recognition of individual motivations and shadow qualities, enabling the withdrawal of projections onto others and opening the door to real relatedness.

In the New Testament the Holy Ghost (or Holy Spirit) appeared at Pentecost in the form of tongues of flame on the heads of the Virgin Mary and the Apostles: 'Suddenly there came from heaven a sound as of a violent wind which filled the entire house in which they were sitting; and there

3 Paraclete: 'literally "he who is called to one's side" [...] commonly translated by "consoler"' (Catechism 1994: 160).

appeared to them tongues as of fire; these separated and came to rest on the head of each of them' (I Acts 2. 2–3). Unlike the destructive fires of hell harrowed at the death of Christ, the fire of Pentecost is creative. In his challenging and comprehensive study of why we tell stories, Christopher Booker agrees that the Holy Spirit 'represents the dynamic power of the Self' and argues that it 'must by definition include a strong, if disguised, feminine component' (2005: 621–2), which is the essence of relatedness. The higher development of the feminine requires 'much subtlety and individual feeling into the situation' and 'a superior way of judging [a] situation' (von Franz 1993a: 213–14). Similarly, Booker defines the feminine value – necessary for wholeness in both men and women – as 'true feeling for others *and* the wider awareness which permits true understanding, an appreciation of the totality of the situation and how everything is properly connected' (2005: 257). Following the descent of the Holy Spirit at Pentecost, the apostles were able to communicate with everyone whatever language they spoke: 'They were all filled with the Holy Spirit and began to speak different languages as the Spirit gave them power to express themselves. [...] there were devout men living in Jerusalem from every nation under heaven, and at this sound [of a violent wind] they all assembled, and each one was bewildered to hear these men speaking in his own language' (Acts 2: 4–6). There is thus tremendous power in the coming of the Holy Spirit – 'a violent wind' – but it is a creative power which promotes community and mutual understanding.

There are examples in Martín Gaite's work of these interpretations of the Holy Spirit and Pentecost, as in the suggestion of a new future in *Castillo* and the transformation of fire in *Pastel*, in the startling shift in emphasis from outer to inner in *Caperucita* and in the new relatedness at the end of *Reina*. All of these works have been described as fairy tales,[4] and

4 See, for example, Mercedes Carbayo-Abengózar: 'en los años 90 Martín Gaite escribe dos versiones revisadas de dos cuentos tradicionales: *Caperucita Roja* y *La reina de las nieves*. Ambas versiones están ya localizadas en el tiempo, en nuestro tiempo. Son cuentos urbanos, contemporáneas' [in the 90s Martín Gaite wrote revised versions of two traditional fairy tales: *Little Red Riding Hood* and *The Snow Queen*. Both versions are located in time, in our time. They are contemporary urban tales] (1998b).

it is in fairy tales that the individuation process is most clearly depicted, in symbolic form. As Christopher Booker argues: '[Fairy tales] reflect the patterns whereby humanity can transcend the limitations of the ego to make contact with the Self' (2005: 640).

Fairy Tales

Martín Gaite's interest in fairy tales dates from her childhood and is recorded in essays in *El cuento de nunca acabar* [The Never-Ending Story], in her own fairy tales and in her translating the fairy tales of Charles Perrault, *Bruno Bettelheim presenta los cuentos de Perrault (seguidos de los cuentos de Madame D'Aulnoy y de Madame Leprince de Beaumont)*. She fails to see meaning in most of the traditional fairy tales she read as a child and addresses her concerns regarding these in *Cuento* (1988a) in essays written around the time she was translating Perrault's tales (1980). She praises only a handful of fairy tales: *Tom Thumb* for being an active hero and for the fact that, unlike all the wealthy characters who get all the help they need, he is poor and has to depend on himself; *Little Red Riding Hood* because it did not have the standard happy ending (and, therefore, she disagrees

---

Likewise Lissette Rolón Collazo: 'Con la publicación de *La Reina de las Nieves* de Carmen Martín Gaite se completa el perfil del cuento de hadas en esta producción' [With the publication of *The Farewell Angel* by Carmen Martín Gaite, the fairy-tale profile in her output is complete] (2002: 159). *Reina* – 'un conte de fées contemporain' [a contemporary fairy tale] (Le Scoezec Masson 2003: 86–7) – was also included in a conference on *La littérature pour enfants dans les textes hispaniques* [Children's literature among Spanish texts] on the grounds that although 'il n'est pas destiné à un public d'enfants [...] si on élargit le champ à la littérature qui plonge ses racines dans l'enfance, le monde de l'enfance, le poids de l'enfance, *la Reina de las Nieves* en fait indubitablement partie' [it is not intended for a young audience [...] if one widens the field to literature which plunges its roots into childhood, the world of childhood, the force of childhood, *The Farewell Angel* undoubtedly belongs there] (Moner & Pérès 2004: 241).

strongly with the Grimms' ending in which the eponymous heroine and her grandmother are rescued safe and sound from the wolf's belly); and *Puss in Boots* (1988a: 146). The last of these is her clear favourite because of the way the cat invents a story to save his master and is so committed to it that it is believed, his plan works and his master's fortunes are transformed. However, Martín Gaite fails to mention that the cat is quite menacing, threatening the workers in the fields if they do not fall in with his plans, that his master is extremely handsome, which is what wins him the attention of the king's daughter, or that his master does nothing, leaving everything to the cat, just like all the other heroes who, in the writer's eyes, do not lift a finger to help themselves. Nevertheless, her praise for the cat illustrates a crucial aspect of many of her own works, namely the importance of telling your story to yourself first and of believing in it.

Her criticisms of other fairy tales include too much reliance on the physical attractiveness of their protagonists – 'son indefectiblemente hermosos o de impresionante apariencia' [they are unfailingly beautiful or impressive-looking] – and on their unrealistic endings, namely

> El premio de una boda con personaje de alcurnia o el casual descubrimiento de los orígenes nobles y aún principescos del propio personaje tan desvalido y huérfano de los favores de la fortuna en los umbrales del relato. (1988: 104)
>
> [The reward of a wedding with a personage of noble birth or the casual discovery of the noble or even princely origins of the very character who was so destitute and devoid of fortune's favours at the start of the story.]

She seems to agree with feminist criticism which argues that fairy tales teach girls to be passive in the expectation that their lives will have a similar outcome to the fairy-tale heroines, 'In the past twenty years, feminist critics have written relentless attacks on the best-known fairy tales claiming that the gender stereotypes they present initiate girls into a code of female passivity that overvalues physical beauty' (Soliño 2002: 30), and the claims that 'the fairy-tale world [...] defined success as marriage to a rich, handsome prince' (Ibid. 26). Martín Gaite further suggests in 'La cenicienta' that the effect of the emphasis on beauty and marriage to a prince is that the tales fail to help the child reader to make a real connection between the fairy-tale world and his own:

> Jamás, después de escuchar esta historia, se le podrá ocurrir al niño hacer un paralelo entre la Cenicienta y la criada de su casa, aunque también ésta se pase el día a vueltas con el fogón, la escoba y el estropajo, duerma en un cuarto mal ventilado y escuche palabras desabridas. (1988a: 105–6)
>
> [After listening to this story, it will never occur to the child to draw a parallel between Cinderella and the maid in his house, even though she too might be spending the whole day with the stove, the brush and the scourer, sleeping in a badly ventilated room and listening to harsh words.]

In an alternative reading of *Cinderella*, Robert McCully points out how 'she dissimulates with her stepsisters and has hidden the mate to the prince's slipper in her apron' (1991: 54). That she seizes opportunities is also indicated from the first appearance of the fairy godmother, when Cinderella makes suggestions as to what else might be bewitched: 'I will go and see […] if there be ever a rat in the rat-trap – we may make a coachman of him' (Lang 1978: 69). The use of 'we' suggests that she thinks of this as a partnership between herself and the fairy godmother, not as the unequal relationship between a very powerful being and a poor passive kitchen girl. For McCully it is the responsiveness and growing awareness on Cinderella's part which brings about the permanent change: 'Her reward for having recognized that her nature included qualities opposite to simple virtues and an excess of naiveté comes when her fairy godmother restores her to the original state that captures the prince's psychology' (1991: 54), which happens after she has tried on the glass slipper. In short, she achieves her good fortune by being alert and responding to the opportunities that present themselves. And although the relationship is unequal in terms of power, a partnership is possible as Cinderella shows, and this partnership mirrors that between the ego and the Self.

Other critics have challenged the view, shared by Martín Gaite, that the female protagonists of the traditional tales are passive, as in fact,

> fairy tales […] tend to show heroines wide open to receiving and transmitting magic, or taking vigorous action. […] Sisters rescue brothers far more often than brothers save sisters. Daughters rescue fathers or lovers rather than the reverse: Beauty goes into the Beast's castle, prepared to sacrifice her life in order to save her father. […] Gretel […] saves her brother's life by pushing the witch into her own oven. Gerda goes off in heroic pursuit of her playmate Kay in […] 'The Snow Queen'. (Gould 2006: xix)

Alison Lurie adds that 'the contrast is greatest in maturity, where women are often more powerful than men. Real help for the hero or heroine comes most frequently from a fairy godmother or wise woman, and real trouble from a witch or wicked stepmother' (in Bayó Belenguer 2002: 198). This broader perspective on the range of roles permits Lurie to advise that reading a collection of fairy tales is the way to 'prepare children for women's liberation' (Ibid. 198), which contrasts with the view that 'when little girls like Gerda were portrayed as clever, it was only to save their male counterparts from being devoured by an evil enchantress' (Soliño 2002: 26). Martín Gaite's own strong female heroes, who take steps to transform their fate, are, therefore, following in a tradition which includes well-known fairy tales.

Robert McCully, in his reflections on fairy tales, considers that 'favourable outcomes pertain only when characters listen to certain things, follow specific rules, and behave in a trusting fashion toward elements ordinarily overlooked' (1991: 54). In her own fiction, Martín Gaite reveals the importance of characters paying attention. There is Cambof's insistence to Altalé in *Castillo* that she should pay attention as 'los informes vienen de todos lados' [information comes from all over] (Martín Gaite 1992a: 50). This means that Altalé does not reject the needlecase from the beggarwoman nor, despite the pain it causes her, does she share the messages she receives and the discoveries she makes with her teacher and friend, Cambof. In *Reina*, Leonardo does not allow himself to be distracted by the chatter of Ángela, who is not important to him, and instead pays attention to the stinging in his foot which leads to his discovering the newspaper and its report of his parents' death. (1994a: 64). Other works, too, provide examples, such as *Nubosidad* where Mariana is inspired, when talking to herself – 'no hay derecho a que me traiga arrastrada por la calle de la amargura' [he has no right to make my life a misery (literally: drag me along the street of bitterness] (1992b: 70) – to leave Madrid and head to the house of her friend, Silvia, in the *Calle de la Amargura* in Puerto Real (Ibid. 70).

Both Martín Gaite's and feminist interpretations regard the occurrences in fairy tales far too literally. Fairy tales can also be seen as symbolic representations of inner processes which yields a very different interpretation. This would be the view of Jungian analysts such as Marie-Louise von

Franz who has written extensively on traditional fairy tales from a Jungian perspective and, after many years, concluded that

> all fairy tales endeavour to describe one and the same psychic fact, but a fact so complex and far-reaching and so difficult for us to realize in all its different aspects that hundreds of tales and thousands of repetitions with a musician's variations are needed until this unknown fact is delivered into consciousness; and even then the theme is not exhausted. This unknown fact is what Jung calls the Self, which is the psychic totality of an individual and also, paradoxically, the regulating center of the collective unconscious. (1996: 2)

The paradox von Franz refers to above lies in the fact that one of the fundamental tenets of Jung's approach is the uniqueness of every human being. As the relationship with the Self is the aim of the individuation process, the close relationship between fairy tales and individuation in the Jungian view is evident:

> Different fairy tales give average pictures of different phases of this experience. They sometimes dwell more on the beginning stages, which deal with the experience of the shadow and give only a short sketch of what comes later. Other tales emphasize the experience of animus and anima [...]. Others emphasize the motif of the inaccessible or unobtainable treasure [i.e. the Self] and the central experiences. (von Franz 1996: 2)[5]

Christopher Booker takes a similar perspective, arguing that 'the archetypal ending of stories where a hero and heroine come together in perfect union symbolises something much deeper than just a marriage. It is the image of complete human integration' (2005: 419). While Booker refers here to all stories, von Franz expresses doubts even about analysing what she calls 'literary fairy tales', arguing that fairy tales written by a single author fall into a different category. They are literary or, as she describes them, 'poetical fairy tales' and she is wary of analysing them. Von Franz argues that whereas the Grimm Brothers and others collected oral tales which had been shaped through many tellings by multiple authors, those tales written by a single author 'are not genuine fairy tales, for they contain

5 'In the various religions and mythologies [the Self] is symbolized by the image of the "treasure hard to attain"' (von Franz 1990: 1).

to some extent the problem of the writer' (1995b: 99). She states that, while it would be interesting to study them, she is inclined to 'keep away from poetical fairy tales' (Ibid. 99), citing as an example Hans Christian Andersen, on the grounds that he experienced a psychological problem which is reflected in the tales:

> Andersen's [fairy tales] mirror the specific religious problem of his country. He had a gift for showing what was going on underneath and produced almost genuine fairy tales, but he was highly neurotic, he never got away from his mother, and he never married. His stories have a predominantly tragic atmosphere: the connection with the anima cannot be made, just as it was not made in Andersen's own life. (1995b: 99)

The tragic atmosphere can be seen in tales such as *The Little Mermaid* and *The Steadfast Tin Soldier*. However, *The Snow Queen* is a much more positive tale which, Andersen recalls, 'came out dancing over the paper in a few days' (Wullschläger 2000: 3), which suggests much less ego involvement in the writing. Martín Gaite described a similar experience in writing *Pastel*: 'Lo había escrito en un estado de absoluto *trance*' [I wrote it in a state of complete trance] (Calvi 1990: 171). Wullschläger also suggests that the tale is 'among [Andersen's] least autobiographical works' (2000: 247), thus removing it from the other stories which von Franz claims reflect a more personal problem.

Christopher Booker claims that fairy tales 'in psychological terms [...] provide as perfect a reflection of the underlying archetypes of storytelling as anything we find in more self-consciously sophisticated forms of literature' (2005: 640). It might be argued that Martín Gaite's work come under the heading of 'more self-consciously sophisticated forms of literature' and that her fairy tales are not traditional stories which have developed through many tellings and re-tellings. However, they all have a link with traditional or well-known fairy stories. María Elena Soliño sees *Castillo* as a re-telling of *Snow White* and, as well as containing a number of elements from that traditional tale, it also reflects aspects of *Sleeping Beauty*. *Caperucita* is self-evidently a re-telling of *Little Red Riding Hood*, while *Pastel*, which Soliño regards as re-telling *Sleeping Beauty*, contains an important motif from the original version of that tale as well as other magical aspects and references to elements of traditional *cuentos*. Finally,

Reina is dedicated to Hans Christian Andersen, whose fairy tale *The Snow Queen* acts as a constant reference point for the protagonist, Leonardo Villalba, although Andersen's magical story is a literary rather than a traditional tale. All of Martín Gaite's fairy tales depict aspects of the Jungian individuation process and there is a sense of progression in individuation across the four stories.

CHAPTER 2

'Los informes vienen de todos lados': Dreams in *El castillo de las tres murallas*

Introduction

> [*El castillo de las tres murallas*] es un cuento para niños, aunque no para niños muy pequeños. Es un cuento para niños de ocho a diez años en adelante. [...] Creo que puede tener bastante interés también para los adultos. (Medina 1983: 186)
>
> [*The Three-Walled Castle* is a story for children, although not for very young children. It's a tale for children aged from about eight to ten years onwards. [...]. I think it could also hold quite a bit of interest for adults].

The complexity of Martín Gaite's fairy tales clearly removes them from the grasp of a mere childhood audience and the publication in Spain of *Castillo* along with *Pastel* and *Caperucita* in Siruela's *Colección las tres edades (de ocho a ochenta años)* [Three Ages Collection (from eight to eighty)] supports the Spanish writer's assessment, as Cusato also notes (1996: 482 n.4).[1]

Most critics seem to agree with Joan Lipman Brown's assessment of *Castillo*: 'Martín Gaite has invented a work that is enchanting, lovely and timeless. *The Three-Walled Castle* is, quite simply, a perfect fairy tale' (1987: 171). However, taking a different approach, Eunice Myers claims that it depicts a 'sad, mythic world' (1984: 47), and argues that 'the ending is too

1 Sandra L. Beckett points out the contrast between the approach taken by the Spanish publisher and that of other countries, particularly France and Germany, where *Caperucita* was targeted at a juvenile audience, although in 1998 the German publisher of the children's version brought out a separate edition for adults (2009: 193–4).

ambiguous to be described as a happy one' (Ibid. 48). Others disagree with this assessment of the ending with Esther Bartolomé considering that the story 'culmina en el desenlace feliz y mágico que le corresponde' [concludes with the happy and magical ending which befits it] (1982: 56), while Brown asserts that 'at the story's close, goodness has triumphed over evil' (1987: 169). Although it is a lovely fairy tale, there is some ambiguity in the ending of *Castillo*.

In an interview in 1991, Martín Gaite claimed that 'una de las estudiosas más serias de mi obra en los Estados Unidos, Ruth El Saffar, considera que *El castillo de las tres murallas* es mi mejor libro' [one of the most serious scholars of my work in the USA, Ruth El Saffar, considers *The Three-Walled Castle* to be my best book] (1991a: 7). This is quite a claim and one which seems unlikely to be shared by all or even the majority of critics. El Saffar also makes interesting observations on the structure of *Castillo*, particularly with regard to the waxing and waning of the power of Lucandro and the pivotal role of the central chapter – the fourth of seven – as representing both the apex and nadir of the story, as it contains both the birth of Altalé and the departure of Serena.

The Fairy Tale

Castillo is the story of a very rich man, Lucandro, with an obsessive mistrust and fear of being robbed. His attitude means he rarely leaves the black marble castle which he has built on top of a mountain and which is protected by three walls and a securely locked gate. The black colour of the marble, while dramatic and rich, associates it with death. Lucandro shares his home with Serena, a beautiful woman whom the local villagers have never seen; an old wise man, Cambof Petapel, who lives in the highest tower of the castle; and a powerful Malay slave, Tituc. Serena has a personal maid, Luva, who figures later in the story, after Serena has given birth to a daughter, Altalé. Lucandro keeps Altalé away from her mother. Serena writes down her dreams and her fidelity to the dream world leads to her running away with Altalé's handsome music teacher, Gisel. Altalé develops into a feisty little girl whose dream is to find her mother, yet who has pity for a father who is slowly turning into one of the creatures – the *brundas*, half–fish, half-rat – which act as a warning system from their place in the moat just outside the castle wall. Altalé, like her mother, responds to her dreams and other signs, following Cambof Petapel's advice that 'los informes vienen de todos lados' [information comes from all over] (50). Fired by her example of standing up to Lucandro, many of the villagers – who have long suffered poverty, hunger, even starvation as a result of the poor harvest from Lucandro's worst lands – move onto better lands and prosper. Altalé's dreams lead her to leave the castle on her fifteenth birthday in the company of Amir, a reincarnation of Cambof Petapel, while the abandoned Lucandro completes his transformation and joins the other *brundas* in the moat.

Some aspects of *Castillo* may be regarded as corresponding to Cervantes's story 'El celoso extremeño' [The Jealous Extremaduran] (2009: 33–76) in which a husband, Carrizales, gives his wife Leonora many riches and keeps the household enclosed in a grand house. In Cervantes's tale a musician comes to the house, a black slave is the means of access, and the husband dies. However, there are many differences between the two tales. Lucandro's concern is primarily with the security of material things, although he also treats people as if they were objects. Unlike the young Leonora, who is delighted with her new materially rich lifestyle, Serena does not enjoy Lucandro's gifts. Carrizales in Cervantes's story does not allow the male of any species to cross the inner threshold of the house, hence the 'musician' (who is really a young gentleman with some musical ability) gains access to the house through persuasion and deceit. In contrast, Lucandro invites the music teacher, Gisel, to live in the castle in order to avoid Altalé having to leave it to take lessons. Despite his mistaken belief that he has been betrayed by Leonora, there is wisdom in Carrizales's recognition of his foolishness in locking up his wife and household, whereas Lucandro has no self-awareness. Finally, Carrizales's death from a broken heart seems tragic and his wife, genuinely sorrowful, refuses to marry the musician, preferring to enter a convent. Serena, on the other hand, leaves the castle with the music teacher eleven years before Lucandro, rather than dying, is transformed into an inhuman form of life.

Snow White and Sleeping Beauty

Castillo has been described as a re-writing of the traditional fairy tale *Snow White* (Soliño 2000: 96–8) and it contains a number of elements from that traditional tale, as well as from *Sleeping Beauty*. Serena has been compared to Snow White's mother: 'Like Snow White's mother, [Serena] looks out the sewing-room window as it snows' (Soliño 2002: 98). Snow White's mother, the queen of that faraway land, looks out of the window at the falling snow before her child is born. Pricking her finger and seeing the drops of blood on the snow, 'she thought to herself: "If only I had a child as white as snow and as red as blood, and as black as the wood of the window frame!"' (Grimm 1996: 161). Shortly afterwards Snow White is born with the same characteristics desired by her mother – the only fairy-tale heroine in the best-known stories not to be blonde. Altalé resembles Snow White physically, with her pale skin and black hair and eyes, but her mother saw the snow start to fall shortly after the birth of Altalé and the wish Serena makes is more profound, it is for her daughter's whole life: 'Que entienda sus sueños mejor que yo entiendo los míos. Y que los pueda seguir siempre' [May she understand her dreams better than I understand mine. And may she always follow them] (39). In a further contrast to the fairy-tale queen, Serena closes her eyes against the snow, turning her attention inwards, which is the world she values more. The overriding importance of the inner world is something Martín Gaite emphasises repeatedly in her writings, both in her notebooks and her novels: 'Lo único importante es atender a las transformaciones internas' [All that matters is paying attention to the inner changes] (2002a: 425).

In the well-known Grimms' fairy tale, Snow White's stepmother disguises herself and tempts the girl three times. The temptations are concerned with Snow White making herself more attractive or reminding her of her own attractiveness – a comb for her hair, a bodice lace of many-coloured silk and 'a rosy and beautiful apple' (Grimm 1996: 168).[2] Snow

2 The tale and the girl are called Snowdrop in some editions of the Grimms' fairy tales including the one referred to here.

White resists none of these temptations and, in his interpretation, Ronald Murphy asserts that she dies and does not regain life in this world, but is carried off to an eternal place: 'The good dwarfs are able to rescue her from the consequences of the laces and the comb, but not from the consequences of eating the apple. "She was dead and she remained dead"' (2000: 127). When Snow White dies she is placed in a glass casket on top of a mountain, visible to all, whereas Altalé lives in a black marble castle, invisible to all outside.

Murphy also concurs with Bruno Bettelheim's interpretation that 'the three temptations are all attempts to deceive Snow White into accepting her mother's concept of the nature of personal beauty' (2000: 126). Snow White's death is seen by Murphy as the inevitable outcome of giving in to the temptation 'to exchange her spiritual sense of what about her is worthwhile, to adopt material criteria only' (Ibid. 127). This situation can also be described as choosing the ego over the Self, which would mean turning away from the path of individuation. In *Castillo* Altalé also faces three tests and Serena's wish is to provide her daughter with the means of facing and passing those tests all by herself. The number three 'has to do with a process of development in time' (von Franz 1997a: 206). Four and its multiples indicate psychic wholeness: 'The number four as the natural division of the circle is a symbol of wholeness in alchemical philosophy, and it should not be forgotten that the central Christian symbol is a quaternity too' (Jung 1964a: 391). Snow White fails her tests and is, therefore, unable to attain the wholeness in life which would follow, which supports Murphy's perspective. Altalé, on the other hand, passes the tests and is, therefore, able to continue on the path of wholeness.

As well as *Snow White*, Serena's response to her baby daughter recalls *Sleeping Beauty* and those tales in which fairies make wishes for the newborn child at the christening. Serena interprets the absence of fairies as there being something missing, for which she must compensate by acting as fairy godmother to her own child. This dual role makes Serena a special character in Martín Gaite's panoply in which relationships between mothers and daughters are often fraught with tension and power struggles, while the godparents, being more detached, are able to intuit the godchild's needs and intervene at exactly the right moment and in the right way. This is the case with Sofía Montalvo in *Nubosidad variable* [Variable Cloud] who receives a red dress from her godmother and with Sara in *Caperucita* who is given books and a map of Manhattan by a godfather-like figure.

Martín Gaite's story shares other, more profound parallels with the story of *Sleeping Beauty*. In that original fairy tale, the king orders the destruction of all the spindles in his kingdom. Marie-Louise von Franz describes the spindle as 'a symbol of femininity' (1993a: 44), although in the same lecture she argues that 'within the weaving activity, which is essentially feminine, the spindle is a phallic thing' (Ibid. 49). In this latter regard, she links the spindle with the kind of pointed remarks that wound and claims that they are made by both women and the anima which, rightly, includes men in this kind of behaviour. One can see that both interpretations are possible – the spindle is associated with femininity and it also has a link with the masculine. In *Castillo* Lucandro tries to prevent Altalé from having too much contact with Serena because of his fear of her feminine influence, which he describes as filling the child's head with 'ideas locas' [crazy ideas] (45).

Briar Rose (Sleeping Beauty)'s father accepts only the light aspect of the feminine and the tale emphasises the girl's 'positive' qualities: 'She was so beautiful, modest, kind and clever' (1996: 32). The task which falls to Briar Rose is the integration of the rejected aspect in order to achieve wholeness both for herself and the kingdom. In *Castillo* the feminine aspect personified by Serena is not only kept away from Altalé but departs from the castle, leaving the key to the child's future freedom in her sewing-room for Altalé to discover. In Briar Rose's sleeping and waking Brenda Crowther, very positively, observes 'a victory of inner over outer experience' (2013: 6). She interprets *Sleeping Beauty* as a tale of the development of new feminine life and wholeness and a new relatedness to the masculine aspect (2013: 20) which corresponds very closely to the outcome of *Castillo*.

Symbols of the Self

In *Castillo* there are a number of symbols of, or connected to, the Self, which is a typical feature of fairy tales. First there is Cambof Petapel, 'el sabio oriental que [...] tenía más de cien años' [the wise man from the East who [...] was over a hundred] (19), who lives in the highest tower of the castle and believes he has experienced various lives including a pirate, a soldier and a princess. According to von Franz, 'the "wise old man" [is] a typical personification of the Self' (1964: 196). On the other hand, von Franz counsels against identifying characters in fairy tales too closely with aspects of the individuation process, claiming that it results in '[getting] stuck in projection' (1997b: 14), so while Cambof Petapel can be regarded as a symbol of the Self, he can also be described simply as a spiritual aspect. Ruth El Saffar describes Serena as 'the incarnation of the spirit world' (1982: 48) but Serena, trying to find her way in the dark – literally and metaphorically – is still rather unconscious and this role is much more appropriately filled by Cambof.

Unsurprisingly, Cambof is depicted as having an attitude quite different to that of Lucandro – he has no interest in material things, never feels bored or worried and reconciles opposite qualities in that his skills and interests embrace both art and science, including carving wooden figurines and watching the stars. However, he is also a problem figure as no one, including himself, can any longer read his writing (which is in a language he invented), he has forgotten who he is, and Lucandro pays no attention to his advice. In short, he is no longer influential. Cambof, therefore, is a spiritual principle that is worn out and in need of renewal. His previous rebirths suggest that he represents an aspect which is continually being renewed, which is also typical of images of the Self.

Joan Lipman Brown comments in her short essay on *Castillo* that, 'in essence, *The Three-Walled Castle* represents the conflict between spiritual values and materialistic values' (1987: 169). Von Franz points out that 'in many tribes there is a split between medicine man and king or chief – that is, between spiritual and worldly power' (1996: 53–4). Here

Lucandro represents the worldly power, equivalent to the figure of the king in many fairy tales who would represent collective consciousness. Von Franz explains that

> the idea behind the division of power was to keep the two separate, so that the religious aspect should have the possibility of renewal, and organization should keep to its own duties. In this way it might be possible to keep balance in the opposites, the tendency toward the continuity of consciousness and the necessity for constant inner renewal. The drawback is the danger of a quarrel and split between the two powers, which really belong together in the psyche. (1995b: 28–9)

This is essentially the problem posed in *Castillo* where the problem is not a quarrel but a lack of any real communication between the two, and domination by the material aspect with the spiritual having no influence. The location of this spiritual aspect in the castle emphasises the problem of isolation and lack of communication as Cambof lives in the highest tower and a tower represents 'the tendency to split off or wall off' (Kapacinskas & Robert 1992: 71).

The spindle in the tale of *Sleeping Beauty* was also in the highest tower of the castle. Associated with the feminine, it confirms that this aspect was split off from the life of the castle. The 'good fairies' all wished light and positive gifts for the child, which was one-sided, yet it was the 'curse' of the rejected fairy that enabled her to grow. Brenda Crowther suggests that, although the thirteenth fairy did not wish lightness for the child, in fact 'with her dark rage [she] brought the light of consciousness' (2013: 21). The acceptance of a more complete feminine nature expanded wholeness and ended the one-sidedness which had previously prevailed in the palace. In Lucandro's castle it is the spiritual aspect that is cut off and ignored and which will provide the opportunity for renewal and growth.

The mountain on which the castle is built is also a symbol of the Self – 'the mountain motif [...] denotes the Self' (von Franz 1996: 129) – and can in addition represent 'a place of orientation' (Ibid. 128) and 'the goal of a long quest or the site of the transition into eternity' (Ibid. 129). Thus it represents an ideal place for these two aspects, the worldly and the spiritual, to meet and find a new orientation and thereby be renewed. Furthermore it has been associated with the mother goddesses, for whom it represented a home (von Franz 2002: 15), and, therefore, it has a connection with the feminine. Elsewhere mountains are described as being 'midway between heaven and earth, they were a place where men such as Moses could meet their god' (Armstrong 2005: 23), and in the Judaeo-Christian tradition as 'the place of revelation' (Martini 2000: 34). Moses received the Ten Commandments on Mount Sinai; the Transfiguration of Christ, Moses and Elijah took place on a high mountain; and Christ was also tempted by the devil on a mountain. The transfiguration scene is significant in Martín Gaite's retelling of *Little Red Riding Hood* (Chapter 4), while Christ's temptation by the devil finds a parallel in *Castillo* in connection with both Lucandro and Altalé.

The Temptation of Christ

This story in the New Testament tells of Christ's response to three temptations by the devil. The story illustrates the values of Christ and his openness to wholeness. The first two temptations are to turn stones into bread to demonstrate his divine power and to throw himself off the roof of the temple to show that he will always be saved by angels. It is the final temptation, which takes place at the top of a mountain, which is relevant to Lucandro: 'Next, taking him to a very high mountain, the devil showed him all the kingdoms of the world and their splendour. And he said to him, "I will give you all these, if you fall at my feet and do me homage." Then Jesus replied, "Away with you, Satan! For scripture says: The Lord your God is the one to whom you must do homage, him alone must you serve"' (Matthew 4. 8–10). In complete contrast to Christ, Lucandro, who only values the material world, seems to have obtained the riches offered by the devil. Standing at the top of the mountain, like an ego rising above the Self, Lucandro declares, full of pride and self-satisfaction: '"Todo esto es mío. [...] Todo lo que está a mis pies ahora, es mío"' [All this is mine. [...] Everything that is at my feet now is mine] (34). The result of Lucandro's identification with the ego means the failure to realise his own uniqueness and even the loss of his human nature. This is in keeping with Christopher Booker's assessment of 'the essence of Jesus's message', namely the development of 'self-awareness to recognise just how all-pervasive a part egocentricity plays in all our human thinking and behaviour. Only through this self-understanding can we properly appreciate the other "centre" in our nature: and how far egotism holds us back from "hitting the mark", in realising that which we have the potential to become' (2005: 618). Christopher Booker sees this Gospel story as an example of the opposition between the ego and the Self and considers that 'in rejecting the three temptations out of hand, Jesus shows he is so completely identified with the Self that he has no ego to be tempted' (2005: 617). Martín Gaite expresses a similar desire – to be centred not on the ego, but on the Self (though she does not use this term) – when she writes in an entry from the early 1970s in her *Cuadernos*:

> Quiero tejer de nuevo mis palabras, mi paciencia, olvidar mi yo. El 'yo' deja su marca en el mundo destruyendo. No quiero invadir el mundo con el pus de mi yo, quiero ser luz para los otros, olvidarme de mí como antes, ser arcaduz, puente, estar, podar mi yo. (2002a: 175)
>
> [I want to weave again my words, my patience, forget my ego. The 'ego' leaves its mark on the world by wrecking it. I don't want to go into the world with the pus of my ego, I want to be a light for others, forget myself as before, be a channel, a bridge, just be, trim my ego.]

The idea of the ego as a destructive force is depicted vividly by Martín Gaite in *Reina* in Leonardo's dream about a steamroller which is out of control, crushing everything in its path.

The Negative Animus

In fairy tales characters are not usually fully developed: 'Fairy-tale style is characterised first and foremost by a simple, unshaded opposition between black and white, good and evil' (Lüthi in von Franz 1997a: 75). In *Castillo*

Lucandro is depicted almost entirely as a negative figure, with an obsessive fear of the passage of time, of death and of freedom, with a mistrust of almost all other human beings and an overwhelming love of material things. Lucandro, as the controlling, stifling agent, can also be interpreted as the negative animus, who keeps a woman from life: 'The dark side of the animus is a demon who would pull women away from life, cut them off from it' (von Franz 2002: 77). Serena wished to travel in order to alleviate her boredom but Lucandro is afraid to let her go or to leave the castle himself. When advised by Cambof Petapel that Serena would benefit from getting away from the castle, Lucandro refuses to accept that she is not happy: '"No," dijo. "Yo creo que no le gustaría. Así que no se lo voy a preguntar"' ['No', he said. 'I don't think she'd like that. So I'm not going to ask her'] (38). The original meaning of Satan is to obstruct, which is what Lucandro does, although his intentions will be thwarted.

At the same time, this kind of desire to travel, to escape has been described, somewhat controversially, as a possible sign of animus possession: 'Not realizing that the problem is an inner one, [animus-possessed women] assume that if only they can go about more, spend more money and surround themselves with more friends, their life-hunger will be assuaged' (von Franz 1993a: 183). To some ears this may sound like an argument made to stifle a woman. Yet Martín Gaite herself made the same kind of criticism of those who try to resolve an inner problem through outer activity. She also challenges the common desire to run away from situations which are difficult or not to our liking or to make some dramatic change – of job, or house, or partner, for example. Quietly, she argues that 'El que se quiere escapar de un sitio lo mejor que puede hacer es no moverse de ese sitio y escaparse transformándolo' [The best thing someone can do when they want to get away from a place is to stay there and get away by transforming it] (1994b: 119). This requires courage to face oneself and one's own contribution to the situation and recalls the Jungian emphasis on consciousness and on facing the shadow aspects of the personality.

Serena is not interested in having lots of material goods and half understands that the inner world might provide some answers, as she tries to write down her dreams. However, writing them in the dark means that the following morning she cannot read them. This suggests that she is still quite unconscious and dominated by the animus, since it is her fear that she will be discovered by Lucandro which prevents her from turning on the light. Thus the negative animus controls access to Serena, whose private dressing and sewing rooms are reached by a spiral staircase from their shared bedroom. In the palace of Sleeping Beauty an old woman spins in a tower room reached by a spiral staircase, cut off from the rest of the life there. In a spiral, progress is not so direct, but the journey is more complete because each stage of progress retains a greater connection with the preceding one. Serena goes up to her rooms and withdraws to these, so her own progress lies through a higher level, through the spirit, which is what the development of the story confirms. However, in these initial stages Serena is 'sneaking a life'. In her analysis of the fairy tale *The Red Shoes*, Clarissa Pinkola Estés describes women who live their creative lives in a hidden way as 'sneaking a life', which, she claims, occurs 'when a woman suppresses large parts of self into the shadows of the psyche' (1998: 234). She claims that 'women with poor marriages do this' (Ibid. 238). It may ultimately be destructive as 'sneaking is good for a captured woman only *if* she sneaks the right thing, only if that thing leads to her liberation' (Ibid. 238). The development of the story suggests that Serena is sneaking the right thing.

The Peacock

That Serena has been sneaking the right kind of life is confirmed by the way she responds to opportunities that offer greater freedom. When she becomes pregnant, she takes the opportunity to withdraw from Lucandro and to live and sleep in her own two rooms. This is a first step towards freedom, to acting on her instincts and the beginning of individuation. The bed she chooses for her sewing-room 'tenía incrustado en la cabecera un pavo real en colores tornasolados' [had a peacock in iridescent colours inlaid in the headboard] (37). As 'an early Christian symbol of the resurrection and of Christ' (von Franz 1996: 29), the peacock can be regarded as a symbol of the Self, in light of the connection made between the Self and Christ. The resurrection also connects it to Cambof Petapel in Martín Gaite's definition of reincarnation as 'muertes seguidas de resurrección' [deaths followed by resurrection] (2002b: 263). Another symbolic attribute of the peacock is that it 'stands for "all colours" (i.e. the integration of all qualities)' (Jung 1963: 287), which associates it with individuation and the Self as a representation of wholeness.

There is a further link in that 'in order to hatch its eggs, the peacock seeks a lonely and hidden spot' (Jung 1963: 292, n.131), which connects it to Serena's withdrawal to her own rooms before the birth. However, there is also an important difference between the bird and Serena as the peahen 'does not introduce her young to their father until they are fully grown' (Ibid. 292), whereas in *Castillo* Lucandro takes Altalé away from Serena very soon after the birth and endeavours to prevent contact between the two. Like Briar Rose's father, who was determined to keep his daughter away from spindles and spinning, Lucandro tries to protect Altalé from feminine influences. Yet, almost incredibly, despite the curse that in her fifteenth year Briar Rose would prick herself on a spindle and fall asleep for a hundred years, on the day of her fifteenth birthday the king and queen are absent from the castle. This may be due to arrogance or over self-confidence that, safe in the castle and with all the spindles destroyed, the young girl can come to no harm. But, by leaving the castle, they leave their daughter free to explore unrestrained and to find her way to the room in an old tower where an old woman spins flax with a spindle and the curse can be fulfilled. Thus the wholeness missing from the kingdom and, therefore, collective consciousness, can unfold and the king's absence could, therefore, be attributed to the Self.

Similarly, in several ways in respect of Altalé, Lucandro can be seen to have acted unwittingly as an agent of the Self. First, when he takes Altalé from her mother, he gives the child a special octagonal room in the highest tower. On the one hand there are resonances of Rapunzel in her tower. However, as the room is octagonal it is a symbol of wholeness, and it is also next to Cambof Petapel's room. Secondly, Lucandro appoints Cambof as the little girl's sole tutor which brings her in close contact with the spiritual principle from a very early age. It is Cambof who urges Lucandro to appoint a music teacher for Altalé in order to allow her to develop her considerable musical talent. Lucandro's fear of contact with the outside world means that he only agrees to the appointment on condition that the teacher comes to live there. This arrangement is the catalyst for the freedom first of Serena, later of Altalé. Martín Gaite claims that 'Cambof [...] es el verdadero autor de la ruina del castillo de las tres murallas' [Cambof [...] is the real creator of the ruin of the three-walled castle] (2002b: 263), and it is true that he is involved in all of these actions along with Serena and Altalé. However, Lucandro's attitude, despite its apparent negativity, is also crucial to their development and success as it is he who brings the music teacher to the castle. The Self acts through all of the characters whether or not they are aware of it and thus Lucandro can be described as an unconscious agent of the Self – he believes he is acting in his own interests, but he is thwarted in ways he could not foresee.

Dreams

The Jungian approach to the dream is that it represents a particularly important manifestation of the supernatural. Dreams have figured in Martín Gaite's fiction since her short stories published in the fifties and continued through the novels. They range from half-remembered fragments to long and complex dreams promising change in the dreamer's life. Characters also respond to their dreams in different ways. In *Balneario* where the narration of the dream takes up almost two-thirds of the novella, the dreamer, Matilde, treats it as a diversion from her dull life, a transient experience with no further meaning. In a later short story, 'Lo que queda enterrado' [What Remains Buried], María's dream depicts symbolically the problem she refuses to face in her life, the death of her baby daughter and her consequent fears for her new pregnancy. It is arguable that Sofía's dream at the start of *Nubosidad* is the catalyst for everything that happens to her subsequently. The response is the key, sometimes simply staying with the atmosphere of the dream, as Sofía does, is sufficient for changes to occur.

In the individuation process 'only dreams can point the way, for this development follows a purely inner bent or is determined by destiny' (von Franz 1997a: 222). Recognising how difficult it can be to understand the meaning of a dream, von Franz concludes that 'it feels like a divine act of grace when a dream provides a clear answer [...]; but often the dream symbols themselves are so complicated that one gets tangled up trying to interpret them' (Ibid. 309). In contrast, the most important dreams depicted in *Castillo* differ from many dreams in everyday life (and from Serena's earlier dreams) in that they do not appear to be symbolic but their message is immediately understandable to the dreamer, usually because someone known to, and beloved of, the dreamer speaks directly to them. Discussing voices in dreams, whether from a person or as if coming from nowhere, Jung said that he had 'often met with the objection that the thoughts which the voice represents are no more than the thoughts of the individual himself' (1970: 39). Jung disagreed with this, arguing that 'the voice gives me certain contents, exactly as if a friend were informing me of his ideas. It would be neither decent nor truthful to suggest that what he says are my own ideas' (Ibid. 39). This is the way Serena, Altalé and Cambof respond to their dreams, accepting the message given to them and not interpreting it as their own. It is true of the dream Serena has in the garden, where she has fallen asleep on the day the servant Tituc is due to return from the city with Altalé's new music teacher. In the dream her daughter, Altalé, who is aged four at the time, appears as a girl of fifteen, with a clear message for her mother, telling her to stay in her sewing-room until further notice. Altalé appears very agitated, shouting and crying, begging her mother not to let anyone see her. Significantly, she tells Serena that 'Es por mi bien' [It's for my own good] (43). Of the three walls surrounding the castle, the middle one, where Altalé appears in the dream, is red. Red is the colour of feeling and this wall is described as being highly resistant to weathering even by extreme cold or wet, reflecting the unbreakable bond between Serena and her daughter. In respect of the number symbolism, the sum total of the digits of Altalé's age in the dream is six which, if we follow Jung's theory, is the number concerned with marriage and the relationship between the sexes, anticipating the development of the story. In Jungian theory, the love relationship between a man and a woman involves 'a six-fold relationship of *four* figures, namely, of the man and his anima and of the woman and her animus' (von Franz 1980: 139).

In her analysis of *Castillo* from a Freudian perspective, Marjorie Sánchez argues that Serena loses interest in Altalé when Lucandro takes the little girl away from her (1991: 43). Nevertheless, Serena's desire not to be disturbed is related to her wish to do what her daughter requested in the dream. Saying she does not want to be disturbed makes it easier for her to fulfil the requirement to stay in her rooms until further notice. Although Serena submitted to Lucandro's taking away Altalé, it was clearly contrary to her wishes for when Altalé was born Serena had hoped to keep the child with her: 'Abrigaba la esperanza de que hiciera poco caso a Altalé y le dejara a ella encargada de su educación' [She harboured the hope that he would pay little attention to Altalé and would leave [the child's] upbringing to her] (40). However, she found that Lucandro saw the child as yet another possession and 'comprendió [...] que acabaría por quitársela, como todos los regalos de valor que le había hecho' [she realised that he would end up taking her [Altalé] away from her, as he had done with all the valuable presents he had given her] (40). Serena's decision that her daughter should not see very much of her also results from her love for Altalé. Despite Lucandro's prohibition that Serena should not take Altalé out without permission, one day they go out into the magnificent garden and sail in a little boat on one of the moats. Lucandro's furious reaction, which causes the child great distress, also contributes to Serena's decision not to try to see her daughter again: 'Serena había decidido que Altalé no tuviera que volver a llorar por su causa' [Serena had decided that Altalé should not have to cry again on her account] (43). In a very different interpretation, Marjorie Sánchez considers that Serena blames Altalé for her own lack of freedom: 'Ya no le import[a] su hija, a quien ve como la causante de que no realice su deseo' [Her daughter, who she sees as the cause of her not achieving her desires, no longer matters to her] (1991: 66). This wish, claims Sánchez, arises when Serena learns that a music teacher is coming to the castle to teach Altalé and the news 'despierta en ella el deseo de huir, de ser libre, de irse con el desconocido y escapar de la prisión y de su carcelero' [awakens in her the desire to flee, to be free, to go away with the stranger and escape from the prison and her jailor] (1991: 57). Sánchez argues that Serena immediately represses this desire, that the dream in the garden is a direct result of the repression and that the girl of fifteen in the dream might even be Serena herself (1991: 66). Taking the argument regarding repression even further, Sánchez suggests that the young woman in the dream could even represent the music teacher (66). However, the reader is told that 'Serena supo que aquella muchacha [en el sueño] era Altalé, aunque tenía como quince años'

[Serena knew that that girl [in the dream] was Altalé, even though she was about fifteen] (43) and there is no suggestion that she could represent the music teacher or Serena herself. The development of the story, including the importance of Altalé's fifteenth birthday, is consistent with Serena's initial understanding of the dream.

Drawing on Freudian dream theory, Sánchez claims that Serena's dreams are nothing more than repressed desires (1991: 56), arguing that the message from the young woman that Serena should wait in her rooms until further notice demonstrates the strength of these desires (Ibid. 66). However, the outcome of Serena's dream in the garden is that she locks herself away in her rooms more completely than before, and that she expects the 'nuevo aviso' [new notice] to come from Altalé who, according to the Freudian interpretation, Serena resents and blames for her lack of freedom. Also, in the dream Altalé seems confident that her mother will act in her interests when she appeals to her that 'es por mi bien' [it's for my own good] (43). Hernández Álvarez, recognises that Serena is following the instructions of a dream and considers that the separation is necessary for the child's development and is in keeping with the development of the hero (2005: 151). Both this temporary separation of Serena from her daughter and the more sustained absence soon afterwards create the kind of effect caused by the death of mothers in fairy tales: 'The mother's death is the beginning of the daughter's process of individuation' (von Franz 1993a: 167), which corresponds to the development in Martín Gaite's fairy tale.

Finally, before leaving the castle some time later, Serena, as we learn near the end of the tale, writes a message for Altalé to find when she is older, and uses her dream as guidance to the timing. Serena also appears to Cambof Petapel and her daughter in dreams, and both respond to her requests. In Cambof's case, Serena's appearance leads to him postponing his death until Altalé is fifteen, which suggests that Serena is very close to the supernatural world and is 'related' to others at a very deep level, which is a different image to the resentful, ego-driven creature depicted in Sánchez's analysis. In another quite different interpretation Sánchez also considers that Serena feels 'cólera' [rage] and 'odio' [hatred] (1991: 54) towards Lucandro, although she also recognises that Lucandro inspires in Serena 'miedo y lástima' [fear and pity] (Ibid. 55).

Serena's Response to the Dream

Serena's obedience to the instructions in the dream means that she stays in her rooms for more than a month. Nor Hall argues that 'withdrawal is a preparation for emergence' (1980: 98) and recalls that 'many fairy tales show women sitting through years of hiddenness, a kind of dark incubation in which something grows. Usually they have to weave or knit in the meantime' (Ibid. 95). Serena embroiders and reads, hardly eats, becomes listless and loses a sense of time and interest in life. Even though there is a purpose in her withdrawal, it is difficult to maintain a constant awareness of the source of such a situation – we are told that by the end of this time she could not remember the details of the dream. Nevertheless, Serena's withdrawal, although it seems related to death, is also closely linked to life: 'Organic life has its own time. It is moon-related, slow, moist, changing in the dark, periodically open – ready for new contents to enter – and periodically sealed off' (Hall 1980: 93). The time spent in her room in response to the message in the dream corresponds to a period of sealing, which precedes the next stage when she will be ready for new contents. Serena's fidelity to the dream and, in this interpretation, to the Self, is absolute. When Lucandro comes to invite her to hear Altalé play, Serena checks in her notebook the details of the dream regarding the timing of her leaving her room, to make sure that it is acceptable: 'La chica de blanco le había pedido que permaneciera encerrada en el cuarto de costura hasta nuevo aviso. Sin duda éste era el nuevo aviso' [The girl in white had asked her to stay shut away in the sewing-room until further notice. Undoubtedly this was the new notice] (45). The fact that Serena describes the figure in the dream as 'la chica de blanco' [the girl in white] and not Altalé seems likely to be due to her listlessness and other effects of the withdrawal.

While Lucandro is waiting for Serena's response, a black bird perches on the iron railings outside the sewing-room. Black birds can symbolise 'dark, destructive fancies and ideas' and represent 'an image of death and [...] an image of the soul' (Jung & von Franz 1971: 269). Ravens and crows are also traditionally depicted as messengers and as having the gift of prophecy. Serena shudders at the sight of the bird, suggesting she is fearful of what it might represent, and, intuitively, she asks about the music teacher. The development of the story, with Serena and the music teacher meeting then fleeing the castle together, confirms the link between Gisel and this image of death. It is a symbolic death – a dying to a former way of life – and, at the time the bird appears, it is something of which both protagonists are unaware, hence the colour black, which is the typical colour of unconsciousness. The birds are also linked to Apollo, the sun god, and Lucandro 'odia el sol' [hates the sun] (52), which suggests that their appearance may be connected with something hostile to his way of life.

At this stage, in her approach to life Serena is not acting in accordance with her ego wishes but with something much deeper. Von Franz likens this approach to the Christian injunction on the need to become like a child in order to enter the kingdom of Heaven: 'In truth I tell you, unless you change and become like little children you will never enter the kingdom of Heaven' (Matthew 18. 3). Von Franz challenges the simplistic interpretation of these words: 'Sometimes one sees that Christian civilization has preferred to believe that one should remain the little lamb of Jesus in order to reach the Kingdom of Heaven, but actually what is required is the restoration of an unreflecting capacity for obeying the Self' (1995b: 109). Such a state is achieved through individuation and the development of relatedness between the ego and the Self. It may sound passive in von Franz's description but it requires awareness and participation, like Cinderella and the fairy godmother and the man in the joke related in Chapter 1. Similarly, in Serena's case withdrawal and introversion are not the result of weakness or passiveness but of fidelity to this deeper aspect of herself.

The Re-emergence of Serena

When Serena is preparing to go to see her daughter and hear her play, she resembles an initiate preparing for a ritual, dressing very slowly and carefully. The silver shoes she chooses are related to the feminine and also to knowledge (Bayley 2006: I, 154 & II, 314), and, according to Nor Hall, the symbol of a new beginning, which fits this situation exactly: 'Silver is a feminine metal, the colour of the new moon, recipient of other [planetary] influences, symbol of new birth and purity' (1980: 146). The violet dress she chooses and the flowers of the same colour which she puts in her hair are significant because violet combines both blue and red, representing respectively the spiritual/thinking and feeling aspects – which are opposites in Jung's polaric structure – and thereby denote wholeness. Violet can also be described as representing wisdom, for, as Jung has argued 'where wisdom reigns there is no conflict between thinking and feeling' (Jung 1963: 249). The link between the colour and the dress, which are both associated with the feminine, points forward to a very favourable development for Serena, not in the masculine area, which might have included a new activity or some kind of creative work, but in the feminine field of relatedness. Because she has a sense of this being an important occasion, her awareness is heightened together with her capacity to respond. Martín Gaite describes the journey to her daughter's room as involving long corridors and many stairs, a journey which Serena relishes as significant in itself. A similar journey is made by Sorpresa in *Pastel*, and both recall the much longer journey by Matilde in *Balneario*, which has a much less positive outcome. As Serena has been guided to this point by a dream, it looks as though the new situation is intended by the Self.

The music teacher, whom she meets for the first time when she goes to hear Altalé play, is significant both as the means by which Serena escapes to a new life outside the castle (each drawn to the other by the physical beauty so disparaged by Martín Gaite in her essay on Cinderella), and for the song he sings which tells 'la historia de un prisionero que oía cantar a los pájaros a través de las rejas de la cárcel' [the story of a prisoner who heard the birds singing through the bars of his prison] (47).[3] Nor Hall describes music as medial (1980: 236) which is appropriate in the context of Serena and Gisel's response to one another. While the song reflects Serena's immediate situation, it will also be an aspect in her daughter's escape eleven years later. María Elena Soliño claims that Altalé 'brings about this first encounter of her mother with her new lover and approves of Serena's

3 This may be the well-known ballad 'El prisionero' [The Prisoner] in which a prisoner knows the time of day only 'por un avecillo / que [le] cantaba al albor' [through a little bird / who sang [to him] at dawn] (Smith 1964: 207). In contrast to *Castillo*, where the birds are caged and later freed, the *avecillo* is shot by a crossbowman.

adulterous union' (2002: 99). However, Altalé is four when Serena leaves the castle and, although it is the child's wish that her mother hear her play, this could have occurred, as Serena suggested, by Lucandro bringing their daughter, without the music teacher, to Serena's rooms.

Von Franz emphasises the importance of the need to escape the negative animus which Lucandro seems to represent: 'Women cannot fight the animus by *killing* him [...]. The male hero in myths fights, overcomes, conquers the monster. The feminine follows the path of individuation by suffering and escaping. It is enough if a woman can walk out into the human situation, rebuild human relatedness, relationship' (2002: 20). Paoli describes Lucandro as 'l'incarnation du mal, aussi bien pour Serena que pour sa fille Altalé' [the incarnation of evil, as much for Serena as for her daughter Altalé] (2007: 200). Nevertheless, he has unwittingly provided the means for Serena to escape, by insisting on bringing the music teacher to live in the castle and also by taking away Altalé and thus freeing Serena to go through her withdrawal/introversion and subsequent escape. From one perspective it looks so cruel and inhuman (and of course the animus is not human), but from another it is the essential pre-requisite in this case for any development. Analysing another fairy tale, von Franz comments that 'if a woman hasn't gone through the experience of being trapped by the demon animus, she has only unconscious thoughts. It is the demon who provides her with the ladder to escape. What was negative becomes positive' (2002: 21). Here Lucandro plays the role of the demon.

In keeping with the Christian injunction regarding not resisting evil, Serena does not fight Lucandro but escapes him by being faithful to her dreams and her inner self and begins the process of his downfall. This thwarting of Lucandro's power first by Serena, and later Altalé, is achieved through love, through eros. Firstly, by the attraction, which is the first manifestation of relatedness, between Serena and Gisel. Secondly, by the love of Altalé for her mother and also by her attraction to Amir and vice versa. In her analysis of another fairy tale, von Franz comments that 'the one who has Eros instead of a power attitude wins against the other party' (1995b: 300), which seems to be just what has happened here.

Finally, it is essential to emphasise the voluntary nature of this period of Serena's withdrawal, and that both the withdrawal and the flight which follows are the result of Serena's response to the dream. To ignore this aspect is to deprive the experience of the meaning with which it is charged. Serena's departure is not the result of ego wishes, of a self-indulgent desire, but of obedience to the Self. It is this important aspect which is overlooked by those who claim that 'only a firm belief in her right to happiness gives Serena the strength to escape' (Soliño 2002: 96), or the publishers in the United States of America who 'censored and refused to publish a translation of *El castillo de las tres murallas* as immoral because an oppressed female character escapes her crippling marriage by fleeing with the man she loves' (Ibid. 94). In addition to those fairy-tale heroines like Gerda in *The Snow Queen* who are clearly active, those who appear to be less active, such as Cinderella, nonetheless demonstrate change and growth. Serena acts when she withdraws to her rooms and waits, as she does again when she leaves. It is the one-sidedness of our Western culture which sees the external patterns of behaviour and not the inner motivation, and judges accordingly.

Abandoning the Child

Perhaps one of the surprising aspects of the story is that Serena leaves her young daughter behind. Robert McCully has written of *Hansel and Gretel*, where the children are also abandoned, though in a more cruel way: 'The tale conveys that this kind of uncaring parent may exist. There are mothers today who show an impassive face to their motherhood' (1991: 14). In other fairy tales the natural mother dies, making way for a cruel stepmother whose wickedness has to be overcome by the heroine. In this story the child is first taken away from her mother by a father who is mistrustful of the feminine. Then the mother abandons the child by escaping the confines of her home with the music teacher. 'If the mother dies, that means, symbolically, a realization that the daughter can no longer be identical with her, though the essential positive relationship remains' (von Franz 1993a: 167). Although Serena does not die, she is completely absent from Altalé's life, and the child develops very differently from her mother. Furthermore, in the dream which set in motion the events leading to Serena's departure, Altalé advised her mother that her request was for her [Altalé's] own good, suggesting that Serena's withdrawal and subsequent flight are closely linked with the child's well-being. In addition, the abandonment of children in fairy tales always marks the beginning of the key development, opening the door to the experience necessary for transformation to take place. In this case, the absent Serena acts as a focus for Altalé's rebelliousness against her father which is also a typical feature: 'In fairy tales where the mother is dead or has disappeared [...] she typically becomes the helpful instinct for the daughter' (von Franz 2002: 32).

The Structure of the Feminine Psyche

In her study of the structural psychology of women, Toni Wolff, the noted companion and collaborator of Jung, identified a polaric structure in which two pairs of aspects are evident: Mother and Hetaira/Companion, on what she called the personally related pole; and Amazon and Medial, on the impersonally related pole (1956). Serena is prevented by Lucandro from living the Mother aspect of the pole, and is thus freed to live its opposite, the Hetaira, with the music teacher. In her study of these four aspects, Nor Hall comments that, in contrast to the emphasis on the Mother and Amazon aspects noted by Toni Wolff at the time of her original draft in 1932, 'the Hetaira and Medial women were held in greater esteem in the Middle Ages and perhaps during the Renaissance. Once again it looks as if the part, or pole, that is repressed returns with great unwelcome force and confusion' (1980: 153). Hall comments on the reaction to this development: 'Few are the mothers or elders who have taught us the ways of the hetaira, or to value her consciously. Nonetheless, as tired masks and roles fall away, it may be that 'she of the sea', the love goddess who can be educated or drawn to the work of relationship, is floating up to disembark again in our culture' (Ibid. 153–4). Like anything that is unfamiliar, these roles are looked on negatively by the prevailing collective culture. Outside the fairy tale, and as can be seen frequently in the media, Serena's behaviour would in some quarters be criticised in light of prevailing collective values, more approving of the two more familiar aspects of Mother and Amazon, and tending to disapprove of situations in which a woman 'relates to man for his own sake, not as father to her children' (Claremont de Castillejo 1990: 65).

The Effect of Serena's Departure

Serena's flight with Gisel has an impact on all the principal inhabitants of the castle. In the case of Lucandro, he ages and takes to drink. Altalé holds onto the dream of seeing her mother again even though, because of the years that have passed, the image of her mother has faded. Jung has argued that 'the truth is that which helps us to live' (1977: 288), and the child's dream of being reunited with her mother represents Altalé's truth: 'Sabía que iba a aparecer, no podía vivir sin aquella certeza' [She knew that [Serena] would appear, she could not live without that certainty] (49–50). In the years following her departure Serena's presence grows in her daughter's imagination and dreams as does her longing to see her mother again.

The reaction by the villagers of Belfondo to Serena's departure is less marked. They had not been aware of Serena's existence until some merchants stopped at a village inn to rest, and it had filled them with hope that she might intercede on their behalf with Lucandro. Even the report by one of the merchants on their return through the town that Serena seemed unhappy and not interested in the things Lucandro was buying for her failed to dim their faith in her as a potential mediator. The role they designated for Serena is similar to the manner in which Catholics have traditionally considered the Virgin Mary, as a mediator of God's grace. In the case of Serena, this faith is clearly unfounded as she appears to neither know nor care about their lives, being too occupied with her own struggle for life in the claustrophobic castle. When they learn of her departure, the villagers transfer their faith to the other female figure, Altalé. This faith is better founded as the stories of Altalé's rebelliousness against her father encourage the villagers to move into Lucandro's better lands and prosper. When they were prevented from cultivating richer land, from growing more and better food, they were literally starving and dying. According to von Franz 'loneliness, poverty and hunger are stressed, typical states that result from animus-possession' (1993a: 183). Once again, it was Lucandro who mercilessly refused to allow them to move to better lands, and they seemed, as it were, paralysed by fear into obeying him despite the often fatal consequences (27). As El Saffar notes, 'the starving townspeople are a sign of Lucandro's own inner impoverishment' (1982: 47). Booker argues that 'the outcome of the personal drama of the hero and heroine often has repercussions which affect many more people than just themselves' (2005: 272). This was the case with Sleeping Beauty when all of the people and creatures in the castle woke up after she did and it is also evident in the developments in *Castillo*.

The villagers learn about life in the castle because Luva, first Serena's, later Altalé's maid, brings stories from the castle to the village and is thus the source of their knowledge of Altalé's rebelliousness and Lucandro's growing weakness. Her story-telling has a very positive outcome and she does not betray secrets in the way servants seem wont to do in traditional tales. Instead she gossips. According to Hall, 'Gossip is worth listening to: it means "god speaking through a woman"' (1980: 189). Luva's tales are certainly worth listening to from the villagers' point of view. This development is facilitated by Tituc's lessening fear of Lucandro which means that he now dares to give the key to other servants in the castle so they, too, can go down to the village.

Tituc and Luva play a significant role in the story as they unite castle and town, moving, literally, between the highest and the lowest. Rolón-Collazo describes Luva as the 'educadora-madre de Altalé' [Altalé's teacher-mother], a 'mujer audaz, decidida' [bold, determined woman], whose role is crucial: 'Le brinda la formación necesaria para que la niña pueda colaborar en la liberación de los belfondinos' [She affords [Altalé] the necessary education to enable the child to contribute to the liberation of the people of Belfondo] (2002: 147). Tituc is described as a slave. Von Franz says of the character of a slave in fairy tales that it is 'a frequent carrier for projection of the naïve, uncivilized, lowest level of awareness. The betrayal of a secret by a slave or someone lowly is a common motif' (2002: 30). In contrast to this more general depiction, Tituc is discreet. He also combines gentleness with physical strength, and is closest to the earth, through his gardening and farming, and to reality, all of which contrasts with his being from the East, more generally associated with a spiritual outlook. The physical threat he represents through his considerable size and his reputation for being unbeatable is only potential, having never been tested. In short, he reconciles pairs of opposite aspects and qualities. He is thus a true mediating principle. Furthermore, he is the fourth character named at the start of the story, after Lucandro, Serena, and Cambof Petapel (Luva is only mentioned later). The fourth aspect in Jungian psychology is considered to be the least conscious, and the door through which unconscious contents can enter. So it is appropriate that it is Tituc who brings the outsider, the music teacher, into the castle, and in a coach drawn by Lucandro's two horses, the black and the white.

Altalé's Tests

The first test Altalé has to undergo, at the age of eight, is one which her father had failed. Lucandro, basking in his material wealth, is represented as having acceded to the kind of temptations by the devil which Christ had resisted. Years later, Lucandro plays the devil's role in relation to his daughter:

> La llevó Lucandro a una sala magnífica en el sótano llena de joyas, de esculturas y de vajilla de un cristal precioso veteado de oro, [...] se había puesto de rodillas delante de ella y le había dicho: 'Todo esto es tuyo, Altalé, si no vuelves a nombrármela [a Serena].' (57)

> [Lucandro took her to a magnificent room in the basement full of jewels, sculptures and precious glassware veined with gold, [...] he had knelt before her and said: 'All this is yours, Altalé, if you don't mention her [Serena] again.']

In reply, Altalé smashes the glassware, making clear that all she is interested in is the return of her mother. That the room is in the basement is significant because the cellar is associated with the collective, with collective values – here with the obsessive materialism which Martín Gaite shunned: 'Yo pienso que en estos tiempos se da demasiada importancia a todo lo que se consigue a base de dinero. Creo que el culto al dinero que existe hoy es excesivo' (1999a) [I think that these days too much importance is given to whatever is achieved through money. I think the cult of money that exists today is excessive].[4] Although the room is full of many objects, it is the glass that Altalé focuses on, smashing it. Glass is cold, hard, brittle, and breaks easily; it is associated with 'being partly cut off, not intellectually, but emotionally' (von Franz 1993a: 158). Lucandro is trying to persuade Altalé to transfer her feelings from a real, warm human being – her mother – to a lot of objects, with which there is no possibility of relationship. Discussing the story of the temptations of Christ, David Cox [...] sees them as 'part of the preparation of Jesus for the work he was to do' (1975: 13). Lucandro, in testing his daughter, also serves to strengthen her resolve, for, by breaking the glass Altalé is symbolically refusing to allow her emotions to be imprisoned and she is also refusing in general to give up her dream of finding her mother in return for wealth or possessions. Furthermore, if we recall Snow White's glass casket in which she lay dead, Altalé's smashing of the glass suggests that she, unlike Snow White, will break out of the prison that holds her. Snow White succumbed to all the temptations, which were related to prizing the material over the spiritual. Here Altalé not only refuses her father's request but destroys the objects he employs in his temptation. In this way she ensures he cannot use them again and also discourages him from similarly tempting her in the future in view of the value he places on them and his protectiveness towards them. Thus, in rejecting this temptation, Altalé is freed and strengthened to go forward and embrace the subsequent tests, which will lead her into the realm of the feminine, to wholeness, relatedness, and freedom.

Altalé is a *chica rara* [strange girl], rebelling against the dominant collective materialistic value. In both the wish bestowed by her mother at her birth (that she understand her dreams) and Cambof Petapel's advice

4 Further criticisms of money in Martín Gaite's work include its rejection by Miss Lunatic in *Caperucita* and the obsessiveness with money of Sofía's husband, Eduardo, in *Nubosidad* through which he loses his sense of fun (1992: 14).

about being aware and alert, Altalé is urged to listen to, and act in accordance with, the Self. To be, in effect, a hero. Serena, too, acted in accordance with the Self and, as a result, was removed from the scene. She was not strong enough to stand up to the negative animus and, had she stayed in the castle, the story is likely to have remained undeveloped. Furthermore, 'Serena [...] has more power in her absence than perhaps she might have had had she remained' (El Saffar1982: 49).

Having passed the first test others follow and for these Altalé is given guidance which comes from a beggarwoman. The beggarwoman could be Serena in disguise although Martín Gaite insists that 'la identidad de esta mujer queda a juicio del lector' [the identity of this woman is left to the reader's discretion] (2002b: 132). She appears as Altalé's fifteenth birthday approaches, and, unseen, throws through the rails of the gate an ivory needlecase. Inside, in the place of the needles, is a message: 'Ha llegado la hora de que estés bien atenta a tus sueños. Y de que los entiendas tú sola' [The time has come for you to pay close attention to your dreams. And to understand them by yourself] (63). Robert McCully claims that 'wise figures in fairy tales simply *know*. Their beggary demeanour shows they live close to nature. They make those they encounter aware' (1991: 35), which is exactly the role this beggarwoman plays for Altalé. The needles recall Sleeping Beauty who pricked her finger on a spindle at the same age as Altalé. Here, however, not only are there no needles on which she might prick her finger and fall asleep, but she is called by the message to a new consciousness. According to Hall, 'to sleep for a hundred years because a spindle or distaff was turned against you would mean that you were "cursed" by the feminine side of the family. [...] Depending upon a girl's relationship to her mother and her mother's relationship to her own sexual nature the pubescent girl will bloom or suddenly fade' (1980: 197). From our knowledge of Serena, the expectation would be that Altalé would bloom.

Altalé's next test comes when, the night after receiving the message, she dreams that 'Serena era una de las estatuas del jardín. Le hablaba y le decía que se pusiera a excavar al pie del tilo que había detrás de su pedestal' [Serena was one of the statues in the garden. She spoke to her and told her to start digging at the foot of the lime tree behind her pedestal] (64). The leaves of this tree are heart-shaped, linking it to love and eros, and also the reputation of the tea made from its flowers (*tila*) – well known in Spain as calming and relaxing – links it with Serena (serenity) and contrasts it sharply with an increasingly agitated Lucandro. The gold key Altalé finds under the tree is also significant as gold is the only metal which won't rust or corrode, and it is associated with the sun (detested by Lucandro), as well as with eternity (von Franz 1996: 82–3) and wisdom (Bayley 2006: I, 154). For Neumann the key is 'the emblem of the Goddess who is mistress of birth and conception' (1963: 170), and, appropriately, here it is dug out of the earth. The Goddess Neumann is discussing here is Artemis/Hecate, and specifically in her role as 'mistress of the way down and of the lower way' (1963: 170). This description connects it with individuation and Jung's concern with completeness rather than perfection: 'This means that you have to come down, and that means a relative lowering of the level of the personality so that this lower level may not remain quite as dark as it was before. [...] But one has to sacrifice a certain amount of striving for perfection in order to avoid building up too black a counterposition' (von Franz 1993b: 59). An example of this kind of sacrifice would be when Altalé decides to stop going to visit Cambof Petapel so that she can fulfil the instruction to understand her dreams herself. Although believing that her decision will be misunderstood she is, nevertheless, willing to suffer the experience as continuing to visit would mean carrying on a pattern of behaviour in order to satisfy the demands of the ego, however altruistic her behaviour might appear to an outsider.

When Altalé sees the gold key she is careful to follow the instruction in the beggarwoman's message to understand everything herself by dissembling with Tituc who she has asked to do the digging and snatching it up while his back is turned. Martín Gaite criticised fairy-tale protagonists such as Sleeping Beauty and Cinderella: 'Ninguno colaboraba en las aventuras que les estaban destinadas por el autor ni se les ocurría nada de su cosecha para poner fin a aquella situación angustiosa' [Not one of them collaborated in the adventures which the author intended for them nor did they think of anything themselves which would put an end to that distressing situation] (1988a: 146). Such criticisms resonate with the views of critics today who argue that the female characters are passive, silent, resigned, waiting for their prince. Nevetheless, Martín Gaite herself records in 1962 in her notebooks how, like the protagonist of her prize-winning novella *Balneario*, Matilde, at times she waited for solutions to appear from out of the blue: 'Recuerdo cuando iba al parque hace unos años. [...]. De fuera pensaba que me iba a venir, como el maná, la liberación' [I recall when I used to go to the park some years ago [...]. I thought liberation would come from outside, like manna] (2002a: 50). Similarly later, in 1977, she writes, 'siempre esperaba, secretamente, algún acontecimiento que cambiara mi vida' [I was always waiting, secretly, for some event that would change my life] (Ibid. 425).

Robert McCully considers that, far from being passive, Cinderella grows and changes in the course of the story. He argues that she was initially too naïve: 'Cinderella was abundantly endowed with compassion, but of an undifferentiated sort' (1991: 55). After midnight she returns to her original state, which he describes as '[relapsing] into the old self-effacing habits of thought' (Ibid. 53). It is only through the development of guile that Cinderella is able to rise up to the challenge of her new self. This is seen, for example, when the stepsisters return from the ball only a short time after Cinderella herself, and she opens the door 'rubbing her eyes and stretching herself as if she had been just waked out of her sleep' (Lang 1978: 71). She even jokingly asks one of her stepsisters to lend her some clothes so that she can go to the ball the next day and see the beautiful mystery princess, and was 'very glad of the refusal; for she would have been sadly put to it if her sister had lent her what she asked for jestingly' (Ibid. 71). Altalé's dissembling with Tituc connects her to Cinderella through the guile which both display.

The quality of the metal of the key Altalé finds is closely related to what it opens – Serena's rooms – leading to another key and another treasure, Serena's notebook. It is this which confirms that her mother always knew they would be reunited, and when. Despite the difficulty Altalé finds in understanding Serena's writings, she is reluctant to seek Cambof's help because of the instruction to work it all out for herself. Although she misses Cambof, Altalé continues to be faithful to her dreams and other guidance, just as Serena was faithful to her dreams. The voluntary detachment of both Serena and Altalé from someone they love in order to follow their own path illustrates the loneliness of individuation and the courage and insight required.

Altalé's Final Test

The last test comes on Altalé's fifteenth birthday, the day on which the story ends, beginning with Serena telling her daughter in a dream to set free all the caged birds, with the promise that 'será la última prueba' [it will be the last test] (68). While it appears simply to anticipate Altalé's own impending freedom, along with that of her father and Cambof Petapel – for whom freedom also comes through transformation – it is more subtle than that. Birds represent thoughts, ideas which have not yet become real, not been earthed: 'Birds in general represent intuitive hunches [...] and have therefore to do with involuntary thoughts which are revealed to be true' (von Franz 1995b: 49). Altalé can set them free because the time has come for her to leave the castle in search of her mother. In the days leading up to her birthday her obedience to her dreams and intuitions, to the Self, is absolute, even when it brings a certain loneliness, such as her avoidance of Cambof Petapel. Yet this, too, can be seen in the fullness of the story as part of the preparation for her to move to the next stage with a new companion and advisor.

Beside the tests, there are other links here with the story of *Snow White*. In the traditional tale, three birds – the owl, the raven and the dove – watch over the dead/sleeping girl in her glass coffin 'out on the hill' (Grimm 1982: 80). Murphy argues that the three birds symbolise three spiritual traditions: the owl of the Greek goddess of wisdom, Athena; the raven of Woden, the Germanic god; and the dove of Christianity symbolising the Holy Spirit (2000: 131).[5] The three birds in *Snow White* watch over the dead girl before she is resurrected. Wisdom in Lucandro's castle is represented by Cambof Petapel who, in one of his incarnations, had been an eagle. Cambof has postponed his death to care for Altalé. The black bird which alighted on Serena's balcony on the day she met Gisel, would correspond to the raven – it acted as a reminder or warning to Serena to follow the dictates of the dream which was for the good of Altalé. Finally, there

5 The dove was the also the bird associated with Aphrodite, the Greek goddess of love.

are many unidentified birds living in cages in Altalé's bedroom, but one is singled out for the intelligence of its gaze. It is the color of fire and Altalé treats it as a friend. At the end of the story, when Altalé is preparing to leave the castle, she releases this favourite bird from the balcony of her mother's sewing-room. From there it flies to the prison constructed by Lucandro following Serena's departure, and returns with a message from the prisoner, Amir. In this role the *pájaro de fuego* [firebird] recalls the dove in the Old Testament which Noah sent out after the flood and which returned with an olive branch. The firebird messenger would, therefore, correspond to the dove watching over Snow White as it facilitates Altalé's departure from the castle. The bird's association with fire also links it to the Holy Spirit, which Christians believe appeared as tongues of fire at the first Pentecost.

The message Altalé receives from Amir asks her not to cry but to go down to the outer wall as 'nada es lo que parece' [nothing is what it seems] (70). A little earlier Cambof had brought Altalé a birthday present and

> lo último que vio Altalé fueron los reflejos de un anillo con piedra azul que llevaba siempre en el dedo índice. Cerró los ojos porque eran tan fuertes que la deslumbraban. Cuando los abrió, Cambof se había ido. (68–9)
>
> [the last thing Altalé saw were the glints from a ring with a blue stone that he always wore on his index finger. She closed her eyes because they were so strong that they dazzled her. When she opened them again, Cambof had gone.]

She has a similar experience when she releases the bird which flies to the window of the prison where Amir is being held, closing her eyes against the same blue glints from a ring on the index finger and, on opening her eyes, finds that the hand has disappeared. So each time she closes her eyes, dazzled, the scenes change. Just before leaving the castle she visits Cambof and finds him dead but no longer wearing the ring. Martín Gaite teases us with the transfer of the ring, anticipating the end of the story. A ring is 'a symbol of union. In its positive meaning, it stands for a consciously chosen obligation toward some divine power, that is, toward the Self' (von Franz 1996: 91). Lifeless, without consciousness, this obligation is no longer meaningful for Cambof, but it looks as though Amir has taken on the role.

The Transformation of Lucandro and Cambof Petapel

The differing responses of Serena and her daughter to Lucandro's gradual transformation illustrate the difference between them. It was Serena who first noticed how like the *brundas* he was becoming, and her response was a mix of pity and fear. Serena is afraid of Lucandro in general, particularly of his discovering the things that matter most to her, so it is not surprising that she should feel some fear. However, it also ensures that Lucandro will not receive any support from his wife should he wish to remain human as fear inhibits love. Cambof Petapel, too, is content to let the development go ahead on the grounds that, while his appearance and behaviour may seem monstrous in his present form, they might appear natural if he were transformed into a *brunda*. In contrast, Altalé, rebelling fearlessly against her father, feels only pity. Altalé is freer than her mother to see 'the other' – in this case, Lucandro – as he is. Nevertheless, Cambof Petapel considers Altalé's feeling for her father to be wasted, and Lucandro is clearly unresponsive to sympathy as he fails to recognise his situation. However, Cambof Petapel is also a principle in need of renewal. In Altalé's more compassionate response lies the suggestion of the future development of this principle.

Lucandro's development, or deterioration, involves shunning the light – a symbol of consciousness – whether this comes from the sun or from Altalé's eyes. This seems to represent an unwillingness to face or to engage with the reality both within and around him. The unconscious seeks to become conscious and it can only do so where human beings take an attitude of respect towards it. Where it is resisted it can break through with disastrous consequences, as Nor Hall warns in connection with the goddess, who is a personification of the Self: 'If she is not welcomed (or worse, is devalued and kept outside the outer walls) she will break the doors down and come in to individual or cultural consciousness in a negative, devouring, [...] way' (1980: 18). The other main characters in *Castillo* develop a positive attitude towards the unconscious through their attention to dreams and their alertness to other messages. Lucandro closes himself to all but his own ego drive for power over his family and the villagers, turning his back on the unconscious. Following the desertion of his wife and then the rebelliousness of both his daughter and the villagers, he tries desperately to retain some control. Just as he seeks to live in the dark or the night, so he lives the darker side within him in by trying to instil fear, building a prison as a deterrent and also to detain those who disobey him. When the unconscious breaks through it increases his lack of awareness of the reality around him, causing him to reveal signs of disorientation, even madness. Inhuman behaviour and evil result in this kind of isolation, which has nothing in common with the period of solitude which Serena experienced.[6] Eventually the unconscious swallows him when his transformation into a *brunda* is completed and he drops, appropriately, into the water of the castle moat – symbol of the unconscious – and into a role in which all that is required of him is to instil fear in strangers, thus fulfilling the desire he had as a human being.

Erich Neumann, in his study of the development of the relationship between human beings and the inner feminine, argues that the unconscious is always experienced as feminine. In contrast to those who develop a conscious, creative relationship with the unconscious, there are others who undergo a different, regressive transformation as a result of the encounter: 'The ambivalent female mana figure may guide the male or beguile him. Side by side with sublimation stands abasement, as, for example, where man is transformed into an animal, where the human is lost to a superior bestial power' (1963: 305). We saw earlier how Lucandro appeared to have

6 In *Memories Dreams Reflections* Jung tells the story of a woman who visited him once to confess that years before she had murdered a female friend in order to marry her husband (1983: 143–5). The husband died soon afterwards, her daughter got away from her, her favourite horse 'shied and threw her', and her favourite dog became 'stricken with paralysis'. She felt 'morally done for' and obliged to confess. Interestingly, in light of Martín Gaite's attitude to psychiatrists discussed in Chapter 1, Jung says that the woman 'wanted to find a person who could accept her confession without prejudice' and that 'the person would have to be a doctor rather than a professional confessor'. The reason for this is partly the same as Martín Gaite's reason for rejecting psychiatrists and partly that the priest would be a bad mirror: 'She would have suspected a priest of listening to her because of his office, and of not accepting the facts for their own sake but for the purpose of moral judgement' (Ibid. 144).

behaved like one who had succumbed to the temptation to wealth and power which Christ had resisted; how, after ignoring the needs of his soul and his wife, he, in turn, turned tempter and was defeated by his young daughter. Finally he is defeated by the (feminine) unconscious which he has so long neglected. Martín Gaite, through the wise man, Cambof Petapel, puts a positive spin on the transformation of Lucandro, but there is no doubt that it is a lower state and a regression.

Because of the transfer of the ring, discussed above, and the voice of Amir, which is exactly the same as the old wise man's voice, it appears that Cambof Petapel is reincarnated in Amir, the young handsome stranger who encouraged the villagers to take Lucandro's better lands and to be free. Martín Gaite later confirmed this to be the case when she referred to 'Amir, avatar juvenil de Cambof' [Amir, youthful incarnation of Cambof] (2002b: 263). The index finger is used for pointing, indicating, showing the way, while the colour blue is identified as 'depicting spiritual contents' (Jung 1960: 211 n.122), and as 'the symbol of the truth' (Bayley 2006: I, 211). This suggests that the traditional, non-materialistic, meditative spiritual aspect which had lost all influence, is transformed into a spirited, energetic and passionate young man knowledgeable about the physical world, who promotes a sense of self-worth among the villagers, encouraging them to take the better lands and put an end to their hunger and poverty. Unlike Lucandro's response to Cambof, the villagers listen to Amir and respond to his words. Thus, apart from a short period when Amir is imprisoned by Lucandro, the spiritual aspect is no longer confined to a tower and withdrawn from the world, but goes out into it, and is concerned with truth and justice. With the transformation of Lucandro into an animal, Altalé would now represent the worldly or material aspect, and these two figures – Amir and Altalé – are working together. The relatedness between these two aspects was initiated very early in the story when Lucandro, again not realising the significance of his actions, created a room for his daughter in the tower, close to that of Cambof Petapel.

There is further meaning in the index finger: 'The thumb, stout and strong, denotes the Chief Person of the Godhead; the third finger, taller than the others, denotes Christ, the most important Person in man's salvation; and the second finger, as between the others, denotes the Holy

Ghost proceeding from the Father and the Son' (Bayley 2006: II, 334–5). This connects the spiritual aspect in *Castillo* with the development of Christianity – the Age of the Holy Spirit – which has its parallel in the individuation process as was discussed in Chapter 1.

The Ending: Positive or Negative?

Martín Gaite has referred to *Castillo* in talks and also in her *Cuadernos* where she records a dream she had about her first fairy tale. In the dream she told her mother that 'lo mejor está al final, todo se entiende al final. Es una especie de jeroglífico' [the best comes at the end, everything can be understood at the end. It's a kind of puzzle] (2002a: 522). In a simple reading of the tale, this is a reasonable assessment. However, in the Jungian approach to the fairy tales one of the starting points is to look at the number of characters at the beginning and end of the story. Typically there are often three at the start and four at the end (symbolising wholeness), or where there are four at the start there is usually a problem, for example they may be all male or all female, and so there is a lack of balance, or one of them might be ill. In *Castillo* there are four characters identified at the start (Lucandro, Serena, Cambof Petapel, and Tituc), while at the end two remain in the castle (Tituc and Luva), and another two leave (Amir and Altalé). In Jungian terms the ending does not represent the attainment of wholeness and, while in some respects it explains earlier events in the story, in others it obscures.

When Altalé leaves the castle to go to the Muralla Erizada as directed by the message, she climbs up a rope alone and is carried down a ladder by Amir. A rope is a much simpler means of climbing, and one which is less easy to manoeuvre, yet Altalé was able to climb it easily. All the dedication and determination she has shown in following her own heart and instinct, her fidelity to her dreams and, thereby, the Self, make this ascent easy. There is a gate in the wall, which Altalé knows how to open, yet Martín Gaite has created this potentially more challenging means of leaving the castle, which carries its own symbolism. Altalé has already walked down the 365 steps of the castle, but at this outer wall her past and future lives seem to be depicted in the climbing and descending. Whereas the rope can be used for many other purposes including fastening and hanging, the ladder is only used for climbing up and descending. A ladder is associated with integrating contents into consciousness (Jung 1953: 61), and also with uniting the highest and the lowest. Therefore, it appears that Altalé must now realise her dreams and achieve wholeness in the outside world, an interpretation which is supported by her walking away from the castle. The path of light which opens in the snow for the young couple, easing their path, also denotes consciousness. The castle garden resembles the Garden of Eden, which was a place of unconsciousness before Adam and Eve ate the apple from the Tree of Knowledge of Good and Evil, following which they were unable to remain there. Adam and Eve were tempted and failed the test. Lucandro failed the test before he moved into the castle and we saw how he grew in unconsciousness, so his 'development' is regressive. Altalé was tempted with riches and passed the test, so her leaving is a positive move. Thus, leaving the castle and the garden could be seen as a move towards a higher level of consciousness which, initially, would appear as a new and tentative state.

This ending provides a further link with the story of *Sleeping Beauty*. Brenda Crowther argues that when Sleeping Beauty awakens following the prince's kiss, the feminine life of the kingdom – so neglected by the king, her father, in his rejection of anything that was not conventionally 'good' – is redeemed: 'The Eros quality of the kingdom is redeemed, the darkness is integrated into the light, the pairs of opposites are united and the level of collective consciousness is raised' (2013: 20). For Crowther, what comes into consciousness is 'the new feminine constellation of life' (Ibid. 20). This ending corresponds to *Castillo* in the relatedness of Altalé and Amir in which neither one is dominated by the other.

On the other hand, a more negative interpretation could be supported by the fact that the couple seem to head west. This was the direction towards which Serena looked from her window. Now as the young couple walk away from the castle, Altalé sings Gisel's song, asking which is the way to freedom. In response Amir indicates the top of the Ladera de los Lobos.

Thus, they would be walking towards the sunset. Amir had also pointed in this direction from his prison when Altalé was in her mother's rooms singing Gisel's song about freedom. According to Neumann, discussing the archetypal symbol of the underworld, 'the sun sinks down in the west, where it dies and enters into the womb of the underworld that devours it. For this reason the west is the place of death' (1963: 158). Von Franz interprets sunset as 'the blocking out of consciousness' (in Boa 1994: 60), in contrast to sunrise – 'that symbolic location from which arise new enlightenments and revelations of the collective unconscious' (von Franz 1997a: 41).

The transformation of Cambof Petapel into Amir, and his joining with Altalé seemed to suggest that this is a new revelation of the collective unconscious, uniting the two principles, reconciling the opposites – material/spiritual, female/male. In the light of this interpretation, the ending suggests that freedom would lie in death or unconsciousness, a response which carries a certain hopelessness unless, like Murphy, one interprets it as the heaven to which the Prince/Christ took Snow White for he considers that Snow White really did die, without any resurrection in this life (2000: 127). Then there is the fact that it is snowing. Symbolically, this could mean that the environment is too cold, that is, not favourable, for this new symbol to flourish, and, therefore, it may need to wait in the unconscious until the time is ready for it to emerge. In Chapter 1 the impact of progress in individuation on community was discussed and identified as relatedness through the Self. Discussing 'the image of a human community produced and governed by the Self' von Franz cautions that 'since this is not yet [...] a realized goal of humanity, it appears in most myths as a postmortal goal, that is, one still in the Beyond, hidden in the unconscious' (1980: 178), which seems to be the outcome here.

Furthermore, that Altalé does not climb down, but is carried by Amir, despite the fact that she has already made by herself the more difficult ascent via the rope, is a little surprising. Martín Gaite's novels often contain motifs from the *novela rosa* [romantic novel] genre, and this may be one of them. On the other hand, having identified Amir and Altalé respectively as representing the spiritual and material aspects which are now united, the fact that Amir carries Altalé down the ladder could also suggest that the spiritual part is now the stronger and 'carries' or leads the other. This would also support the interpretation that this is a new way of living, a higher level of consciousness, which belongs to the future

As discussed earlier, the number symbolism at the beginning was four, including a weak feminine aspect and two ruling principles in need of renewal. At the end there are only two figures in the castle, Tituc and Luva. The whereabouts of Serena, Gisel, Altalé and Amir are unknown, and their story develops elsewhere, with the signs suggesting that it continues in the unconscious. Two is an incomplete number, but the number of *brundas* increases to thirteen following Lucandro's transformation. The internal sum of 13 (1+3) is four, so this looks like another example of wholeness at the end but, again, only in the unconscious, symbolised by the water of the *Foso de las Brundas* [Moat of the *Brundas*], and, therefore, appears to represent a kind of failure. In the castle, apart from the two servants, there is also the lifeless body of Cambof Petapel which might suggest, to those who did not know otherwise, that the spiritual aspect is dead. Then there is the transformation of Lucandro which, again, to those who had not seen him fall into the moat, might look simply like a disappearance. To an observer it would appear that all that remained was a stage of emptiness, barren and unspiritual.

Nevertheless Neumann, in his interpretation of the story of 'Eros and Psyche' from the tale by Apuleius, describes sunset as the time 'when the sun returns home, when the masculine principle approaches the feminine' (1971: 100). Noon would represent the time when the powers of the masculine principle were at their highest and most destructive, burning, drying out, 'rabid and ruinous' (Ibid. 100). But 'it is not always high noon, and the masculine is not always deadly' (Ibid. 100). So the time of the sunset is also a time when the feminine can 'enter into a fruitful relation, that is to say, a love relation, with the masculine' (Ibid. 101), which corresponds to the popular romantic view of sunset. Thus Serena's looking towards the sunset from her balcony can be seen as a desire for such a relationship, which seemed impossible with a husband who rejected eros in favour of power. This view is further supported by the number symbolism of Altalé's age – one plus five is six, the number concerned with marriage and the relationship between the sexes – and also by the renewal of the new spiritual principle, and the unification of opposites in Altalé and Amir. As discussed above, Amir's carrying Altalé down the ladder could also indicate that the spiritual principle was the leading aspect, and this interpretation is supported by Amir's pointing the way. Both interpretations of the heading west are possible since anything new is born first in the unconscious. Therefore, the possibility exists that the new spirit may be swallowed up in the unconscious before it has had a chance to develop or, like the sun, it may emerge again from the east. The story leaves open the question of whether the new developments indicated will emerge again in the future.

CHAPTER 3

¿Cómo crecer? The Process of Individuation in *El pastel del diablo*

Introduction

Carmen Martín Gaite suggests two ways of reading *Pastel*: as a child making up stories or as 'el proceso recordado de mi vocación de narradora' [the remembered process of my vocation as a storyteller] (2002b: 264). Critics suggest other interpretations. María Elena Soliño considers that 'we can read *Caperucita*, *El castillo*, and *El pastel* as autobiographical texts to the extent that they portray the difficulties, and possible triumphs, of a girl coming to writing in a patriarchal society such as Franco's Spain' (2002: 104). Others see the journey in the story-within-a-story as a Grail Quest (Hernández Álvarez 2005) or as the initiation quest of the hero in Joseph Campbell's *The Hero with a Thousand Faces* (Myers 2003–4).

Connections have been made with other works by Martín Gaite including *Castillo* (Hernández Álvarez 2005: 157), *Las ataduras* (Jiménez 1992)[1] and the writer's first longer work, *Balneario*. Although there are links between the two, *Balneario* represents aspects of an individuation process which is unrealised, whereas in *Pastel* a successful individuation process is represented vividly and in some detail in symbolic form. This reading is compatible with the view of both writer and critics that *Pastel* represents Martín Gaite's development as a writer, since individuation, being concerned with the development of the unique individual, includes the realisation of one's vocation.

1 In her talk, 'Galicia en mi literatura', Martín Gaite also draws parallels between Sorpresa in *Pastel* and Alina in *Las ataduras* (2002b: 128–30).

The individuation process is ongoing, as the Jungian psychoanalyst and writer, Murray Stein, writes: 'Individuation is never finished or completed, because there is always more unconscious potential to bring into the personality's full integration [...], we must also conclude that an imago, once filled out after midlife has been traversed, shows the indelible outlines of the "whole person"' (1998: 38). Stein defines imago as 'a living, evolving psychic structure with roots in the archetypal unconscious and ultimately in the self. It both frees people to be what they most deeply are, and it defines who and what they are and what their lives are about. [...] Once we grasp a person's imago, we understand something essential about them. We see them whole' (1998: 133–4). At the end of the inner journey which Sorpresa makes in *Pastel*, the reader sees her whole, and those indelible outlines to which Stein refers are clearly visible.

Reconciliation of Opposites

The problem of the opposites is an important aspect of the individuation process, arising in both the encounter with shadow figures – the unknown and sometimes undesired aspects of oneself – and with the contrasexual element – animus and anima – whose opposite nature is self-evident. What is sought in the process is the reconciliation of those opposites: 'The goal of individuation is the synthesis of opposites, once they have become conscious, in the self' (Jaffé 1986: 119). This is the approach taken by Martín Gaite generally, for she seeks more their reconciliation than polarisation and this, von Franz argues, is the province of the feminine (1997a: 14). This was evident in the ending of *Castillo* and is particularly significant in *Pastel*, where the development of Sorpresa through the process of individuation depicted in the tale illustrates the creative outcome which occurs when opposites are reconciled. This reconciliation can also be associated with the Christian Feast of Pentecost when, after Christ had ascended into Heaven, the Holy Spirit descended on the apostles and Christ's mother in the form of tongues of fire, for Sorpresa transforms potentially destructive flames into creative fire through individuation.

The Setting

Whereas the settings of traditional fairy tales are generally non-specific, the setting of *Pastel* is recognisable as a small Spanish village with its church and priest, its grandee, but no school of its own.[2] It has in common with traditional tales that the time is not specified, but it is less vague than *Castillo*. The village is untouched by modern technology, it is a place where cars and gramophones are luxury items available only to the very rich. This is also true of a good education, since the little girl, Sorpresa, has to leave school aged only ten when the schoolteacher finds himself unable to teach her anything else, and there is no alternative option available to her family.

Marie-Louise von Franz says of older parents that 'such a situation – for instance, when the parents marry late or have no children for a long time – often brings on tragic difficulties' (1996: 190). Sorpresa's parents, like so many in traditional fairy stories, longed for a child for many years. However, Sorpresa appears to bring them mostly distress since after her birth they seem less happy and disagree about the child's welfare. The mother, Remigia, whose ambitions for her only child are narrow and conventional – that she should marry and have children – tries to impose a traditional lifestyle on her daughter, believing that Sorpresa can be made to learn to accept her *destino* [fate]. For the young girls in the village this means an early marriage, and like Lucandro's attitude to Serena's potential influence on Altalé, Sorpresa's mother welcomes the idea of her daughter marrying 'un hombre honrado y trabajador que le quitara de la cabeza todos los pájaros que se le habían metido en ella' [an honourable and hardworking man who would get rid of all the featherbrained notions that had got into her head] (89).

Destino is used here in the opposite sense to that associated with the process of individuation in which a person discovers her real *destino*, which

2 David González Couso, who has undertaken several studies of *Pastel* and *Caperucita*, highlights the setting of *Pastel*, along with *Retahílas* and *Las ataduras*, in the Galician village, San Lorenzo de Piñor, where Martín Gaite spent so many summers as a child and young woman (2008c).

would be her unique role in life. Here the collective, opposed to any kind of individuality or expression of uniqueness, prescribes what every young woman (and man)'s place in life will be, and can, therefore, be said to be opposed to individuation. Whereas Altalé rebels against her father, Sorpresa's fate is to rebel against her mother and the dominant collective values promoted by the collective feminine, which are stifling to her dreams of freedom and creativity. In contrast, her father, much more positively, searches for the means to give his daughter the books that will stimulate and develop her, although it proves to be an impossible task because of their relative poverty.

Power in the village resides with the priest and *el señor de la Casa Grande* [the owner of the Big House]. *El señor* represents the worldly principle, typical of the king in fairy tales, and holds the same kind of fascination for the villagers as Lucandro. However, while he provides a source of employment for some, he does not wield the same kind of power over their lives. The villagers are aware of his moral shortcomings – according to Sorpresa's mother, '[lleva] mala vida' (92) [he has a dissolute lifestyle] – which might be expected to make him, for the villagers, inferior to the spiritual principle. However, the spiritual principle, represented by the priest, defers to *el señor*, which leads to the latter's playing a role in the naming of Sorpresa. Because it does not figure in the list of saints' names, the priest consults *el señor*, who is well-travelled and well-read, about its acceptability. *El señor* advises that, although he hasn't heard of Our Lady of the Surprise, she ought to exist in view of the Virgin Mary's propensity for appearing suddenly to those who seek her help.

This imaginative response means that Sorpresa is given the name her parents chose for her. It is, therefore, to intelligence, learning, culture, and the confidence born of these, to which the priest defers. The role played here by *el señor* corresponds to the one he will play later in the story in Sorpresa's imagination. The priest initially looks to the law, the rules of the Church which prefers children to be given the name of a saint.[3] According to Nor Hall, an approach which is concerned with rules and laws excludes the

3 'In Baptism, the Christian receives his name in the Church. Parents, grandparents and the pastor are to see that he be given a Christian name. The patron saint provides

feminine, which would be more concerned with the individual situation. The Church is an authority in the world and the teaching on baptismal names is a Church law. *El señor* looks at the *meaning* of the word, which links him to the highest level of the Jungian creative animus. Jiménez emphasises the similarities with the man in black in *Cuarto:* 'Ambos personajes están rodeados de un intrigante halo diabólico que los hace atractivos y poderosos' [Both characters are surrounded by an intriguing satanic aura which makes them attractive and powerful] (1992: 88–9). And both can also be described as positive animus figures or creative spirits.

As critics have commented, in *Pastel* there are aspects of the same fairy tale which was reflected in *Castillo*, namely *Sleeping Beauty*. Both couples had a daughter after much waiting and longing. The king and queen 'went to all the waters in the world; vows, pilgrimages, all ways were tried, and all to no purpose' (Lang 1975: 54). Similarly, Sorpresa's parents prayed for a child and made vows. Both children were given splendid christening parties. However, in *Sleeping Beauty* the thirteenth wise woman (or the eighth in some versions) was overlooked and not invited to the royal christening. This rejection led to her cursing the child, saying 'that the Princess should have her hand pierced with a spindle and die of the wound' (Lang 1975: 55). Only the softening by the twelfth wise woman, who had not yet made her wish, turned death into sleep: 'Instead of dying, she shall only fall into a profound sleep, which shall last a hundred years' (Ibid. 55). At Sorpresa's christening, there is only one wise woman, Balbina, who predicts Sorpresa's fate: 'Hará preguntas que no le sabrá contestar nadie y deseará siempre todo aquello que no puede tener' [She'll ask questions that no one will be able to answer and she'll always want what she can't have] (83). Balbina's role is not to bring good or ill to the child but simply to say what she sees, not a curse but a prophecy, which is a function of the medial feminine. In Toni Wolff's polaric structure of the feminine psyche, with its poles of Mother/Hetaira or Companion and Medial/Amazon, the medial feminine mediates knowledge from unconscious to conscious: 'In the unconscious, time has no meaning and all things are already known'

---

a model of charity and the assurance of his prayer' (Catholic Catechism 1994: para 2165).

(Claremont de Castillejo 1990: 70). Balbina seems far from being an evil or even supernatural figure, but very human, and she plays the drum at village funerals. In addition, unlike the original fairy tale, at Sorpresa's christening no one was left out.

As if to ensure that there is no further delving into the enigmatic prediction – which the child's parents were determined to do – Martín Gaite kills off Balbina on the day of the christening. Having played her part, Balbina goes off into the trees to enjoy some wine and cakes and is found dead the next day. However, despite being a baby in a cradle at the time, Sorpresa's view of the day and of Balbina are quite different. As she grows up and hears the many versions her father tells of the event, she creates her own image of Balbina, converting her in her imagination into a typical fairy-tale witch whom she blames for everything:

> El personaje que tenía la culpa de todos los males se llamaba la bruja Balbina. Era una vieja harapienta de ojos amarillos y nariz ganchuda, tocada con un sombrero puntiagudo. (153)
>
> [The one who was to blame for all the ills was called Balbina the witch. She was an old woman in rags with yellow eyes and a hooked nose, wearing a pointed hat.]

Thus Sorpresa recreates the story in a way that brings her closer to the traditional fairy-tale heroine with whom she has been compared, imagining that she has been cursed in her cradle by the dark figure of Balbina. As a *curandera* [wise woman], Balbina resembles the Grimms' twelve invited guests who are described as wise women rather than fairies, along with the thirteenth who was uninvited. It is the thirteenth wise woman's response to the rejection that has coloured her image in the minds of listeners and readers and represented her as being intrinsically evil, a real witch.

'The witch is an archetypal aspect of the Great Mother. She is the neglected Mother Goddess, the Goddess of the earth in her destructive aspect' (von Franz 1995b 126). She has in common with the thirteenth wise woman in *Sleeping Beauty* this aspect of being ignored. Yet the rejected wise woman can also be seen as the source of the redemption of Briar-Rose/Sleeping Beauty and of the whole of the life in the palace. Briar Rose had to integrate and relate to the shadow aspects rather than living only the one-sided aspects favoured by her father. Sorpresa does live out a number of characteristics that are rejected and frowned upon by the adults in the village as not being typical of their view of the feminine: her liveliness, her lack of interest in marrying young (or even in marrying), her energy and independence represent aspects which they, like Briar Rose's father, reject.

In contrast to the rejected wise woman, Balbina's prediction related specifically to unanswered questions and unfulfilled desires. Sorpresa's challenging of this fate harbours positive aspects. Hernández Álvarez sees Sorpresa as the new Perceval who goes to the *Casa Grande*/Grail Castle to ask the all-important questions: '¿Cómo crecer, cómo transformarse, cómo vivir, cómo contarlo?' [How to grow up, how to change, how to live, how to tell it all?] (2005: 158). The growth in consciousness associated with Adam and Eve's eating the apple and having to leave the Garden of Eden is denied to Perceval who has 'failed by *not* eating of [the Tree of Knowledge], by *not* asking, *not* becoming conscious of the mysterious thing that he has seen' (Jung & von Franz 1971: 181). In Hernández Álvarez's parallel, therefore, asking her burning questions should lead Sorpresa to greater consciousness, which would also be the effect of individuation.

When Sorpresa is obliged to leave school, her father, like the priest, sees *el señor* as the source of a solution as he has lots of books – again, the connection with the word. Eunice Myers interprets the father's intention differently, as 'looking for financial support rather than books' (2003–4: 411), and the text permits both interpretations. However, her suggestion that the mother fears *el señor's* erudition seems less well-founded. It seems more likely, as Carbayo-Abengozar indicates, that 'no quiere que Sorpresa vaya a la casa grande porque el señor lleva "mala vida"' [she doesn't want Sorpresa to go to the Big House because the man of the house has 'a dissolute lifestyle'] (1998a: 137). While Sorpresa's mother is happy to earn some extra money by working in the *Casa Grande* when there is a party, she seems afraid of being dependent on *el señor*, and particularly of any contact between him and her daughter. This decision, which leaves the ten-year-old child without further educational opportunity, is heavily criticised by Soliño:

> Why should a smart child cause fear? Beyond merely embarrassing the teacher, her status as an unsatisfied non-conformist makes her a threat to the established order in which men and women each perform their specific roles without questioning the system. In addition, both the teacher and Sorpresa's mother believe that at her age she should focus her attention more on learning to be a good wife than on books. (2002: 102)

While Remigia's attitude is clear, the teacher takes a quite different view in his conversation with Zenón, Sorpresa's father: 'Talento tiene mucho, y creo que podría dedicarse a los estudios. Pero necesita libros, muchos más libros de los que puedo darle yo. Y también otros profesores' [She has a lot of talent and I think she could get an education. But she needs books, many more books than I can give her. And also other teachers] (88).

Hernández Álvarez rightly believes that Sorpresa has a vocation which she alone has to live and that cutting ties with traditional education are part of achieving this (2005: 157). The way forward is indicated in that when she is thrown back on her own resources her love of telling stories grows. Finding one's true vocation is an important outcome of the individuation process, as von Franz confirms: 'The true process of individuation – the *conscious* relationship with [...] one's own psychic center – usually begins with an injury or some state of suffering, which represents a kind of vocation that is not often recognized as such' (1997a: 300).

The Individuation Process

Von Franz's claim that the individuation process begins 'with [...] some state of suffering' in which 'the ego feels it is being obstructed in the fulfilment of its will or desires' (1997a: 300) is confirmed in *Pastel*. The obstruction occurs for Sorpresa when she is left alone by her best friend, thwarted in her desire to grow up, and criticised as 'mala' by her parents and others in the village. One expression of Sorpresa's difference from other girls her age is her friendship with fifteen-year-old Pizco which is founded on their love of story – on her part, inventing and telling, on his, listening. When Pizco, irritated, criticises her on *la noche de San Juan* [St John's Eve], telling her she should stay at home and help her mother instead of spending her time up in the hills, he is only repeating what he has heard others in the village say. Yet Sorpresa isn't bad or evil, just different to the others in the village, a *chica rara* [strange girl]. However, she represents a shadow figure for her critics – strange, unrecognised, containing lots of energy, vilified, not valued, and she becomes the target for their collective projection. The effect on Sorpresa of the accumulated criticism from her parents, the priest and the women in the village is that she threatens to live out the projection by really being bad, 'más mala que el diablo' [worse than the devil] (104). This desire is born of a rage against all those who criticise her for being just that. Fernández Hoyos sees parallels between the attitude of the villagers and Martín Gaite's *malos espejos* which she cites:

> 'Son miradas [...] que no se aventuran a internarse [...] Son miradas que abominan lo intrincado' [1982: 19]. [...] Esas miradas son precisamente las que dominan en un pueblo como el de Sorpresa. (2004: 573)
>
> ['Theirs are eyes [...] that dare not go deeply into anything [...] Eyes that detest anything complex' [1982: 19]. [...] These are exactly the kind of prying eyes that predominate in a village like Sorpresa's.]

In her compassionate study of the feminine psyche, *Women Who Run with the Wolves*, Clarissa Pinkola Estés describes the damage done to Janis Joplin by her community, which echoes Sorpresa's situation:

> Her creative life, innocent curiosity, love of life, somewhat irreverent approach to the world during her growing-up years were mercilessly vilified by her teachers and many of those who surrounded her in the 'good-girl' white Southern Baptist community of her time. Though she was an A student and a talented painter, she was ostracized by other girls for not wearing makeup and by neighbors for liking to climb a rock outcropping outside town and singing up there with her friends. (1998: 234)

The result of all this unjustified criticism, according to Estés, was that 'she could no longer tell when enough was enough' (1998: 233), and this lack of instinct led to her death at a young age. While the culture is different, it is not difficult to see the same kind of attitudes surrounding Sorpresa in her own community and the negative, aggressive-defensive response they provoke in her. Claremont de Castillejo claims that the deepest darkest shadow in women is that of the witch, which she describes as the desire for power (1990: 41–2). Sorpresa's wish to be really bad seems to be born of a similar desire, and the strength of the affect accompanying the declaration suggests there is a real danger of her acting out this destructive aspect of herself. Sorpresa's distorted image of Balbina also indicates that this shadow element is being projected onto the *curandera* [wise woman].

Pizco's criticism of Sorpresa opens up a gap between the two friends which is widened by Sorpresa's pride. He has accused her of being jealous of him because she is too young to go to *la noche de San Juan* celebrations and, not to be outdone, she pretends she is going to the *Casa Grande* to help her mother in the kitchen there. Having eavesdropped on her parents' conversations and overheard discussions about the *Casa Grande*, the fascination of that forbidden place is increased in her imagination. The rupture with Pizco makes a seamless transition to the story she will spend much of the night inventing and which begins with her choosing the road on the left and running along it without looking back, an early indication of the story's important theme of not looking back. Their descent of the hill also anticipates the rest of the story, with Pizco taking a longer, easier cattle track and Sorpresa a more dangerous route. This prefigures Pizco's following a more typical way of life, one which is both silly and sad in Sorpresa's eyes (161). In contrast, Sorpresa, in true *chica rara* fashion, will follow her unique path – the path of individuation, with its loneliness and unpredictability. Hernández Álvarez again sees separation as a necessary part of the hero's development (2005: 158).

The Story-within-a-Story

As in a number of other novels and stories by Martín Gaite, this embedded tale takes place at night and through the night. This contrasts it with the main story where the events are depicted for the most part during the day or in the early evening. Night, dark, suggests the unconscious and the encounters which Sorpresa has with various figures parallel the encounters of the ego with aspects of the unconscious. As in *Castillo*, these aspects may be symbolised by human figures, as well as by inanimate objects.

It is argued by Jungians that the process of individuation is not chosen by the ego – it is the Self which compels the ego to embark on the journey. Some fairy tales, too, warn of the dangers of seeking contact with the unconscious for personal gain. That Sorpresa finds the main door to the garden of the *Casa Grande* opens without any effort suggests she is being invited in. This is confirmed by the fact that, when almost immediately she changes her mind, the door, which has closed by itself behind her, remains closed and she is unable to find the means to open it. Before she is able to enter the house itself, the number three figures prominently: in the three black limousines sitting outside and three landings on the stairs up to the door. The number three 'has to do with a process of development in time' (von Franz 1997a: 206), which is appropriate for the start of an adventure. Also, three is regarded as 'a creative flow' (von Franz 1995a: 260), which seems a positive indication of what may follow. The symbolism of the door knocker in the shape of a lion is also important. Lions, like tigers, can represent 'negative, destructive emotions' (von Franz 1990: 23), as in Sorpresa's desire to be really bad. Eunice Myers, citing Joseph Campbell, claims that the lion knocker is 'a typical guardian of the first threshold' (2003–4: 413). Campbell's argument is that 'the approaches and entrances to temples are flanked and defended by colossal gargoyles: dragons, lions, devil-slayers with drawn swords, resentful dwarfs, winged bulls [...] to ward away all incapable of encountering the higher silences within' (1968: 92). However, this house is full of sound and Sorpresa seems to be being invited in. Sad music is coming from the house and sadness, with its associations with tears and, therefore, water, represents a contrast to the fiery rage she has recently expressed. Hall considers music to 'mediate the unknown' (1980: 236). If further proof were needed that this encounter with the unconscious is invited, the door is sufficiently ajar for Sorpresa to slip through with ease.

In these first stages, both outside and inside the house, the darkness is broken by some light. This may be the light of the full moon or, where the trees are so thick that the moonlight cannot penetrate, the artificial light of the globe lights at the bottom of the steps. Then there is the torch held by a wax model in the first room Sorpresa enters which also holds a tray of small, coloured drinks which glow. The moon, the globe lights, and the torch are like flashes of consciousness, while the drinks, described as 'licor' [alcohol], are a means of accessing the unconscious artificially, hence the light they give off is fuzzier. Alcohol is also a means of opening the door to the unconscious and of gaining courage, and this is its effect on Sorpresa for she feels less afraid, less timid. The liquid in the glasses is of different colours and the glasses themselves have golden letters inscribed on them – Sorpresa chooses one with the word 'más' [more], which seems to be linked to her desire to be grown up. Critics have noted the similarity between this scene and aspects of *Alice in Wonderland* where Alice drinks various liquids and grows or shrinks as a result (Hernández Álvarez 2005: 159 n. 23 and Jiménez 1992: 86). In addition to recognising the influence of Lewis Carroll, Jiménez also sees another connection between this scene and Martín Gaite's best-known work, with the coloured drinks resembling 'la cajita dorada con pastillas de colores que el "hombre de negro" ofrece a C. en *El cuarto de atrás*' [the little golden box of coloured pills which 'the man in black' offers C. in *The Back Room*] (1992: 86).

The wax model is dressed in red velvet with silver shoes. As discussed in connection with *Castillo*, red is associated with feeling and silver with the moon and the feminine. In *Castillo* Serena chose silver shoes and a violet dress when preparing to go to hear her daughter play. Thus the wax figure appears to symbolise feminine qualities of feeling, but she is not a human figure, suggesting that at this stage these qualities are not sufficiently developed. The figure could be a shadow aspect, in general the part of the unconscious first encountered in the individuation process. The room itself is octagonal, like Altalé's room in the tower in *Castillo*. The number eight symbolises wholeness, and the symbol is strengthened by the fact that the room contains eight mirrors: 'the number eight, like the number four, indicates psychic wholeness' (von Franz 1997a: 183). Jung pointed out that: 'The number four as the natural division of the circle is a symbol of wholeness in alchemical philosophy, and it should not be forgotten that the central Christian symbol is a quaternity too' (1964a: 391). Mirrors have many uses, both generally and in Martín Gaite's work. In general they symbolise reflection: 'The mirror symbolizes the much-needed faculty of true, inward-looking "reflection"' (von Franz in Jung 1964b: 217), and from now on Sorpresa does seem to stand back and grow in awareness. On the other hand, the song she sings while dancing around the wax figure before leaving the room, is full of resolve, emphasising the importance of going forward and not looking back or even around her. The act of reflection requires looking back, but here Sorpresa is seeking more not to be distracted from her task. The room is empty of furniture and has no windows. It is not a place to stay, but to pass through, taking strength for what lies beyond. The red velvet curtains separating the mirrors also suggest that it is feeling, the heart, eros, which is important here whichever way you look at it.

Sorpresa's question to the wax figure is about the location of the kitchen, where her mother is working. Not getting a reply gives her time to develop through subsequent encounters, so that when she sees her mother later she hides, content now to make her own way. However, first she has to leave the room with the mirrors. The fact that she only sees the door within one of the mirrors after going round the room several times – inspecting it carefully, looking at the details – is a typical way of solving a problem. At this point she addresses her reflection in the mirror, as Matilde did in *Balneario*, but in quite a different way. Matilde in the hotel bedroom addressed her shadow in the mirror: 'Yo soy ésa, yo soy tú' [I am her, I am you] (Martín Gaite 1984: 234), as if she were inferior to the shadow in the mirror. She feared that the figure in the mirror was mocking her: 'Matilde advierte [...] que la de dentro tiene en los ojos un poco de burla' [Matilde notices [...] that the one in the mirror has a slightly mocking look in her eyes] (Ibid. 233). Matilde envies her shadow 'porque le parece que sabe más cosas que ella' [because she seems to know more than Matilde] and with the envy comes a power attitude, the opposite of eros: 'Y entonces se ríe [...] y le gusta ver que la de dentro se ríe y hace los mismos gestos, como una esclava' [And then she laughs [...] and it pleases her to see that the one inside [the mirror] laughs and makes the same gestures, like a slave] (Ibid. 234). Nevertheless, when she is ready to join her friends downstairs Matilde simply admires herself in a dress she is wearing for the first time (1984: 245–6), which signals her turning her back on the difficult challenge posed by individuation. Sorpresa, on the other hand, addresses the figure in the mirror simply as an image of herself, encouraging herself to continue with her adventure (112). There is a positive relationship here between ego and shadow which is absent from the much earlier novella.

Outside the room Sorpresa finds a black and white corridor. As with Lucandro's horses in *Castillo*, black and white represent the opposites, and this corridor which leads to the next room seems to indicate the nature of the next challenge. The animus is the personification of the contrasexual element and *el señor*, whom she meets in the next room, is the opposite to Sorpresa: old, where she is just ten; a man; rich; well-travelled; and bored. Dressed in loose black satin with an embroidered top and with bare feet, he presents a dramatic figure which contrasts significantly with the little girl with her worn sandals and crumpled socks. Drunk and depressed and used to giving orders, he represents an enormous challenge to Sorpresa. She survives this initial encounter first of all by being very polite, then by being true to herself, which is the key to her successful passage throughout this journey. Her responses show that she keeps her feet on the ground as when she replies to his dramatic declaration that he's dying by asking him not to die, and when he asks melodramatically who would care whether he lived or died, responds that it would matter to her. Up till then, too, she has spoken quietly but, coming up against something really important to her, she speaks much more clearly. *El señor* illustrates a predilection of Martín Gaite when Sorpresa reflects that his black eyes remind her of a wolf. Reflecting popular attitudes, Michael Ferber states that 'the wolf seems to be the most feared and despised mammal in literature; a good wolf is extremely rare until recent times' (1999: 240). Martín Gaite, on the other hand, takes a consistently positive view of wolves: from Sorpresa who feels sorry for them, to Sara's view in *Caperucita* that the wolf in her story book has a nice face, and Guillermo in *Nubosidad* with his '*cara de lobo*' [wolf-like face], which both Mariana and Sofía find attractive.

This important dialogue between *el señor* and Sorpresa is saved from sentimentality, from the worst features of the *novela rosa* [romantic novel], by the little girl's single-mindedness, by her refusal to abandon her own grasp on life in the face of such overwhelming surroundings. The well-lit, large room with its three balconies is furnished in a way which is very different from Sorpresa's own home, being full of books, sculptures and furniture as well as a gramophone. The reason for Sorpresa wanting *el señor* to live is not merely so that he will open his eyes and look at her again, but that the room seems ideal for telling stories. Thus, by behaving naturally and by treating him with respect and courtesy, she evokes a similar response from *el señor* who ceases to regard her merely as someone who can be useful to him (by bringing him another bottle of champagne), and instead begins to look at her differently and really see the person in front of him. Furthermore, Sorpresa has not simply argued that she wants him to live because he is a human being and, therefore, must be worthwhile – good enough, but it does not lead anywhere. She has gone further than this, implying that as he is a human being he must have stories to tell and share. In this, Sorpresa anticipates Miss Lunatic in *Caperucita*: 'Cada persona es un mundo' [Each person is a whole world] and 'todos tenían alguna historia que contar' [they all had a story to tell] (1992c: 87).

The music Sorpresa heard on entering the house seems to be coming from the room where she discovers *el señor*, and this fits well with his later admission about the nightmares and dark thoughts in the form of flocks of black birds which assail him for 'music has always been a religious means for man of driving away evil thoughts and evil spirits' (von Franz 1997a: 127).

Sorpresa draws continually on the stories she knows well and whose heroes she wants to emulate. When asked to give a message to Ricardo she realises that it would be helpful to know who he is but that in stories the hero is expected to find out everything and overcome all the challenges unaided. Her determination not to return by the same path is extended to the means of entering and leaving rooms. From this second room, Sorpresa leaves by a small door lined with blue silk. The fact that it is small suggests it could be easily overlooked, and noticing such things is what sets fairy-tale heroes apart from more ordinary folk. The blue silk makes it seem special, more intimate. Blue is the colour associated with spirit and also with thought which, according to Jung's polaric psychological typology, is the opposite to feeling, the aspect first encountered by Sorpresa. The other pole holds intuition and its opposite, sensation.

The third room, reached by a similar but longer corridor, is full of noisy people who are moving or sitting and 'vestidos de forma tan singular' [so strangely dressed] (118). Thus, Sorpresa is not noticed and sensibly heads for a round table in the centre of the room in case one of the bottles is champagne. She is on a quest, but the passage is difficult, there are many interesting people to distract her attention and the temptation to let herself go with the crowd seems a very pleasant option. This is similar to Matilde's reaction in *Balneario*:

> Era muy grande la tentación de quedarme con ellos, y parecía todo tan sencillo [...]. Quizá tan sólo consistía en girar y girar [...] con los mismos pasos que ellos daban, sin perder el compás del ritmo de todos. (1984: 220–1)

> [The temptation to stay with them was very great, and it all seemed so simple [...]. Perhaps all that was required was to go round and round [...] taking the same steps that they did, without getting out of step with the rest.]

Jung recognises the attractiveness of collective behaviour compared with consciously following the individuation process: 'In society we lose the feeling of personal responsibility and can swim with the current. One feels safe in the multitude' (1977: 688). Writers who describe individuation insist on the loneliness of the process. Because loneliness is a very difficult condition to bear, the temptation will arise to look back, to try to go back to a previous situation, or even just to expend energy in trying to resist the changes instead of investing it in the more difficult task to which one has been drawn. Sorpresa is attracted by a rocking seat on the terrace from where she can also see the hills by the light of the moon, including the *Perro Dormido*, the hill where she and Pizco had met so recently. The fact that the only others on the terrace are two couples who pay no attention to her only serves to heighten the sense that she is alone and, looking back at the hills, she is seized by the temptation to feel sorry for herself and to cry.

Story is the key once again when, in keeping with the theme of not looking back, she remembers, at just the right time, the tale of Lot's wife in the Bible who looked back as they left Sodom despite being warned by God that she should not, and, as a result, was turned into a pillar of salt. Campbell links the story of Lot's wife with other tales including *Sleeping Beauty*. For Campbell the biblical story and the fairy tale have in common the experience of being spellbound as a result of an inability to move on to the next stage, to the new experience. He distinguishes between the parallel experiences he describes: 'Some of the victims remain spellbound forever [...] but others are destined to be saved' (1968: 63). Lot's wife falls into the first category, Sleeping Beauty into the second. Sorpresa takes a lesson from the biblical story and this, together with the parallels already drawn between her life and the fairy tale, suggest that, like Sleeping Beauty, she will find freedom and fulfilment; she will not be trapped in the unconscious or fail in the process of individuation. Sorpresa's reaction was to a familiar sight, something close to home. Ronald Murphy discusses the dangers of returning home from both a psychological and a spiritual perspective in his analysis of the fairy tale *Hansel and Gretel*: 'Bettelheim has noted that to go back home would be to regress psychologically [...]. The same is true when reading the story spiritually. It would be most unfortunate for the children [...] to regress to the premoral, selfish state of their parents' (2000: 57–8). Here, too, Sorpresa needs to move beyond the narrow, constraining world of her parents into a way of life which is appropriate for her.

Von Franz argues that 'salt symbolizes the wisdom of Eros, its bitterness together with its life-giving power – the wisdom acquired by feeling-experiences' (1996: 130): 'Salt is a part of the sea and has the inherent bitterness of the sea. The idea of bitterness is also associated with tears and with sadness, disappointment, and loss' (1996: 129). She also suggests that 'the connection between petrification and bitterness' comes from the fact that 'bitterness is a kind of hidden affect, or rage, but turned within, and it has a stiffening effect upon the personality' (1990: 137). Lot's wife was no longer human, but made of salt, suggesting that in her case bitterness had won out; there was no longer any scope for discernment or development, or for wisdom. Wisdom is still beyond Sorpresa, but her refusal to look back and her determination to continue with her tasks – of finding the champagne and giving Ricardo the message – keep her on her path. They seem small tasks, not heroic feats, but doing the things you have to do as well as you can is part of Martín Gaite's philosophy, inherited from her mother: 'El secreto está en no tener prisa y en atender a cada puntada como si ésa que das fuera la cosa más importante de tu vida' [The secret lies in not rushing things and in attending to every stitch as if the one you're making now was the most important thing in your life] (1987a: 114). With this resolve, Sorpresa returns to the third room somewhat changed, no longer dizzy or overwhelmed by the confusion of the collective unconscious represented by the activity within the room, and able to focus clearly on what is happening. Her attitude recalls the behaviour of Sofía in *Nubosidad*, who, attending a cocktail party where she knows no one, decides that 'en vez de decir "Estoy como un pulpo en un garaje; ¿qué pinto yo aquí?", te pones a mirar con atención y ya estás pintando más que nadie' [instead of saying, 'I'm all at sea, what on earth am I doing here?', you start looking attentively and find you count for more than anyone] (1992b: 80). 'Mirar con atención' [looking attentively] also represents an important aspect of Martín Gaite's approach to life.

And just as Sorpresa finds she can bring order into her own way of seeing and behaving, someone begins to organise the great crowd of people in the room, bringing inner and outer into harmony. That the experience on the terrace has effected a major inner change is further confirmed by the fact that she now hides when she sees her mother, whereas when she first entered the house she had sought directions with the specific intention of finding what was familiar. This need to avoid being seen by her mother also ensures she does not fall into the crowd again, to be organised by the leader as one of the collective, but remains with her individual quest.

Because this is an individuation process, which involves the Self, what seem like sensible approaches by the ego might be thwarted, for reasons which may only become clear much later. Sorpresa is prevented from reaching the round table for two reasons. The first is to avoid the danger of meeting her mother who, shortly after the child has gone out onto the terrace, appears in the room to collect dishes and glasses. The second is that Sorpresa has to go much deeper and face a greater challenge before she can return to the room with the gramophone and, therefore, she must find the champagne elsewhere.

As always, there is a paradox, for, just as Sorpresa is congratulating herself at having escaped two dangers related to her past– the threat of tears and her mother – and likening herself to the heroes of the stories she loves, she is discovered by those putting up scenery. She blames her failure to heed what she knows to be right on looking back at what she had escaped rather than forward to the next challenge (122–3). Nevertheless, she responds as always with her natural politeness and willingness to help. And the helpfulness, as happens so often in fairy tales, is rewarded: having piled up three boxes to climb onto (she has also already come through three rooms/three encounters successfully), she then jumps down and discovers another small door which might have been overlooked and which enables her to move on to the next, very different, and more dangerous stage.

The Descent

It becomes clear why it was important that Sorpresa should not find a bottle of champagne in the third room when she finds herself going much deeper into the unconscious by means of a long narrow and worn spiral staircase. This is a typical image of Martín Gaite who, in her *Cuadernos*, writes:

> Tengo que pararme, aunque cueste, volver a lo interior, al *neverending*, me está haciendo daño la falta de concentración. Tengo que atreverme a bajar al sótano con el candil encendido, aunque me tiemble la mano. (2002a: 394)
>
> [I must stop, however difficult, return to the inner world, to the *neverending*, the lack of concentration is hurting me. I must dare to go down to the basement with the oil lamp lit, even if my hand is shaking.]

In her lively and comprehensive study of life-writing in Martín Gaite's notebooks and later novels, María José Blanco suggests that the references to the *neverending* refer to Martín Gaite's work on her collection of writings, *El cuento de nunca acabar*. While this seems to be true of some of her comments, statements such as the one quoted above suggest that *neverending* may also refer to the unconscious, while others such as 'Me voy a meter de lleno en el *neverending*. Es la única salida verdadera' [I'm going to go straight into the *neverending*. It's the only real solution] (2002a: 397), could refer to either. Hernández Álvarez describes the movement in *Pastel* as a descent not only to the depths of the house but also of Sorpresa's own being, 'para merecer subir después hacia la luz' [in order to be worthy of then going up to the light] (2005: 161). According to von Franz, 'life cannot go further before first going downward' (1990: 49), and she further asserts that 'you cannot get near the Self and the meaning of life without being on the razor's edge of falling into greed, into darkness, and into the shadowy aspect of the personality. One does not even know if it is not necessary sometimes to fall into it, because otherwise it cannot be assimilated' (1990: 49). Eunice Myers concurs, citing Perera's 'description of the Goddess's initiatory descent in order to reunify the upper and lower parts of the self' (2003–4: 416). Unusually, in *Pastel* it gets lighter the deeper Sorpresa goes, but it is a poor and unadorned light made by a couple of bare lightbulbs and comes from the wine cellar into which she is descending. So this fourth stage takes her just where she wants to be in order to fulfil at least one part of her allotted task.

Wine is a symbol of the spirit (von Franz 1996: 140). Without the light, it is unlikely Sorpresa would have discovered the wine cellar or any way out other than retracing her footsteps, which would have yielded only a partial experience. Because of the light she quickly finds the champagne bottles, drawing on her experience of seeing the one her father brings home on birthdays. Champagne is a kind of treasure, used to mark important occasions. *El señor* wants another bottle so that it will take away the darkness and depression he feels. In this respect it is artificial and has only a temporary effect. But its associations, its special nature, and the symbolism of wine as spirit make it a more positive experience. It is not unique, there are lots of bottles, and Sorpresa takes one, any one. Yet the way in which she looks about to make sure no one else is near, snatches a bottle and then runs away, associates it with Prometheus, who, according to Greek mythology, stole fire – a symbol of 'emotion [which] is the chief source of consciousness' (Jung 1959: 96) – from the gods. Sorpresa's deepest desire, to grow up, means to her to understand difficult things, which is akin to the higher consciousness symbolised by the fire snatched by Prometheus.

Despite the fact that she has been asked to bring back a bottle by someone she considers important and who seems to own the house, she views the taking of the bottle as stealing. It is a psychic stealing, taking something stored in the deeper levels of the unconscious and bringing it up to a higher level. There are a number of fairy tales in which the hero is required to steal something, though they usually put all their energies into the task and do not express moral qualms. Generally it depends on who is doing the stealing (or in some cases the killing). On the other hand, fairy tales reveal a general pattern of behaviour and are not meant to be interpreted literally but treated as symbolic. Eunice Myers believes that when Sorpresa steals the champagne 'the reader naturally remembers her telling Pizco that she wants to be bad, complete with horns and a tail' (2003–4: 416), but there is no bravado in Sorpresa's action or reaction. So far Sorpresa has progressed by remaining conscious, by holding on to her human aspects, by being herself, and her attitude to taking the champagne continues this approach. Nevertheless, snatching it and running off as fast as she can also leads to her getting lost and going round in circles unable to find the way out. Hernández Álvarez compares this experience with that of the Grail Knights: 'Como los caballeros del Grial erraban solitarios y perdidos, ahora corre Sorpresa por los túneles obscuros' [Just as the Grail knights wandered alone and lost, now Sorpresa runs along dark tunnels] (2005: 162). On the other hand, as Jiménez recognises, it is also reminiscent of a scene in *Balneario*, particularly the scene in which Matilde wanders through labyrinthine corridors (1992: 88). A labyrinth is a place with 'a way in and a way out and a journey to be made between the two, that takes time, perseverance, patience and courage to work out' (Robinson 1979: 27). It is also 'a universal symbol of man's search for meaning' (Ibid. 38), with very different outcomes for Matilde and Sorpresa, illustrating the difference when consciousness participates in the search as a partner. In Matilde's case, the search remains largely unconscious.

The running and the circling in the shock following the theft bring Sorpresa back to the wine cellar from the opposite side, as if to enable her to start again on the return journey but this time looking at things from a different angle. Once more, by looking carefully she sees a third opening, so getting lost has afforded the opportunity for adjustment and the development of a calmer approach, having gathered her wits, which is essential for the next encounter.

Encounter with a King

One of the characteristics of the animus is that he deceives. Coming through the opening Sorpresa has identified as a possible way out, she sees a king wearing a crown and a cloak. A king in the depths of the psyche would be an important figure, representing the ruling principle. His red cloak is typical of his role but, in keeping with the symbolism of the colour, also suggests feeling, eros, warmth, emotion, and fire. On the other hand, red also has negative associations of death, war and evil: 'Red, which is not only the positive color of fertility but also the color of calamity, evil, blood, death, the desert, where, thousands of years later, the Devil appeared to tempt the elect' (Neumann 1963: 171).

Jung identified four stages of development in both anima and animus. Emma Jung, making reference to Goethe's *Faust*, argues that in the case of the animus 'power corresponds very well to the first stage, the deed follows, then the word, and finally, as the last stage, meaning' (1981: 3). By coincidence, the king's lines – particularly '¡Olvidaos de ese disfraz de niña atemorizada [...] y haced que despierte vuestro corazón de mujer!' [Forget this disguise of a frightened child [...] and let your woman's heart awaken] (126) – cause Sorpresa to think he has the answer to her most important question, how to grow up. She has first been delighted by his role of king, then notices how tall and handsome he is. Suddenly the situation becomes meaningful to her personally and he appears to represent the potential source of meaning. The importance of the situation is described as like opening a drawer 'del que salían volando pájaros de oro' [from which golden birds flew out] (126), which appears to be the beginning of an important projection of the highest level of the animus. The gold is the key to the value that is placed on this question being answered, and on all her unanswered questions receiving a response.

The king carries a mirror and papers. A mirror can be used to admire one's appearance, to see oneself, and even to find out something. In this case the king uses it for all three purposes, though primarily the first two. The papers could represent learning, which here can be interpreted literally as they contain his lines for a play, which he is trying to memorise. Herein lies a warning as to the nature of this figure: he is self-regarding, and his best words are not his own, they don't come from within himself. At first Sorpresa is overawed by the king, thoroughly deceived, though again her courtesy prevails as when she asks him to wait a moment so she can put the bottle on the ground in order to give him her full attention. And again her own authenticity calls up the reality of the other, for he shouts at her in his own, very different voice, telling her not to interrupt him, which gives Sorpresa the first hint of his duplicity.

Sorpresa asks her question which, unsurprisingly, he fails to answer and his impatience to return to his friends provokes an explosion of rage from the little girl – '¡Creí que los reyes serían distintos! ¡Váyase al infierno! ¡Le odio!' [I thought kings would be different! Go to hell! I hate you!] (128) – which is just the right response in the circumstances as it stops him from leaving and allows him to provide important information. First she learns that he is Ricardo, at which point he returns to his 'acting' voice which she initially found so attractive. However, experience has taught her that he is not to be trusted completely. She has learnt very quickly to see through the deceptions of this animus figure who appears royal, but is a fake and would fascinate her and take her away from her task. He suggests she go up and watch the play which would mean retracing her steps, getting caught up in collective activities, possibly even being seen by her mother, and thus failing in the process which she has begun so well. Ricardo is a bad mirror, as O'Leary and Ribeiro de Menezes point out: 'Martín Gaite suggests that, with his self-satisfied and patriarchal attitude, [Ricardo] is an "espejo malo", or inadequate interlocutor, for Sorpresa' (2008: 255).

The unconscious is full of shades, deceptions, and temptations, and Sorpresa responds well to the challenges, keeping herself aware, responding to each new piece of information, weighing the reality she encounters against her initial expectations, and adjusting her vision accordingly. All of this enables her to be confident as she runs away from Ricardo without looking back. This is a courageous decision for her to take given her propensity to be helpful and responsive, and, thus represents an important step in the process. It is also a typical aspect of the journey, as Neumann points out: 'This firmness of the strong-willed ego, concentrated on its goal, is expressed in countless other myths and fairy tales, with their injunctions not to turn around, not to answer, and the like' (1971: 112–13). Sorpresa's references to typical events in the stories she has read suggest she is well aware of this, as she reveals, for example, in her encounter with Ricardo when she realises she is giving away a secret (where *el Señor* is hiding himself), something heroes should never do.

In responding to Ricardo/the king instinctively there are three important developments. Firstly, she learns that the third opening she saw earlier *is* an alternative way out and the king gives her detailed instructions for getting back to *el señor*. Secondly, the reaction of the king to the message causes her to realise the importance of having found *el señor*. Both of these developments help Sorpresa to re-focus on the most important task: returning to the room with the gramophone. Finally, Ricardo twice tries to disparage her importance to *el señor*, ridiculing the notion that he is waiting for her as he never waits for anyone or shows any interest in anyone but himself. Sorpresa knows that at the very least he is waiting for the champagne, that he has told her to be quick, and didn't argue with her assessment of the room in relation to stories and their telling. On the other hand she is intrigued by Ricardo's final description: '¡Se quiere comer él solo el pastel del diablo!' [He wants to eat the devil's cake all by himself] (130). This is her final test in the wine cellar, and she passes it by *not* asking what it means – once again with the help of the example of the heroes of her stories who face tricks and temptations that try to distract them from their task. Not even Ricardo's voice calling her back deters her. In the development of the story through her long conversation with *el señor*, the full importance of Sorpresa's not responding to Ricardo's mysterious words is revealed. Finally, as I mentioned earlier, Sorpresa has been compared with the Grail knight, Perceval, who failed to ask about the things he saw in the Grail Castle. As a result, healing and wholeness were not achieved: 'So much would have been restored if only you [Perceval] had asked' (Jung & von Franz 1971: 174). Here Sorpresa fails to ask a question, but she does this knowingly, consciously.

Conversation with an Ideal Interlocutor

Sorpresa's attempts to engage with *el señor* are rewarded when he confounds Ricardo's description of him and asks her not to leave. Martín Gaite is here depicting story as irresistible even to the most jaded personality. If we consider Sorpresa as a feminine ego on a process of individuation, in this encounter with an important animus figure she is behaving exactly as she should – sympathetic without forgetting her own world or interests. When *el señor* responds further by making a space for her on the balcony opposite him, he seems to confirm their relative positions as opposites: conscious/

unconscious figures, together with the aspects identified earlier. In addition, Sorpresa is sitting on the right-hand side which is associated with the conscious side and hence appropriate for her. The theme of opposites is continued in the two little figures of angels made of iron on the balcony railing: one shooting an arrow, the other immersed in a book. In their study of the goddess myth in the Western tradition, Baring and Cashford identify the age of iron with the polarisation of opposites: 'More generally, in the mythology of the Iron Age, sky becomes exalted over earth, and the paradigm of opposition and conflict grips the consciousness of humanity' (1993: 282). In the story which *el señor* tells Sorpresa later, he and his first fiancée identified themselves with the angels. They broke up, she died, so as opposites they were never united. The little angels turn up again later, when Sorpresa has left the *Casa Grande*, to complete the story in a way which confirms significant progress in the process of individuation.

In *Castillo* Cambof Petapel wore a ring with a blue stone on his index finger and it was interpreted as being connected with the spirit. *El señor* wears a ring with a red stone which connects him to the theme which has been present since the beginning of the analysis of this story-within-a-story: feeling, relatedness, eros. We do not know which finger the ring is worn on, but from their relative positions on the balcony, it seems to be on the left hand, which connects it to the unconscious and creativity, where the goal, the meaning is to be found.

Fantasy and Reality

Within this story-within-a-story and its quest for independence and maturity, Sorpresa, sitting in silence as *el señor* smokes, imagines herself in another story:[4] she is on the deck of a cruise ship, has just met the captain and, naturally, she is grown up and wearing high heels and a silk dress. Estés argues that there are three kinds of fantasy: 'Pleasure fantasy [...] strictly for enjoyment, such as daydreams [...]. Intentional imagining [...] a vehicle to take us forward into action. [...] Then there is the third kind of fantasy, the

4 For a discussion of the different levels within the tale see Merlo 2004a: 186–7.

kind that brings everything to a halt. This is the kind of fantasy that hinders right action during critical times' (1998: 322). Spontaneous daydreams can be treated like dreams and analysed in the same way. On the face of it, Sorpresa appears just to be enjoying herself and thus falling into the first category. It seems harmless. Yet we have seen how reality has pervaded the bigger story and is never far away, and how Sorpresa's grip on reality has enabled her to meet every challenge so far. Imagining herself grown-up is escaping from reality and preventing her from being alert to the possibility of achieving her goal. Whereas Ricardo, acting as a king, had covered her grubby hand with kisses without seeming to notice, she did notice, and was sufficiently alert to the other deceptions (his voice, his changing moods) not to be drawn into the illusion that she was already grown-up. *El señor* is more sympathetic to her than Ricardo, he has made clear that he wants her to stay, she is looking forward to hearing and telling stories, so the whole environment is so favourable that she could lose herself in it and, therefore, get stuck in the process. Sorpresa has been admirable in her honesty to herself and others, and in her awareness. In addition, there have been interventions by others, such as those building the stage, which have assisted her in going forward. Now it is *el señor* himself who brings her painfully back to earth when he asks how old she is. Time has played an important role in the story: on the terrace when she almost turned back as she reflected on the length of time she had been in the house; and when she recalled the urgency of her task to take back the champagne. Having been in danger of losing a sense of reality, this question focused on her personal relationship to time forces her to see her shabby clothes and to wake up.

Martín Gaite is often quoted on the purpose of her writing in relation to reality and fantasy: 'Toda mi literatura oscila entre lo excepcional soñado desde lo cotidiano y al revés' [All of my literature fluctuates between the exceptional dreamed from the perspective of the everyday and its opposite] (2002a: 572). The relationship between the two worlds is also at the heart of Jung's vision of wholeness, in which consciousness, through the ego, plays a full part. Getting stuck in the unconscious, being fascinated by it, is a danger highlighted by Jung: 'Your conscious autonomy begins to disappear, and you get more and more under the fascination of unconscious contents' (1977: 74). The threat of getting lost in fantasy, then being pulled back into reality is a theme of the scene on the balcony. Immersed again in the same fantasy about the ship, when el señor asks her if she likes champagne, she is able to accept an experience previously forbidden by her mother because this is what would be expected of any woman in such a situation. Thus, the scene which follows this decision is only accessible to her through the fantasy, which has given her a different sense of herself.

However, because Sorpresa is aware of her mother's attitude to champagne, she is also conscious of her act of disobedience. Having drunk too much she begins to 'see' all the people she has met in the Casa Grande, including el señor, holding hands in a circle and laughing, but is prevented from joining them by the image of her mother tugging at her skirt and holding her back. Here the image of her mother acts as a sobering presence ensuring Sorpresa does not get swallowed up in the unconscious, unable to distinguish fantasy and reality. As Couso confirms:

> La figura de la madre asiéndole la falda constituye, aun dentro del sueño, el contrapunto real, la atadura que desdibuja lo fantástico y la aproxima a lo cotidiano. (2014: 44)
>
> [The figure of the mother taking hold of her skirt constitutes, even within the daydream, the real counterpoint, the bond that blurs the outlines of the fantastic and brings it closer to the everyday.]

The dangers of this were present even before Sorpresa started drinking champagne when she found the whole experience of the evening quite dizzying, likening it to 'luces que se encienden y se apagan, sin guardar relación unas con otras' [lights that go on and off, with no connection between them] (140–1). This image implies flashes of consciousness, but they are disconnected. The individuation process, with its ups and downs, its groping in the dark, its loneliness, is ultimately about the search for, and discovery of, meaning, of a new value which unites the opposites. Sorpresa has not yet reached that stage.

From the image of her mother reminding her of boundaries, the drunk and dizzy Sorpresa manages to remain sufficiently alert to discover that *el señor* is very different from the romantic image of the captain of the cruise ship she has been fantasising about, and this despite his putting his arm around her and speaking to her very softly. In view of her earlier susceptibility to his wolf-like eyes, this voice, coupled with the champagne, make it almost incredible that Sorpresa is not completely overwhelmed. It is appropriate that the effort she makes to open her eyes – to be conscious – is described as superhuman and she is rewarded with renewed contact with reality, for it is at this point that she realises for the first time that he is old.

This step is crucial. Had she not taken it, she might have succumbed to the next development when *el señor*, also rather drunk and mixing dream and reality, mistakes her for his childhood sweetheart, Cecilia, and hugs and kisses her. From seeing that he is not the man she had imagined, it is a short step to pointing out very forcefully to him that she is certainly not the person he imagines her to be 'como si se arrancara una careta' [as if she were tearing off a mask] (143). The process of individuation is one of becoming a unique individual, an authentic human being. Tearing off a mask would symbolise rejecting a false image, whether it comes from oneself or is projected by someone else. This is the most important step Sorpresa takes, and is the key to all that follows.

When Sorpresa tears off the mask she asserts who she is, making five positive statements – about her size, her age, her desire to be bad and to be grown up, and her wish to tell stories – as well as defining herself in terms of what she is not vis-à-vis *el señor* with his books, large house, champagne, friends, gramophone, and travels, before returning to her main preoccupations:[5] '¡ni he visto el mar, ni me contesta nadie a lo que le pregunto, ni he hecho ningún viaje de verdad, ni he conocido al capitán de ningún barco' [I have never seen the sea, nobody answers anything I ask them, I have never made a real journey, nor do I know the captain of any ship] (143). Then all roads lead back to her deepest desire and she is able to end on a note closer to her recent, real experience, telling him how fed

5 There was a crucial time in Jung's life when he was being assailed by unconscious forces and feared for his sanity, when only the repeated assertion of facts about himself kept him in touch with reality: 'The unconscious contents could have driven me out of my wits. But my family, and the knowledge: I have a medical diploma from a Swiss university, I must help my patients, I have a wife and five children, I live at 228 Seestrasse in Küsnacht – these were actualities which made demands upon me and proved to me again and again that I really existed, that I was not a blank page whirling about in the winds of the spirit, like Nietzsche' (1983: 215).

up she is with everyone lying to her or scolding her and declaring her two, contrasting ambitions: 'porque quiero contar historias de verdad y ser mala y mayor de verdad' [because I really want to tell stories and be really bad and grown up] (143). Sorpresa's earlier declarations of her wish to be 'mala' were in response to the way she felt regarded and treated by the grown-ups she knows. On this second occasion she is under the effects of the champagne, and alcohol, like other drugs, opens the door to the unconscious. The desire to be bad, provoked by the collective shadow cast on her by other villagers, was expressed initially following Pizco's wounding criticisms. Now it comes at the end of the list of declarations of who she is not, and is delivered in a way which is forceful, highly emotional and determined, and hence dangerous to her potential future development.

There is in this scene an element which comes up in a number of fairy tales – that of *not* asking a question, which has already been discussed in connection with Perceval. Although neither Perceval nor Sorpresa asked a question, in the latter case it was the result of awareness, not the forgetfulness of the Grail Knight. In an example which is closer to Sorpresa's experience, the Russian fairy tale *Vasilisa the Beautiful*, Vasilisa is sent by her stepsisters to get fire from the Russian fairy-tale witch, the Baba Yaga. Having been warned by the Baba Yaga that 'not all questions are good. To know too much makes one old!' (von Franz 1995b: 195),[6] Vasilisa asks about the strange sights she has seen outside the house. However, heeding the witch's advice, she does not ask about what she has seen inside, and is rewarded. The young Sorpresa, born with a talent for asking questions, has learnt from experience that there are some things it is not worth asking about as adults will not give a truthful answer. But, although she understands this to be the case, she does not really accept it and holds firmly to the biggest question of all – how to be grown up. According to Baba Yaga,

6 Estés translates it as 'Vasalisa the Wise' and has the Baba Yaga say 'too much knowledge can make a person old too soon' (1998: 75). This connects it with Sorpresa who desperately wants to grow up and is cursed with asking questions which are not answered, that is, trying to obtain knowledge which is denied her. There are other connections between the Vasilisa tale and Sorpresa – the amber and the warmth, and the creative and destructive fires.

getting old before your time is the result of asking questions, so Sorpresa could be on the road to realising her dream just by being herself. But the Baba Yaga's advice is a warning to Vasilisa, and von Franz concludes that 'if Vasilisa had asked the fourth question, the witch would have exploded in anger, and to do that is a kind of defeat, which she would have resented. The one who gets angry has lost' (1995b: 215). The implication is that Vasilisa would not have got the fire she sought, and the witch would probably have gobbled her up. Sorpresa is also seeking fire (the fire of consciousness, although she has also threatened a destructive fire) and, like Vasilisa, she obtains it, with positive results.

At the end of Sorpresa's encounter with Ricardo, he criticised *el señor* for his impatience and self-absorption, and made his strange remark about the devil's cake. By then Sorpresa had experienced the deception in Ricardo's dress, voice and attitude, and so resisted her first impulse, to ask what the phrase meant. Fear that this would distract her from her main purpose held her back. Now on the balcony, asserting who she is and who she is not, Sorpresa concludes with her desire to be like *el señor* and '¡Comerme yo sola el pastel del diablo!' [Eat the devil's cake all by myself] (143). However, she doesn't understand fully what she is saying. Von Franz identified the kind of rage the Baba Yaga could have got into with 'hot evil'. *El señor* initially explodes with anger, but then withdraws into an icy silence, finally emerging with a deep sense of sadness. The reason that he does not stay in the first, explosive stage seems to be two-fold. First, Sorpresa does not attack him with Ricardo's words, but turns them on herself, saying that she wants to be like *el señor*. The criticism is, therefore, deflected and does not wound in quite the same way. Secondly, when *el señor*, furious, demands to know who said this Sorpresa adds 'Pero no lo entiendo bien. Debe ser una adivinanza' [But I don't really understand it. It must be a riddle] (143). In this way she veils herself in the kind of discretion, of respect, which Vasilisa showed, although Sorpresa seems, as always, to be telling the truth. Nevertheless, she is able to make this honest statement because she did not allow herself to be distracted by her own curiosity at that crucially important earlier stage. And her reward is the story of Cecilia and *el señor*, the photo of himself as a child, and the loss of Cecilia which he had not appreciated at the time. Sorpresa's earlier assessment of the room being ideal for storytelling is thus proved to be right.

Ricardo's criticisms, conveyed by Sorpresa, seem to have wounded and reminded *el señor* of his duty towards his guests and his role in the play as, following the story of Cecilia he begins to make himself up like a devil, with a little beard and horns. In other words, he disguises himself as a devil and Sorpresa addresses him as such. Contrary to the associations of the devil with aspects such as greed and desire, he gives Sorpresa a gift telling her that it will teach her to appreciate what she has. As already indicated, he is also an animus figure, and the animus, in some of its negative and even ambiguous guises, can appear devilish. At the beginning, it was not clear how he would behave, so bored and aloof did he appear. In the course of the encounter with Sorpresa he changed, as the animus also changes when faced with a woman being herself (Claremont de Castillejo 1990: 88–9). *El señor* dances round the room in a way that mirrors Sorpresa's dancing and singing in the room with the mirrors. His song is about there being no freedom without evil, which could refer to the importance of integrating the shadow and of accepting it where integration is not possible; of recognising that a one-sided, 'goody-two-shoes' attitude is unreal, incomplete, lacking in substance. It could also mean that there is no freedom without the choice between good and evil.

The Fourth Function

Jung developed a theory of psychological functions, identifying four which formed a polaric structure: Thinking and Feeling, Intuition and Sensation (the latter has also been described as the reality function (Tuby 1977: 6)). The aim of wholeness – and, therefore, of the individuation process – is naturally to develop all four, but in practice there is often an emphasis on one or two, with the third hardly developed and the fourth not at all. Discussing the fourth, or inferior, function, von Franz describes it as the one through which we encounter the unconscious, having as it were a door always open, one which cannot be closed or controlled in the way that the other three functions can as a result of living with them for a long time: 'It remains that door which is not quite shut against the other impulses of the collective unconscious' (1993b: 61). According to Irene Claremont de Castillejo, it is through this door that evil comes: 'The ill-developed fourth function is the gateway through which evil might once more try to explode its way' (1990: 37). At the collective level, she identifies it as the feeling function: 'On the whole the menace to civilization today seems to come from man's over-developed thinking, and the consequent unadaptedness of his fourth function, feeling, which thereby lets in the evil' (Ibid. 39). Von Franz agrees, although she includes all inferior functions in her analysis: 'The little open door of each individual's inferior function is what contributes to the sum of the big collective evil in the world. [...] The sum of millions of inferior functions constitutes an enormous devil!' (1993b: 57–8). The Jungian view of the way to transform destructiveness and provide the answer to the problems of society is that it lies with the individual and depends on the individual growing in consciousness and relating to, rather than rejecting, the unconscious, and taking responsibility for one's own shadow. Irene Claremont de Castillejo insists that 'the only way of developing our lesser functions is to give less energy to the first' (1990: 33). The inferior function is also described very positively as 'a sort of gold or diamond mine of possibilities, a place rich in roots but basically undiscovered' (Mercurio 2011: 24), or as a 'divine spark' which frustrates the ego and, in so doing, affords us the opportunity for growth (Ibid. 27). Tuby describes its 'quality of freshness and vitality' (1977: 17) which results precisely from its closeness to the unconscious.[7]

Sorpresa is very bright, always asking questions, thinking, reflecting. She also loves being outdoors, running around and making up stories. She seems to be extroverted, directed outwards, and her first function appears to be thinking, with the functions of sensation and intuition also partly developed. Therefore, her fourth function could be introverted feeling.

7 This description recalls Gerard Manley Hopkins's poem 'God's Grandeur': 'nature is never spent; / There lives the dearest freshness deep down things'. A couple of lines later the poet expresses his confidence that life will continue renewed 'Because the Holy Ghost over the bent / World broods with warm breast and with ah! bright wings' (1970: 66).

Sorpresa has shown herself to be very polite with strangers, and Jung says this is typical of inferior feeling which, like all the fourth functions, is experienced as primitive, and 'primitive man is extraordinarily polite, he is very careful not to disturb the feelings of his fellows because it is dangerous to do so' (Jung 1977: 20). On the other hand, her being at ease with reality, her ability, for example, to invent and capture the physical reality of her invented *Casa Grande* in great detail, might support the view that her first function is the sensation or reality function, in which case her fourth function would be intuition, and the fact that it is her intuition that will finally reveal her vocation seems to support this alternative interpretation.

La noche de San Juan

Sorpresa's invented story takes place on 23 June, *la noche de San Juan*. Among the many stories associated with this night, one promises that, if you look in the mirror at midnight, you will see the Devil. We don't know exactly what time it is, only that it is dark and late when Sorpresa is watching *el señor* make himself up at the mirror. Although he pays no attention to her, she, on the other hand, sees the devil reflected there.

In many fairy tales the devil is an evil principle which needs to be destroyed. Sorpresa identifies *el señor* with the devil and is unafraid, considering his face to be beautiful. In some fairy tales an evil power has some precious thing which must be rescued: 'This corresponds to the usual pattern of getting the pearl away from the dragon, or the treasure difficult to obtain out of the hands of evil powers' (von Franz 1995b: 270). In contrast, in Sorpresa's story *el señor*, dressed as the devil, gives her an amber stone, telling her to bury it in 'el lugar de origen. Y después invocarme' [the place of origin. And then invoke me] (150). Sorpresa does not have to steal the precious thing as in traditional tales, and it is a gift from someone with whom she has shared stories and silence. Often, too, the treasure is already buried and has to be dug up, whereas here *el diablo* tells her to bury it in order to find the answer to her secret, the treasure she really seeks. So the traditional patterns are being reversed and the opposites are present here, too. Throughout the story-within-a-story, Sorpresa's instincts have enabled her to deal successfully with the various encounters. With the instructions from *el señor*, she runs from the *Casa Grande*, taking, naturally, a different way out.

At the moment in which she realises that *el lugar de origen* means the clearing in the woods where her christening party was held, she feels as though the active angel on the balcony which was shooting an arrow has changed into the other one, which was reading a book. This seems to be the reconciliation of the forces within Sorpresa, which anticipates the end of the story. It is only at this point that we learn of the story Sorpresa has built up of her birth and christening and its impact on her life: in her imagination the clearing is the source of Balbina's curse. When she invokes the devil in order to despatch the witch as *el señor* instructed – '¡Que tu poder retroceda ante el mandato del diablo!' [May your power retreat in the face of the devil's command!] (154) – paradoxically, given the opposition between herself and collective feminine values, she is following a matriarchal custom of her village. In Trimonte the women believed that 'la hechicería y el mal de ojo sólo los puede conjurar el diablo' [witchcraft and the evil eye can only be exorcised by the devil] (153–4). Here a theatrical devil overcomes the destructiveness of an imaginary witch but, on the level of the imagination, both are real to Sorpresa.

The symbolism of amber is closely related to a number of aspects of the story. In Poland amber was thought to ward off evil spirits on *la noche de San Juan*. Amber is warm and soft and, though found in a whole range of colours, the most common is yellow. The warmth associates it with feeling, the colour with the sun and also with fire. Sorpresa's anger and desire for power, if acted out, would have been like a destructive fire, causing mayhem and bringing her no peace. By being contained within the symbol of the piece of amber, and buried in the earth from where its energy can be drawn (amber stores static electricity and was called elektron by the Greeks[8]) this fire can be transformed from destructiveness to

8 Exploring the derivation of 'elektron' scholars have suggested connections with 'helko', to draw or attract, or 'aleko', to ward off evil. Associations with *elektor* in the *Iliad* have also been identified, where it means 'the beaming sun', linking it to the festival

creativity. When Sorpresa buries the piece of amber, she is able to get rid of the witch from her psyche, sending her to hide in the darkness, that is, in the unconscious, and thus freeing herself for a new stage in the individuation process. As discussed previously, creative fire is also associated with the Holy Spirit and with Pentecost.

In Matilde's dream in *Balneario* the funeral procession carried off the negative animus, Carlos. Here the drum roll and canticles moving away represent the funeral of Balbina, the dark shadow, only this time with the drums which were missing from the original procession at her funeral, thereby completing it. As in *Balneario*, the funeral march carries away something which has to die, which is no longer relevant to consciousness. Eunice Myers considers that Sorpresa hears musicians 'returning from the night's festivities' (2003–4: 421), but it seems unlikely that they would play something so solemn. Although in her dream Matilde seemed relieved that Carlos was dead, when she woke she clung to the memory of him and appeared to ignore the end of the dream. Sorpresa, on the other hand, recognises the negative impact of the image of Balbina and enthusiastically despatches her. Thus, unlike Matilde – and Lot's wife – she is freed for the next stage in the process, for the funeral procession despatching Balbina is followed immediately by a very different, but related, experience.

The Vision of the Self

In a woman, the Self, where it is personified by a human figure, is often feminine (masculine in a man). So, too, are shadow figures. It is as if the image of Balbina, representing a dark, collective female shadow, had prevented the emergence of an image of the Self. Such an image emerges now. It is a beautiful woman whose face is partly veiled in a velvet mask, who wears

of the summer solstice, San Juan (<http://museumcatalogues.getty.edu/amber/intro/7/> accessed 1 May 2017).

golden high-heeled shoes and lilies in her long fair hair. Like the Statue of Liberty, she carries a torch. The lily is a symbol associated with virgins. The Jungian interpretation of this word would not be the narrow, 'conventional meaning of virginity as a refusal of sexual experience' (Luke 1981: 48): 'The term "virginity" must refer to a *quality*, to a subjective state, a psychological attitude, not to a physiological or external fact' (Harding 1982: 102). Harding goes on to clarify that '[the virgin] belongs to herself alone. She is one-in-herself' (Ibid. 103), which would be the effect of individuation on a woman. Martín Gaite makes reference to this state on a number of occasions in her *cuadernos*. For example: 'Es todo quedarse quieta, no agitarse, estar-en-sí, si me estoy quieta sirvo, si me agito no sirvo a nadie' [Everything lies in keeping calm, not getting upset, being in yourself, if I am calm I can be of some use, if I get upset I'm no use to anyone] (2002a: 193–4). The physical beauty and the clothes of the apparition contrast her with Balbina, but she is not all light and clarity for, through the velvet mask, she retains an element of mystery. Velvet is a material which appears consistently in Martín Gaite's stories, usually coloured green, as in Serena's notebook in *Castillo* in which she records her dreams, Rebeca Little's comfortable old armchair in *Caperucita* and the settee in Martín Gaite's real *cuarto de atrás* in her childhood home in Salamanca. This vision in Sorpresa's story carries a torch, which illuminates,[9] and she is also associated with several opposites: the materials of her clothes; the hidden face and the torch which casts light. The wax figure in the first room Sorpresa entered in the *Casa Grande* also carried a torch but was inanimate, whereas this is a living, moving symbol, illustrating the progress Sorpresa has made in the course of the story. Some critics claim that the figure Sorpresa describes is herself grown up (Myers 1984: 42). Others have, understandably, seen in this figure connections with the Statue of Liberty and, therefore, with Miss Lunatic in *Caperucita* (Couso 2008a: 397). Couso also sees parallels between Miss Lunatic and Balbina (2008b: 26–7). The figure Sorpresa sees appears to be an image

9 Interestingly, Irene Claremont de Castillejo's image of a positive animus is of 'a torch-bearer: the figure of a man holding aloft his torch to light my way, throwing its beams into dark corners and penetrating the mists which shield the world of half-hidden mystery where, as a woman, I am so very much at home' (1990: 76).

of the Self, as is Miss Lunatic, which represents an alternative connection between the two.

After burying the amber in the earth, instead of acting out a lie by becoming like the villagers' projection onto her, Sorpresa turns inward towards something that belongs to her alone. On the instruction of the devil, and in contrast to her earlier preference for knowledge, she invokes the moon which, according to Hall, has 'two manifest emotional movements: one is active, fiery eruption given to prophecy, rage, possession, and lying (making up a story); and the other, more measured meter given to meditation, dreams, waiting, wishing, lingering' (1980: 10). Sorpresa has not erupted with rage as she had threatened, but, still inspired by the same face of the moon, she chooses 'lying' or fabrication, and, in so doing, she turns, too, towards the other face. Hall also links these two moon faces with the medial aspect of the polaric structure identified by Toni Wolff as representing the structure of the feminine psyche. This aspect, on the 'impersonal pole' (in contrast to the 'personal pole' of Mother and Hetaira/Companion discussed in Chapter 2), is at the opposite end to the Amazon, which seemed to be the aspect Sorpresa was living before her decision to write.

As is well known, *la noche de San Juan* is traditionally a festival of fire, when bonfires are lit and the past can be symbolically burnt away; when the sun – the fire star – is honoured, and there is a sense of fire as a purifier, particularly of sin. It is a festival linked to the summer solstice, when the sun is at its highest and the days are longest. Light has traditionally been associated with good, dark with evil, so this festival has been interpreted as the triumph of good over evil. Symbolically, it could also be seen as the celebration of consciousness over unconsciousness. Yet, as was indicated earlier, the most fruitful relationship between these last two aspects is not that of conqueror and vanquished, but of relatedness and cooperation, since they are mutually dependent. The unconscious needs consciousness for its realisation. Through the unconscious consciousness develops and derives meaning. The process of individuation is concerned with the reconciliation of opposites. Almost from the moment Sorpresa entered the *Casa Grande*, one of the main aspects of her journey was also seen to be concerned with the reconciliation of opposites. Now, on this festival of the sun, linked with midsummer's day, Sorpresa, acting on the words of *el señor/diablo* is focused not on the sun but on its counterpart the moon, the full moon, on which the magical effects of her piece of amber depend. There is also here a further link with the story of *Sleeping Beauty*. Sorpresa's christening took place in a wood – a symbol of the unconscious (von Franz 1996: 120) – and here, too, there is a despised feminine element which needs to be made conscious. Sorpresa's focus on the moon suggests her reconciliation with the feminine is complete as she takes up the prediction of Balbina onto a new level where she can relate to it and transform it. In all this, Sorpresa is true to her feminine nature which, as was indicated earlier, 'seeks more the reconciliation than the polarisation of the opposites' (von Franz 1997a: 14). Discussing renewal and resurrection, Molly Tuby reflects on the symbolism of Christianity and concludes that 'it is through the death of a part of ourselves on our inner cross that resurrection can take place' (1977: 8). The 'death' of Balbina in this case opens the door to resurrection for Sorpresa.

The Return

This reconciliation of opposites continues the next day when Sorpresa sees the real *señor de la Casa Grande* walking home and recalls her invented story.[10] The fact that Pizco is not entertained by the carefully and lovingly constructed tale leaves Sorpresa at a crossroads. Abandoned by her friend who is taking a different direction, then seeing *el señor* who is walking back to the *Casa Grande* and who neither sees her nor knows who she is, the contrast between her imagined and anticipated worlds and reality could

10 A number of critics argue that it is not clear whether Sorpresa invented the story or whether she really went to the *Casa Grande* (Jiménez 1992; Myers 2003–4; Hernández Álvarez 2005). However, Sorpresa states that she 'inventaba despierta en la cama aquel cuento tan bonito' [lying awake in bed she invented that lovely story] (161), and describes it as 'el cuento más fascinante que había inventado nunca' [the most fascinating story she had ever made up] (158).

have turned Sorpresa's fire to ashes. But, in a moment of utter loneliness which almost overwhelms her, she realises she is 'sin más compañía que aquel motorcito invisible que fabricaba imágenes por dentro de su cabeza' [alone with only that invisible little engine that created images inside her head] (162), and which only she could wind up. As Tuby argues, 'born from the greatest pain we can possibly endure consciously, a strange and miraculous renewal can come about' (1977: 8). From the pain of loneliness which Sorpresa experiences, intuition reveals the way out – writing stories. Instead of wallowing in self-pity and using her talents and spirit to create mischief, the outcome is positive although, ever the realist, Martín Gaite ensures her protagonist is aware that her gift is not permanent and unchanging.

In responding in this way in her own world, Sorpresa resembles the Cinderella who has found the lost glass slipper. There is no danger now of her losing herself in her inner world, of her trying to prolong everything past midnight. In Sorpresa Martín Gaite has created a fairy-tale heroine who will make magic: for herself through recognising her gift and giving free rein to it, and for others who will read her stories. The treasure that other fairy-tale heroes find is often made of gold or jewels. Martín Gaite has enabled Sorpresa to find a different kind of treasure – one which does not depend on money or status for its possession. What seems to be missing is the fairy godmother. And yet, according to McCully, 'the fairy godmother is a dream figure who constellates Cinderella's intuition which can lead to an imaginative solution' (1991: 52). Sorpresa's intuition appears as a flash of inspiration in the midst of her loneliness, which leads her straight to the imaginative solution of writing stories. After this inspiration she, like Cinderella, 'must rely on herself for permanent changes' (McCully 1991: 52). At the end, no longer believing that her life can only begin when she is far away from her village, her everyday life is transformed and now offers previously undreamed-of opportunities in a new, exciting and fulfilling way of life; one in which she can answer her own questions – such as 'what is the *Casa Grande* like inside?' – through her writing. Thus, she overcomes the prediction of Balbina. She will have what she most desires – the vocation of writing – and she will find answers to her own questions which are more than satisfactory.

She is no longer deterred by impatience, which has been a predominant characteristic up till now, and the activity – writing stories – is one which she can carry out with all four functions. Earlier I quoted von Franz on the link between individuation and unrecognised vocation. It was not recognised by Sorpresa at the start, but at the end of the story, after all her encounters with the unconscious, she does discover her vocation. According to Hernández Álvarez, the meaning of *comer el pastel del diablo* is 'el gozo de la escritura, algo que se come en solitario' [the joy of writing, something that is eaten alone] (2005: 165).

The story Sorpresa invented about the *Casa Grande* was a departure from her traditional inventions. She drew on something in her own environment, which she had previously disdained, as the starting point for her best story. Thus she fulfils Martín Gaite's view about not running away but staying put to transform a situation and escape that way (1994b: 119). Although while watching *el señor* walking home she realises that there is no point asking him to finish the story of Cecilia as none of it was real unless she creates the characters again. Nevertheless she reconciles the two worlds by first calling on the moon (which had given the amber its magical properties) to witness her resolution to write stories; and, secondly, by promising that the owner of the *Casa Grande* would read them one day, and thus '¡Aprenderé a comerme yo sola, como él, el pastel del diablo!' [I'll learn, like him, to eat the devil's cake all by myself] (163). Thus, Sorpresa withdraws her projection from *el señor* then identifies possible relatedness between them on another level. Furthermore, Sorpresa's promise is to a sleepy moon which appears 'rodeada de un halo color naranja' [surrounded by an orange halo] (163). Orange is produced by mixing red and yellow which correspond, respectively, to the functions of feeling and intuition, both of which have been essential in the process of individuation depicted in the tale and which were identified as the less developed functions.

In the course of the process of individuation depicted in this *cuento* – encounters with shadow and animus figures and the first glimpse of the Self – Sorpresa has discovered the meaning of her life. Those indelible outlines, which Stein described, trace the storyteller she is and will become. The energy which threatened to break out destructively will be channelled into the act of writing. The destructive fire has been transformed into one which is creative, and the revenge-filled flames of hell have become the creative flames of Pentecost. The potentially destructive desire for power buried with the amber has released a different power – 'the power to create beautiful, magical, enthralling stories' (Brown 1988: 98).

CHAPTER 4

El quehacer más importante: Listening as Eros in *Caperucita en Manhattan*

Introduction

The traditional story of *Little Red Riding Hood* exists in numerous versions and has been re-told many times. The image of the little girl in red has captured imaginations over the centuries and continues to appear today in both word and image. Although the basic story of a child or children being eaten by a wolf or monster can be found in the oral tradition in many countries, the versions most familiar to children in the Western world are the tales of *Little Red Riding Hood* (*LRRH*) by Perrault (1697), and the Grimm brothers (1812). While the core of the tale is recognisable in both versions, there are significant differences. Martín Gaite seems to have been familiar with both stories: her translation of a number of Perrault's tales was published in 1980, and she refers to the differing endings in an essay in *Cuento* (1988a: 124). Critics have observed that Martín Gaite's re-telling seems more closely influenced by the Grimm brothers' version because it includes specific warnings by the child's mother (Llorente 2002: n.1 and Odartey-Wellington 2000: 552).

Charles Perrault and the Brothers Grimm: The Different Versions

The focus in the traditional tales is on the little girl who goes by herself to her sick grandmother's house to take her some nourishment. The story tells of her encounter on her journey with a hungry wolf who tricks the child and eats first the grandmother and then LRRH. The little girl in the Perrault and Grimm tales is described as 'the prettiest little creature that has ever been seen. Her mother was excessively fond of her' (Perrault 1998: 27); and as 'a sweet little maiden, who was loved by all who knew her' (Grimm 1996: 116). Nevertheless, in both tales she is especially dear to her grandmother. It is the grandmother who gives her the garment which leads to her name: in Perrault it was a little red hood, 'the kind ladies wear to go riding'; whereas the Grimms' tale identified it as 'a little red velvet cloak'. The father is not mentioned. Of the mother we know very little in the French tale, but the Grimms added an important aspect to their version: LRRH's mother gives her clear instructions on how to behave on the way to her grandmother's house and when she arrives there: 'Go quickly, before it gets hot, and don't loiter by the way, or run, or you will fall down and break the bottle and there won't be any wine for Grandmother. When you get there, don't forget to say "Good-morning" prettily, without staring about you' (1996: 116). The mother's words, while apparently intended to keep the child safe and instil good manners, nevertheless put her in danger.

In the basket of Perrault's LRRH is a custard and a pot of butter. The custard is one of a batch made by the little girl's mother and is intended to nourish her ill grandmother. The Grimms put a cake and a bottle of wine in their basket, with the same purpose. At the end of the Grimms' tale we are told that 'the grandmother ate the cake and drank the wine which Red Riding Hood had brought, and she soon felt quite strong' (1996: 119). As might be expected, in versions of the traditional tale written for children today, 'the wine is often eliminated as being politically incorrect' (Beckett 2002: 35). Also, in other re-tellings the wolf is not killed but only hit hard on the back of its head and shaken until LRRH and her grandmother pop out (Beckett 2002: 38). The little girls in both the Grimms' and Perrault's versions meet the wolf in a wood, and both behave trustingly, giving the animal a clear description of their destination. Perrault's grandmother's house is on the other side of the mill, the first house in the village, whereas the Grimms put the house in the woods, half an hour from the village, and located under three big oak trees, near a hedge of nut trees. The presence of woodcutters working nearby prevents the wolf in the French version from eating the child there and then to assuage his hunger, whereas the Grimm wolf is more cunning and greedy: 'The wolf thought: "This tender little creature will be a plump morsel; she will be nicer than the old woman. I must be cunning and snap them both up"' (1996: 117). The voice of this wolf challenges the caution of the little girl's mother: 'Look at the pretty flowers, Red Riding Hood. Why don't you look about you? I don't believe you even hear the birds sing, you're as solemn as if you were going to school' (1996: 117). In both versions LRRH spends time in the woods picking flowers. Meanwhile the wolf eats the grandmother, disguises himself in her clothes and gets into her bed.

Both little girls go through the well-known question-and-answer session with the disguised animal, ending with 'what big teeth you've got', and both are devoured. However, although Perrault's protagonist is afraid when she hears 'the big voice of the Wolf', she thinks that her grandmother, who has been very ill, has a cold and is hoarse, thus finding a logical explanation to assuage her anxieties. We learn more about the Grimm child's reaction on arrival at the house: 'She was astonished when she got to the house to find the door open, and when she entered the room everything seemed so strange. She felt quite frightened, but she did not know why. "Generally I like coming to see Grandmother so much," she thought' (1996: 117–18). Thus, the little girl's instincts are sound but she does not act on them, having been instructed by her mother in a strict code of behaviour. Following her instinct would have made her much more cautious and wary. Instead, she ignores the sense of strangeness she feels, over-rides her instinct, and is gobbled up. In contrast, Zipes claims that Perrault's LRRH 'trusts her instincts when she speaks to the wolf' and that this leads her into trouble (Dundes 1989: 123), whereas it appears rather that her behaviour is naive. She, too, explains her 'grandmother's' strange voice in a way that falsely reassures her and fails to keep her alert and attentive.

The difference between the endings of these two versions is also well known: Perrault's wolf's hunger is satisfied and he ends with a moral, warning 'young ladies' about 'wolves of every sort and every character [...] who [...] ogle and leer; languish, cajole and glance' (1998: 31). It is Perrault's ending which leads Martín Gaite to exclude *LRRH* from the fairy tales she disparaged for being too predictable in storyline and outcome and having characters which were passive. On the other hand, her attitude to the Grimms' ending, in which LRRH and her grandmother are rescued from the wolf by a hunter, is less accepting: 'A Caperucita algunas versiones posteriores la sacan del vientre del lobo sana y salva, que eso sí que es un pegote' [Some later versions take Little Red Riding Hood out of the wolf's stomach safe and sound, which is certainly a botched job] (1988a: 146). Yet Bettelheim cites Andrew Lang as considering the Grimm's version much more typical and even suggesting that it may have been the original ending:

> Little Red Cap [the Grimms' name for the child] and her grandmother are resuscitated, 'the wolf it was that died'. This may either have been the original ending, omitted by Perrault because it was too wildly impossible for the nurseries of the time of Louis XIV, or children may have insisted on having the story 'turn out well'. In either case the German *Märchen* preserves one of the most widely spread mythical incidents in the world – the reappearance of living people out of the monster that has devoured them. (1978: 318, n.53)

Joseph Campbell – whose well-known study, *The Hero with a Thousand Faces*, Martín Gaite had read (2002a: 78), and who was cited in connection with *Pastel* – claims that the 'popular motif [of a hero being swallowed by a monster] gives emphasis to the lesson that the passage of the threshold is a form of self-annihilation' (1968: 91), that is, it strengthens the argument that the ego must give up its wilful determination to have its own way. For Campbell, the experience of being swallowed and then liberated from the belly of a terrifying creature means that 'having died to his personal ego, [the hero] arose again established in the Self' (1968: 243). This would suggest that *LRRH* is a tale of resurrection or rebirth, which was also Jung's perspective on *Sleeping Beauty* (1956: 242). Such an experience would be part of the process of individuation, and would find common ground with periods of withdrawal such as the case of Serena in *Castillo* or Sorpresa's getting lost in the basement of the *Casa Grande* in *Pastel*.

Interpretations of *Little Red Riding Hood*

Studies of the traditional tales proliferate, including the variations from around the world, along with critical appreciations of the retellings. In the past twenty-five years there have been a number of critically acclaimed studies exploring both the original versions and re-tellings.[1] Most critics concur that the tale points to a sexual encounter between the wolf and LRRH. Perrault's overt moral warned young women against allowing themselves to be seduced by charming, sweet-talking men and thereby ruining their chances of marriage. The German scholar Jack Zipes states bluntly that 'it is because rape and violence are at the core of the history of LRRH that it is the most widespread and notorious fairy tale in the western world, if not in the entire world' (Zipes 1993: xi). He claims that the retellings relate this same interpretation of the tale: 'There is no end to her story: even though LRRH is constantly mutilated by the wolf and dies, she is always reincarnated in some retold form to mark shifts in our attitudes toward gender formation, sexuality, and the use of power' (Ibid. xi).

None of these interpretations of the original versions reflect Martín Gaite's re-telling. As Morales Ladrón asserts, 'Martín Gaite corta de raíz cualquier aspecto que pudiese evocar violencia o erotismo' [Martín Gaite nips in the bud any aspect which could evoke violence or eroticism] (2002: 179). In another, very different interpretation of the Grimms' version by Ronald Murphy, the key lies in the red cap. The red cap or hood in both versions has been interpreted as signifying sexuality; as 'sin and blood' (Zipes 1993: 8); 'harlots, scandal and blood' (Orenstein 2002: 36); 'violent emotions, very much including sexual ones' (Bettelheim 1978: 173); a cap of red roses 'worn in celebrations of May' (Saintyves 1989: 76); and even as the red cap of liberty worn by Republicans (Jäger 1989: 102). However, for Murphy, who believes that Wilhelm Grimm saw 'fragment[s] of ancient religious poetry' in the tales he collected (2000: 78), red 'is the colour of Pentecost', which is 'a sign of the moment of spiritual maturity in a Christian reading of the tale' (Ibid. 74). That the child visiting her sick grandmother carries in her basket not the custard tart and butter of Perrault, but a cake or round flat bread (from the French *galette*) and a bottle of wine, indicates to Murphy that the story has been given a Christian foundation, through the introduction of the elements of Communion (bread and wine). Murphy sees other religious elements in the tale. In LRRH's straying off the path to pick flowers he identifies the legacy of Adam and Eve: 'The warning, "don't

1 Dundes (1989) Zipes (1993) Orenstein (2002) and Beckett (2002, 2008 & 2009).

go off the path, otherwise you will fall" tells the reader that the story will deal once again, as in the case of *Hansel and Gretel*, with the Fall' (2000: 76). The wolf is regarded as the devil: 'In the Grimms' German dictionary we find that the entry under "uses of the word" states that "wolf", under Biblical influence, has primarily been used as an image of Satan' (Ibid. 78); and the grandmother's house is seen as the locus of the struggle between good and evil.[2] Even the symbolism of the oak trees and hazel bushes is cited in support of this interpretation: 'The live oak spreading above, and the noxious hazel below, and the wolf is in league with the hazel, as Red Riding Hood well knows, and is deadly' (Ibid. 80). For the German scholar, the rescuing hunter is Christ: 'The hunter's identity as the Savior, as Christ, is shown in the resurrection of the two women, ancient and new, from the death which comes through succumbing to temptation, sin' (Ibid. 82). This is similar to Murphy's interpretation of the story of *Snow White*, discussed in connection with *Castillo*, where he identified the prince with Christ. It is an imaginative and well-argued interpretation which extends far beyond the more reductive critical approach of Zipes.

While I do not support all of the details of Murphy's argument, the symbolism of the bread and wine is compelling and the scholarship underpinning the interpretation of the location of the grandmother's house persuasive. However, what is striking in the Grimms' version of the tale is the greed of the wolf. The general depiction of animals' reliance on instinct supports the view that they eat when they are hungry. Undisturbed by woodcutters (unlike Perrault's tale), the wolf could have eaten the little girl straight away. Instead, its instinct is overlain with a desire for greater pleasure – satisfying his hunger with the grandmother, then gorging himself on the tastier morsel of the child. LRRH's own instinct for danger, as we have seen, is also overlain, by a desire to please her mother, and in the Perrault version, too, the child explains away her fears and fails to act on them. The hunter, on the other hand, hearing snoring coming from the old woman's bedroom, does not ignore it, but follows his instinct and also his concern

2 'The role played by the serpent in mythology is analogous to the end of the world. [...] In the story of Red Riding Hood, the serpent or fish is replaced by a wolf, because he is the typical destroyer' (Jung 1956: 438 n.87).

for her: 'A huntsman went past the house, and thought, "How loudly the old lady is snoring; I must see if there's anything the matter with her"' (Grimm 1996: 118). Thus, the hunter is the only character who is true to his instinct and who responds to the reality of other human beings – in this case the possibility that the snoring woman is ill – rather than seeing them in terms of his own desires. As a result, the hunter rescues the feminine from the darkness of the unconscious. Murphy's identification of the hunter with Christ, given Jung's identification of Christ with the Self, therefore seems appropriate as it would have to be a very powerful spirit which was capable of such a feat. The ending of the Grimms' tale, however, does not fulfil the promise of the rescue as LRRH resolves: 'I'll never again wander off into the forest as long as I live, if my mother forbids it' (1996: 119).

Red symbolises feeling and, therefore, includes love and eros or relatedness, which are connected to the feminine. Furthermore, in paintings and images, Christ is most often depicted wearing a red cloak. If we recognise that, historical development aside, the fundamental principles of Christianity are love of God and love of self and all other human beings, the Grimms' tale of *LRRH* can be seen as a symbolic representation of the potential powerful effects of Christianity: the liberation of love from the darkness of the unconscious. The importance of instinct and of listening to it is part of the message and can be related to the injunction to be 'cunning as snakes and yet innocent as doves' (Matthew 10. 16). This particular aspect of the teaching of Christ has not been taken up into collective consciousness, which too often, like LRRH's mother (and LRRH herself), sees Christianity as being concerned with right behaviour rather than reliance on, and relationship with, the inner Self. Jung, speaking of Christianity and complaining that 'our myth has become mute, and gives no answers' (Jung 1983: 364), echoes the failure to address this aspect: 'For example, the words are put into Christ's mouth: "Be ye therefore wise as serpents, and harmless as doves." For what purpose do men need the cunning of serpents? And what is the link between this cunning and the innocence of the dove?' (Ibid. 364).

Critics who complain that the story of *Little Red Riding Hood* is too didactic, too focussed on teaching children – particularly young girls – how they must behave, fail to recognise the challenge which the hunter presents. In some cases the hunter is seen as being linked with the mother – 'the protective spirit of the home, secretly related to the protective spirit of the hunter' (Murphy 2000: 83) – whereas the opposite is true. The story of *Little Red Riding Hood*, whatever the Grimms' intention, seems to depict the real meaning of Christianity and Christian communion, and the liberation with which Christianity, with its fundamental preoccupation with freedom and absence of fear, is concerned.

Caperucita en Manhattan

Like the original tale, Martín Gaite's re-telling, *Caperucita en Manhattan*, also lends itself to a range of sometimes contradictory interpretations of this highly regarded novel. It has been described as a search for communication and an ideal interlocutor (Calvi 1992–3) and a search for freedom and identity (Moulin 1997 and Pérès 2004) – all themes common in Martín Gaite's work. The importance of the role of the fantastic in this re-telling of a tale which, in its original forms, does not include any supernatural aspect (Bayó Belenguer 2002: 196), is highlighted in a number of studies. Llorente considers that fantasy conquers reality at the end of the story, and Odartey-Wellington agrees that 'el final feliz de esa novela gira alrededor de la reivindicación de la imaginación sobre la razón' [the happy ending of this novel revolves around the vindication of imagination over reason] (2004a: 220). In contrast, Calvi argues that in Sara's vision of the world, 'il fantastico svolge un ruolo privilegiato, senza però eclissare il senso del reale' [the fantastic displays a privileged role, nevertheless without eclipsing the sense of the real] (1992–3: 66). Several critics observe the key role of the fantastic within the everyday world (Calvi 1992–3: 67; Blejer 2007: 20), and the blurring of the boundaries between dream and reality (Teruel 2006: 149).[3] However, not all critics view the mix of reality and fantasy positively (Martín 1991: 33).

3 This, of course, represents Martín Gaite's entire approach as the 'narrador testigo' [storyteller witness] (Teruel 2008: 9) whose vision encompasses dreams, fantasy, mystery, magic and the supernatural, in addition to external reality.

Several connections between *Caperucita* and other works by Martín Gaite have been identified. Calvi sees clear links with *Pastel* and, in the protagonist, Sara, being at odds with her family, also draws parallels with Alina in *Las ataduras* and David Fuente in *Ritmo lento* (1992–3). Daniella Blejer agrees with the link with *Las ataduras* and, in addition, notes connections with *Usos amorosos de la postguerra española* (1987b) because of Sara's silent subversive struggle (2007: 17). Isabel Roger sees shared aspects between C.'s mysterious visitor in *Cuarto* and the supernatural figure in *Caperucita*, Miss Lunatic, primarily because of 'la ambigüedad, el no saber o no poder resolver si la novela era producto de un sueño o de una visita real' [the ambiguity, not knowing or not being able to decide whether the novel was the result of a dream or a real visit] (1992: 330). Both of these figures also symbolise aspects of the unconscious encountered in the process of individuation, namely the Self (Miss Lunatic) and the animus (the man in black).

Martín Gaite's re-telling is in two parts. The first sets the scene and introduces in some detail all of the characters who play a role in Sara's life – her parents Samuel and Vivian, her grandmother Rebeca and the neighbours the Taylors – as well as describing the dreams of Sara and her grandmother. Martín Gaite creates a pretext at the end of the first part of the book for Sara to stay with the family's neighbours and, hence, find it easier to escape. The second part – *la aventura* [the adventure] – depicts Sara's journey alone to her grandmother's house during which she encounters the millionaire businessman, Mr Woolf. As Couso rightly points out, this part of the tale belongs to a different world:

> Si la primera sección concluía con la lectura de Sara del libro sobre la estatua de la Libertad, el capítulo seis introduce al personaje de Miss Lunatic, que se presenta con una serie de rasgos pertenecientes a un mundo distinto, llámese fantasía, imaginación, o sueño. (Ibid. 26–7)
>
> [If the first section ends with Sara reading the book about the Statue of Liberty, chapter six introduces the character of Miss Lunatic, who appears with a number of characteristics pertaining to a different world, call it fantasy, imagination, or dream.]

Traditional tales usually have rural settings, and Martín Gaite followed this pattern in her earlier fairy tales. As the title of *Caperucita* indicates, this story shifts to the North American metropolis, distinguishing it from both *Castillo* and *Pastel* where time and place were less specific and, in the case of the former, very vague. However, the differences in the responses to the writer's depiction of the setting of *Caperucita* are stark. Martín Gaite relates that a friend said to her 'es que se respire Manhattan aquí, está estupendamente descrito' (1993a: 28) [you really get a sense of Manhattan here, it's wonderfully well described]. In contrast, for Salustiano Martín 'la realidad [de Manhattan] no es así y uno no puede dejar de recordar [...] cómo es en verdad' (1991: 33) [the reality of Manhattan isn't like that and one can't help but recall [...] what it's like in reality].

Like most archetypal tales (and including the Christian story), and in contrast with the glamorous associations of the locus of the title, the heroine comes from the duller, concrete suburb of Brooklyn, where she lives in an unattractive tower block. At the start of the story, Sara shares the attitude of Brooklyn children in general who see Manhattan as exotic and compare it to Brooklyn, which they see as a lost place where nothing ever happens. To cross over Brooklyn Bridge into the exciting, glamorous, luxurious and slightly dangerous world of Manhattan is a collective dream. Fittingly, Brooklyn Bridge acts as a symbolic link between the everyday world and the world of dreams, further supporting the view that the second part of the story, set entirely in Manhattan, takes place on the level of the imagination.

Unlike *Castillo*, where the symbols of the Self were either masculine or inanimate, in *Caperucita* as in *Pastel*, the symbol of the Self is linked to a goddess-like figure, as Miss Lunatic is the spirit of the Statue of Liberty, which the protagonist, Sara, describes as a goddess.[4] In addition, like the traditional tales and her two earlier fairy tales, Martín Gaite's story seems to seek to compensate the collective conscious attitude and values: 'Fairy tales are related to collective consciousness as the dream is related to an individual's consciousness: there is a slight compensatory function which points to certain dangers which are not indicated openly in collective consciousness' (von Franz 1990: 69). Although von Franz is talking about

4 It is typical for the Self to appear in a feminine form in the dreams and fantasies of women.

traditional tales, there is much in this that is relevant to Martín Gaite's stories. In *Castillo* excessive materialism and the consequent alienation from reality were criticised together with an outlook on life which was centred on fear and mistrust. In *Pastel* again it was fear – of difference, of a person living their uniqueness and appearing to flaunt the collective code – which was challenged through the person of Sorpresa. *Caperucita* takes up both of these themes – fear and excessive materialism – and, in addition, proclaims a new way of living. It has been claimed that Martín Gaite 'trata de ofrecer otro camino a los seres humanos' (Martín 1991: 33) [tries to offer human beings a different way], and this is particularly evident in *Caperucita*.

Children being left alone is a typical feature of fairy tales – as Sara realises from her own stories – as this constitutes the core of the adventure. As in *Pastel*, here, too, there is a magical story which takes place on the level of the imagination.[5] However, while forming a distinct part of the book, Martín Gaite uses devices to bewitch the reader into believing that the second part is but a continuation of the first by introducing specific wishes, dreams and plans in the first part which are then developed in the second: Sara dreams of going to live with her grandmother; she wants to see her grandmother wearing her green dress again; her grandmother wants a rich boyfriend; and Sara's family and their neighbours, following an unusually rapturous reception for Sara's mother Vivian's strawberry tart at Sara's birthday meal, plan to go to the famous pastry-shop and tea rooms, *El Dulce Lobo* [The Sweet Wolf], and compare Mr Woolf's strawberry tart with Vivian's.

5 Martín argues that Sara is a continuation of Sorpresa (1991: 33). Martín Gaite would not disagree, as she asserted in an interview 'todas se parecen' [they're all alike] (1991a: 11). The development from *Pastel* to *Caperucita* can also be seen in the depiction of the individuation process in the two stories, although the aspects portrayed are different. Both heroes find their vocation, the way in life that is theirs alone.

Vivian

Whereas we learn very little about Little Red Riding Hood's mother in the traditional tales, in *Caperucita* Sara Allen's mother, Vivian, is a much more prominent figure but one who is also out of touch with her instincts. Critics have identified Vivian as stereotyped and exaggerated: 'Vivian Allen, Sara's mother, is presented in a profoundly negative, indeed exaggeratedly ridiculous, light' (O'Leary & Ribeiro de Menezes 2008: 256). Like LRRH's mother, who told her how to behave on the way to her grandmother's and what to do when she arrived there, Vivian's emphasis is on behaviour and giving instructions to her daughter not to look around her, not to let go of her hand. However, re-tellings of the tale reflect the contemporary situation, and, in contrast to LRRH's mother in the traditional tale, the mother in this Spanish version would never allow her child to travel alone to her grandmother's to take the strawberry tart on a Saturday.

Sara's mother is associated with baking tarts, especially strawberry ones, which has become a ritual, something she does every day after work. However, it is a ritual which is worn out for, instead of considering first the occasion and then what kind of baking might be appropriate for it, she does the opposite, looking for a reason to justify the baking. Thus Vivian Allen fails to respond to the life around her, choosing instead to forge ahead with her own desires, and rendering any special aspect of the strawberry tart stale and routine. Von Franz talks about 'the famous partnership between shadow and animus. The shadow wants to do something in a driven way and the animus provides the right collective justification, and then the whole situation is wrong!' (1993a: 213–14). Vivian is driven to make the tarts and the excuses she makes are very general and not appropriate to the individual situation. This is the opposite attitude to that defined by von Franz as the highest level of the feminine, which would mean 'knowing instinctively what is right *in this special case*, knowing how to act in each individual case' (1993a: 213). The drivenness also means she fails to accept her own needs, such as when she sets about making the tart after getting back from Sara's birthday meal in the Chinese restaurant, just because it is Friday evening and that is her routine, despite being tired. The slavishness of Vivian's adherence to this routine is seen to be even emptier when we learn, through Sara's father, that Rebeca does not like the tart. Vivian's behaviour reflects the relationship between shadow and animus described by von Franz. She is driven by unconscious forces and is unable either to respond to or challenge them – awareness and reason are alien to her. Von Franz argues that it is possible, with a lot of hard work, to 'give the animus subtlety' and this 'would mean finding the attitude which suits the situation' (1993a: 213), but at this stage, in terms of individuation, Vivian remains relatively undeveloped.

Erich Neumann points out that originally all the main activities of primitive peoples represented a kind of ritual, including that of food preparation, and adds: 'One expression of this fact is that these activities were often handed down secretly' (1963: 281). The recipe for the strawberry tart is something Vivian keeps very secret, to the extent that when she has to give it to someone, she alters the quantities so they never get it right. This associates it with ancient rituals, but at the same time it represents a distortion of the province of the Feminine, since here, in order to preserve the secret without openly admitting it, the recipe is transformed to become inedible.

In addition to the ritual of the strawberry tart, there is another, equally meaningless ritual of a cucumber sandwich she leaves for her husband every week together with a note reminding him of this and of where she's going. On the one hand, her husband is happy to fend for himself in the local Chinese restaurant, on the other, a cucumber sandwich, with its associations of daintiness and lack of substance, seems an inappropriate lunch for someone returning from a morning's physical work. The note is clearly unnecessary as Vivian makes the same trip every Saturday, and the formal tone she uses is completely inappropriate. The fact that she does not write it quickly and sometimes sits staring into the middle distance, suggests the strangeness for Vivian of this contact with the written word, and the way the experience seems to open a door to a different level to which she draws near but does not enter, thereby remaining undeveloped.

Vivian seems to be in the grip of something – a negative animus – which compels her to act with scant regard for others or for herself. When she is outside her home with Sara she tries to prevent the little girl from looking too much around her, particularly from looking at other people, whereas Sara feels compassion for those who are alone and ignored by the people around them. Taking refuge in the collective approach, based on fear, Vivian's attitude is the opposite to her daughter, Sara, whose compassion is individual. The little girl is drawn to those who are rejected and ignored by the majority. This evidence of conscious feeling for the other person contrasts with her mother's more unconscious collective attitude. Vivian tries to shut herself off, by creating invisible barriers and ignoring her fellow passengers. However, those wealthier than Vivian also shut themselves up in their limousines and secure homes to keep out other people who they do not trust and with whom they do not wish to engage. Vivian travels on the underground because she has to, so her attitude is not so different from the prevailing collective outlook which is so preoccupied with security and based on fear.

Unlike the hunter in the traditional tale, Vivian's focus is not on the reality of the other person but on an *imagined* need, as when she complains that her mother will not come to live with them and let herself be looked after. In light of Martín Gaite's depiction of Rebeca as a storyteller, as lively, individual, and wishing for a rich boyfriend, Vivian's attitude is ridiculous and bears no relationship to reality, as critics have recognised (Llorente 2002: 4; Odartey-Wellington 2004a: 215; Carbayo Abengózar 1998a: 140).

Vivian is depicted as a character in whom the eros function is faulty and, therefore, represents a principle in need of renewal. She typifies a collective attitude, dominated by fear and by a corresponding desire for power and control. This desire for power, revealed in her thwarted attitude towards her mother and her admonitions to her daughter, are projected outwards instead of being turned inwards to the much-needed separation of the animus and the shadow through the development of a conscious relationship between the ego and the animus. The outcome of such a shift on the inner plane would mean the predominance of eros, not power. This is quite different from the depiction of the relationship between ego, shadow and animus in *Cuarto* (Martín Gaite 1990), where the man in black was identified by Julian Palley as an animus figure, with Carola, the woman who telephones, as a shadow figure (1983: 224). The successful partnership in *Cuarto* is between ego and animus. The phone call from Carola at the end of the novel, in which she criticises the man in black's behaviour, indicates difficulties in the relationship between shadow and animus, whereas his conversation with C. (as animus and ego respectively) results in creative activity – the writing of *Cuarto* – which illustrates the kind of effect such a shift in inner relationships can have. In *Caperucita*, Vivian represents a model of the feminine which is flawed and outdated and which needs to be renewed.

Rebeca Little/Gloria Star

In Sara Allen Martín Gaite has again created a ten-year-old protagonist whose restlessness and dreams are the key to her own development and that of those around her. Sara resembles the traditional LRRH in the strong bond which exists with her grandmother, such that she dreams of going to live with her one day. This bond which crosses the generations appears frequently in Martín Gaite's work.[6] One of the reasons for this strong bond across the generations may be, as suggested by Hall, that grandmothers take a nursing rather than a mothering attitude, one which 'accepts a child as it is, in its weaknesses, and does not spiderlike spin fantasies around it that can immobilize' (1980: 79). As critics have recognised, Sara's grandmother, Rebeca Little does not share her own daughter, Vivian's, qualms about the precociousness of the child's questions about death and freedom, instead encouraging Vivian to send Sara to her so she can give her some answers.

6 Martín Gaite claimed in an interview in 1991 that in *Caperucita* 'hay un ingrediente nuevo, que es el de los cuentos de la abuela, la relación especial que la niña tiene con ella. Y es que creo que son muy frecuentes los casos de niños que están más vinculados a sus abuelos que a sus propios padres. No es mi caso personal, pero lo he visto mucho a lo largo de la vida' [there's a new element, which is the grandmother's stories, the special relationship the little girl has with her. And I think that the case of children being closer to their grandparents than to their own parents is very common. It wasn't the case with me but I've seen it a lot in the course of my life] (1991a: 12). The relationship is present in most of the novels written after *Caperucita*, including *Nubosidad* (Sofía's mother and her daughter), and *Irse* where, as in *Reina*, the relationship is between a grandmother and grandson.

Furthermore, as critics have emphasised (Carbayo Abengózar 1998b: 10 & Morales Ladrón 2002: 177), Rebeca is a healthy, spirited woman, unlike her counterparts in the traditional tales who are recovering from illness.

Martín Gaite's heroine's red garment is a raincoat which, unlike the traditional tales, is not identified as a gift from her grandmother or as a pretty thing. It is functional and burdensome, a raincoat made of oilcloth, which her mother makes her wear even when rain is not forecast. In contrast, the gifts she receives from her grandmother are generous and are in keeping with a child's dreams, reflecting the bond between them. Having won 150 dollars playing bingo, Rebeca throws the money into the air on her return home,[7] and later gives Sara half, telling her to choose one of the evening bags in the wardrobe to keep it in. The blue satin bag embroidered with sequins which Sara chooses is not practical but it is lovely, and ideal for a child whose dream – inspired by a fur-collared coat once worn by her grandmother – is to be a glamorous actress dressed in furs and drinking champagne, which further emphasises the bond between the two. Although the bag is for a grown up, Bettelheim's claim that the grandmother in the traditional tale 'can be viewed as a symbol of a premature transfer of sexual attractiveness' (Bettelheim 1978: 173), does not fit this re-telling. Although her last partner has left her, Rebeca asks her granddaughter after winning the money to find her a rich boyfriend. And it is well known that young girls, such as Sorpresa in *Pastel*, want to be grown up and often love pretty, sparkly things.

Rebeca Little's originality is also evident in her attitude to crime and to ritual, again distinguishing her from her daughter. Rebeca's flat is in glamorous Manhattan, albeit in the poorer district of Morningside.[8] Images of the urban jungle aside, while not in a wood, the flat is opposite Morningside Park, which years before was the place where five women were murdered.

7 Teruel recalls Ana María Martín Gaite telling him how Carmen similarly threw into the air in front of her daughter the money she had earned from teaching during one of her spells in the USA (2006: 150, n.13).

8 As Joan Lipman Brown points out, 'Martín Gaite got a few things wrong, possibly on purpose. There is no "Morningside" neighborhood in Manhattan, only the more prosaic "Morningside Heights"' (2017: 207).

The perpetrator, who was never found, was nicknamed 'the Bronx vampire'[9] and the park continues to be viewed as a very dangerous place which should be avoided at all times. Rebeca's attitude to the park and its reputation are at odds with the collective view. She continues to walk there, reasoning that it must be safe as no prospective criminal would waste their time in such a deserted place. Her response is rational and illuminates the unreason in the collective fear of the park, which runs through the community and is accepted without reflection.[10] In addition, she has an image of the murderer himself as someone very clever and good-looking. In other words, she sees him as a human being and not as the personification of evil. She does not project onto him her shadow, personal or collective. The freedom from fear which such an outlook brings allows her to act as a good mirror – one in which others can see themselves reflected clearly without it being clouded by prejudice or projection. Rebeca appears to be a woman who has made significant progress in the lifelong process of individuation. Her determination to see even a serious criminal as a human being, and one with some good qualities, is also in accordance with Christ's injunction not to judge or condemn others: 'Love your enemies, do good to those who hate you. [...] Be compassionate [...]. Do not judge, and you will not be judged; do not condemn, and you will not be condemned' (Luke 6. 27 & 36–7).

However, Rebeca's attitude is startling even to Sara. Yet without the kind of step Rebeca takes, away from the typical vilification resulting from the projection of the shadow, community is impossible. In *Reina*, Leonardo's grandmother shows a similar sympathy when she asserts that 'ningun malo tiene la culpa de haberse vuelto malo' [no villain is to blame for going wrong] (1994: 101). The folklorist Max Lüthi records the attitude of the Romantic poet Novalis: '[Some tales suggest] that when man overcomes himself he also overcomes nature and a miracle takes place. In one tale a

9 Morales Ladrón comments that 'lo más parecido al símbolo del lobo que aparece en el cuento es el "vampiro del Bronx"' [the 'vampire of the Bronx' comes closest in the tale to the symbol of the wolf] (2002: 178, n.18).

10 Discussing unreason in emotion, John Macmurray gives the example of someone who is 'terribly afraid of a mouse' and argues that such fear 'is not in terms of the real nature of the situation' (1992: 11).

bear is transformed into a prince at the moment he is loved. Perhaps a similar transformation would occur if man began to love the evil in the world' (1976: 81). This represents a leap from loving a creature/person to loving evil. The finer distinction – between the person and the crime – implied in Rebeca Little's attitude, seems to address the problem more precisely. In Jungian terms this would mean accepting one's own shadow and one's contribution to collective life, and recognising one's personal responsibility.

Martín Gaite's reaction to the murder of his children in the early 1960s by a tailor in Madrid and the challenge of the writer to those who were content to label it a tragedy and the tailor as ill or mentally disturbed were discussed in Chapter 1. Taking a very different perspective, Martín Gaite considered that 'algo de tal magnitud no puede existir sin tener raíces en alguna parte, mucho más hondas y reveladoras que la de una mera desgracia familiar' [something of such magnitude could not exist without having roots somewhere, much deeper and more revealing than a mere family misfortune] (2002a: 61). She goes much further than Rebeca, focusing not so much on the perpetrator (who she described as an instrument of God) as on the crime itself. Her view is that it should be regarded it as an act inspired by God for a clear purpose: 'Para ver si los hombres se retiran de una vez a buscar en todo lo que hacen y dicen la relación con tanto, tantísimo espanto' [To see if people will retire once and for all in order to try to find in all they say and do the link with such appalling horror] (2002a: 62). She sees clearly the inter-connectedness of human beings and, as a result of this, the shared responsibility of all. Written more than fifty years ago it is still a perspective that many today would find shocking and incomprehensible. The collective reaction in this case is different from the response to the *vampiro del Bronx* as there is no perceived personal threat from the Madrid tailor. However, one cannot help feeling that Martín Gaite would have insisted that there was a connection in the Bronx case too and that it needed to be understood.

Martín Gaite's perspective, including the idea that God could have a role in this kind of evil along with the shared responsibility of the whole community, is very much in line with Jung's thinking. One of Jung's major preoccupations was with 'the dark side of the Divinity' which he felt had been lost between the Old Testament and the development of the Christian message. The New Testament is full of recognition of the reality of the world and warnings about being wise and wary, and of the treatment which could be expected by those who preached Christ's message, but, as we saw in the analysis of the Grimms' version of *LRRH*, these are often lost under a more superficial cloak of 'being nice' and an emphasis on behaviour rather than on the inner, spiritual attitude. Martín Gaite looks squarely at the evil act in the *Calle Mayor* and argues that for her this more than anything else '[sería] la mayor prueba de la existencia de Dios' [[would be] the greatest proof of the existence of God] (2002a: 62).

In *Caperucita*, in addition to her challenge to collective perceptions through Rebeca, Martín Gaite also subverts the typical response to the portrayal of Central Park in the media and various art forms as a dangerous place to be avoided after dark[11] by describing it an exciting place to be at night, watching out for all the murderers and muggers and hiding from them when necessary. In traditional fairy tales children and other characters are placed in dangerous situations which rarely correspond to the everyday encounters of readers in their own world. Hansel and Gretel meet a witch, LRRH a wolf, other characters fight with mythical creatures, carry out seemingly impossible tasks, and suffer at the hands of wicked members of their family. In her tale Martín Gaite evokes a danger familiar to most readers, then suggests a means of dealing with it. By challenging the tendency of parents and others to coddle, she frees the reader's imagination from the inhibiting fear often induced by the collective attitude. She does not pretend that the dangers do not exist, but she insists that our response to them need not completely constrain our behaviour, that we need not lock ourselves away in our homes, hiding from the things of which we are afraid.

11 Calvi rightly speaks of 'il fascino della Grande Mela, che tante immagini cinematografiche hanno reso familiare anche a chi non l'ha mai visitata di persona' [the fascination of the Big Apple, which so many cinematographic images have made familiar even to those who have never visited it in person] (1992–3: 65). Specifically regarding Central Park, Terry Jones partly challenges the typical depiction through the somewhat bizarre behaviour of his main characters at the end of *The Fisher King*; Chris Columbus puts friendship at the heart of the park in the shape of the Bird Woman in *Home Alone 2: Lost in New York* (1992); while *The Out of Towners* written by Neil Simon and directed by Arthur Hiller (1970) presents a more typical view.

The Renewal of Ritual

In the second part of Martín Gaite's tale, when Sara sets out to her grandmother's house she takes with her the strawberry tart which her mother bakes every Friday evening. As Sara's father had recognised, her grandmother is bored with it and has admitted that she often gives it away. However, on the visit by Sara and her mother described in the first part of the story, which takes place the week before, Sara is first left on her own for half an hour in her grandmother's house, then has a further half hour alone with her grandmother who has just returned with her bingo winnings. The happiness resulting from Rebeca's good fortune and the understanding between the two, together with the temporary absence of the obsessively tidy and unfree Vivian, create a different atmosphere in which both find the strawberry tart tastes delicious. This contrast with the usual experience illustrates that despite the emptiness which all ritual can attain, it can be renewed and given meaning through spontaneity and feeling. Rebeca's explanation – 'Es que no hay nada como una buena conversación y no tener prisa para que sepan ricas las cosas' [There's nothing like a good conversation and not being in a hurry for making things taste delicious] (69) – indicates that what matters is the psychological atmosphere, the feeling and relatedness between persons. The symbolism of the strawberry tart – the redness of strawberries and their heart shape link them with feeling and eros – also supports the interpretation that it is in general the feeling function which is faulty. Vivian's drivenness in making the tart is unhealthy, while the strawberry tart in *El Dulce Lobo* – whose owner is a lonely millionaire – is of a lower standard than it should be.

Animus Figures and Masculine Influences

In addition to the glamorous grandmother, in Martín Gaite's tale there is also a balance of other influences which are missing from the original tales. Unlike LRRH, Sara has a father who recognises his daughter's need to express herself by giving her a big hard-backed notebook from his work where she can draw and scribble. Like Sara's father, Sorpresa's father in *Pastel* also sympathised with his daughter and her interests although he was not able to provide the books she needed. Sara also has another human and very important support. For a few years, the (to her) invisible presence of her grandmother's partner, Aurelio Roncali, provides a lasting spiritual influence. Through his gifts – a jigsaw, three storybooks, and a map of Manhattan – Aurelio guides the child through language and story-telling. In his role as spiritual guide, Aurelio acts as a positive animus figure, a creative spirit, inspiring in her a desire to travel and to read. He is contrasted sharply with Sara's father's friends who only talk about baseball (24).

The fact that Aurelio Roncali is only alluded to and remains in the background before returning to Italy means that he retains an air of mystery. His role in the story is like that of a fairy godfather. The figure of an intuitive adult who sends the right gift at the right time also plays an important role in *Nubosidad*, where the godmother of Sofía Montalvo sends her goddaughter a dress at just the time it is needed (1992b: 235–9). The red dress is appropriate for a young woman ready for her first important relationship, and, equally appropriately, Aurelio sends the child Sara items which develop her mind and imagination.

There are similarities between the role played by Aurelio and the one played in *Pastel* by *el señor de la Casa Grande*, but there are also important differences. While Sorpresa knows what *el señor* looks like, she has no personal relationship with him, whereas Sara has no real image of Aurelio, but he chooses specific gifts for her and is 'related' to her grandmother. Both young girls have a romantic perspective on the men, but Sorpresa, after inventing a story in which *el señor* plays a prominent role, directs her gaze outwards, seeing *el señor* as the recipient of her stories. In contrast Sara turns her gaze inwards, dreaming and imagining, at first asking questions then later, when Aurelio has left and there seems no hope of ever meeting him, keeping quiet, reading her books and studying the map. Aurelio's encouragement to Sara to read, and particularly his gift of the map of Manhattan, play a significant role in the second part of the book as they, along with a book from her grandmother about the Statue of Liberty, facilitate her profound encounter with the magical figure of Miss Lunatic. In this, Aurelio resembles what Jung describes, in his own study of fairy tales, as the archetype of spirit which 'in the shape of a man, hobgoblin, or animal always appears in a situation where insight, understanding, good advice, determination, planning, etc., are needed but cannot be mustered on one's own resources. The archetype compensates this state of spiritual deficiency by contents designed to fill the gap' (1959: 216).

Sara imagines Aurelio's bookshop, Books Kingdom, as a magical world containing miniature houses 'habitadas por unos seres minúsculos y alados con gorro en punta' [inhabitated by tiny winged creatures in pointed hats] (26), which only comes alive at night when the shop is closed. Like Sorpresa, she imagines what she has not seen, and she concludes that to live there all that would be necessary would be the ability to tell stories. Seen in the light of Martín Gaite's assertion in an essay on fairy tales that 'si bien se mira todo es narración' [if you think about it, everything is about telling stories] (1988a: 121), everyone should be able to live in Books Kingdom should they so choose.[12] This represents a considerable shift from the message of *Pastel* where the outcome of finding her vocation is very positive and liberating, freeing Sorpresa from the limitations of her parents' life and the narrow future of marriage and motherhood desired for her by her mother. However, Sorpresa's imagination and writing skills are key to any future success in writing her stories and publishing them. Telling stories is different and, at least in principle, within the scope of everyone.

However, in Martín Gaite's world the quality of the narration is important as is creating the right environment in which stories can thrive. Martín Gaite's criticisms of busy wealthy people who rush in large cars or taxis through Central Park, seeing nothing around them and failing to enjoy life, imply that they would not have time to tell stories as they deserve to be told. The main contrast she makes is between their attitude and that of the children who would enjoy being in Central Park at night but who are often stuck at home watching television. Children and the rich are singled out and contrasted in the New Testament, too. There it is argued that the rich exclude themselves from the Kingdom of Heaven: 'It is easier for a

12 Booker agrees, arguing that 'to a far greater degree than we are consciously aware, we look at the world in terms of stories all the time. They are the most natural way in which we structure our descriptions of the world around us' (2005: 573).

camel to pass through the eye of a needle than for someone rich to enter the Kingdom of Heaven' (Matthew 19. 24). This attitude is contrasted with that of children – 'unless you change and become like little children you will never enter the kingdom of Heaven' (Matthew 18. 3), which was discussed in Chapter 2 as meaning possessing 'an unreflecting capacity for obeying the Self' (von Franz 1995b: 109). The impression given of wealthy people in *Caperucita* seems to be that they would find it just as difficult to get into Martín Gaite's storytelling kingdom, too. In the second half of her story, the writer introduces two characters who epitomise these two extremes: one, a bag lady who loves stories and believes everyone has a story to tell; and a millionaire with a very successful cake business.

Un acompañante mágico

Critics' views of Miss Lunatic differ, with some seeing her as 'una simbiosis de la abuela de Caperucita con la tradicional hada madrina' [a symbiosis of Little Red Riding Hood's grandmother and the traditional fairy godmother] (Morales Ladrón (2002: 176); as a 'sorte de double imaginaire de la grand-mère' [a kind of imaginary double of the grandmother] (Pérès 2004: 157); or as not really existing: 'Su verdadera existencia es dudosa [...]. No hay ninguna razón para no admitirla como una creación de la fértil imaginación de Sara' [Her very existence is doubtful [...] There is no reason for not accepting her as a creation of Sara's fertile imagination] (Odartey-Wellington 2000: 536). Roger shares Odartey-Wellington's uncertainty concerning the reality of Miss Lunatic (1992: 330). It does appear that the second part of the story takes place on the level of the imagination, although the transition between the two parts is seamless. The ending, in which Sara does not return home, may also be due to a desire to maintain the uncertainty about the connection between the two parts.

It is generally recognised that, not only do all fairy tales not contain fairies, but that *Little Red Riding Hood* is hardly a fairy tale at all. Bayó Belenguer points out that 'there is no happy ending and no supernatural magic element' (2002: 196). This is true of Perrault's version, while the Grimm brothers give us the resurrection of LRRH and her grandmother without the intervention of an overtly supernatural figure (although, in one interpretation, the figure of the hunter was regarded as a powerful supernatural symbol). The introduction of a supernatural figure into her re-telling, therefore, represents Martín Gaite's most significant departure from the original tale. In a talk about writing *Caperucita*, the author tells how she was convinced of the need to introduce this figure, just as in a typical fairy tale:

> Yo sabía, casi desde el principio, que para llevar a cabo esta escapatoria Sara Allen necesitaría de la ayuda de un ser sobrenatural, ese 'acompañante mágico' que tantas veces en la literatura sirve de guía a los niños perdidos. (2002b: 149)
>
> [I knew, almost from the start, that to make her escape Sara Allen would need the help of a supernatural being, that 'magical companion' that so often in literature acts as a guide to lost children.]

This resembles the kind of criticism made by Martín Gaite in her essay on *Cinderella* of fairy-tale heroes whose inevitable and invariable escape was always 'mediante el concurso de apariciones providenciales, ayudas mágicas o prodigios inesperados' (1988a: 146) [through the help of providential appearances, magical assistance or unexpected wonders]. However, her own heroes more clearly contribute to their adventures.

Martín Gaite's *acompañante mágico* is no typical fairy godmother, for she has drawn a most unusual supernatural figure who outwardly resembles the kind of person Sara's mother has taught her to ignore in the streets and on the underground. It was this aspect that Martín Gaite chose first: 'Yo había pensado en uno de esos mendigos que se ven tanto por Nueva York. No sabía si iba a ser hombre o mujer' [I had thought about one of those beggars you see so much around New York. I didn't know if it was going to be a man or a woman] (1991a: 10). A bag lady with her pram and bits and pieces that she finds in the city, she nevertheless stands out because of her dignity, her independence and the way she relates to people. And although she is dressed in rags she also has long white hair in a plait and wears a large hat. Earlier editions of *Cuento* were published with drawings by Francisco

Nieva of Miss Mady to illustrate some of the essays. Miss Mady is a figure with long flowing clothes who immediately brings to mind Miss Lunatic: '[*Cuento*] is illustrated with fourteen enigmatic drawings of the character of Miss Mady (a precursor of Miss Lunatic in *Caperucita en Manhattan*)' (Bayó Belenguer 2002: 193–4).

Daniella Blejer highlights Martín Gaite's creation of a beggarwoman representing the Statue of Liberty as an example of the writer's subversive attitude, whereas José Teruel is unperturbed by the choice, referring to 'lo más alto de la representación de la libertad, ya sea en forma de diosa o en disfraz de mendiga' [the highest representation of freedom, be it in the form of a goddess or in the disguise of a beggar] (2006: 146). Robert McCully considers figures in fairy tales who appear as beggars to be knowing: 'They make those they encounter aware' (1991: 35), as was the case with Altalé in *Castillo* when she received a message in a needlecase left by a beggarwoman. These attributes also apply to Miss Lunatic, who describes herself as a beggar, although she barters for a bowl of soup rather than begs. Beckett also notes an important contrast with the traditional tale of *Cinderella*: 'In [Martín Gaite's] fairy-tale novel, it is the fairy godmother who is dressed in rags, but they do not conceal her noble bearing any more than they did Cinderella's' (2002: 318).

Other lonely people are depicted as speaking to themselves, sometimes making speeches to invisible groups of people in a way that seems unconscious and uncontrolled. In contrast, when Miss Lunatic talks to herself it is a conscious dialogue. So, while Martín Gaite has given us a figure who *looks* like someone who lives on the margins of society, Miss Lunatic is also a considerable personality who is conscious precisely because she communicates with the unconscious. Despite being a supernatural figure, she is depicted as being very human, even prone to depression, though her awareness is such that she does not allow dark moods to take her over, but recognises them and reacts by walking tall and focusing her gaze (119). That she has these human weaknesses along with her wisdom and awareness, confirms that, unlike the messages in the traditional fairy tales, nothing, including happiness, is forever and ever and there is no such thing as perfection. According to von Franz, the highest development of the feminine principle 'entails constant watching of one's own shadow drive' (von Franz,

1993a: 212), which is in keeping with the fact that the individuation process is never completed but is the work of a lifetime.

Miss Lunatic's supernatural aspects – her age, ability to be in more than one place simultaneously, her means of travelling to and from the Statue of Liberty, and her role as the spirit of the statue – are, therefore, balanced by very human elements: a bag lady, wearing layers of ragged clothes, pushing an old pram, getting tired and depressed. Thus, she unites the highest – her wisdom, powers and spirit – with the lowest – her raggedy appearance, lack of money and possessions – which, like Tituc in *Castillo*, makes her an especially potent figure. Miss Lunatic can be described as a symbol of the Self. It is to be expected, in the light of earlier discussions of the role of this aspect, that she will, therefore, point the way to renewal. In her values Miss Lunatic resembles St Francis – 'It was only because he possessed nothing that St Francis could feel sincerely a brotherhood with all created things' (Longford 1978: 2) – through whom the expression of Christianity underwent a profound renewal and who was identified by Murray Stein as an exemplar of individuation (2006: 209, note 3). Like all human beings, and also in keeping with the character of the Self, Miss Lunatic carries opposite aspects *within* her. Not just the divine/human opposites, but her tendency to dark moods is balanced by a great sense of fun, such as when she rides on a fire engine and loves ringing the bell.

Nor is it surprising that she should enjoy something illegal,[13] or that she should turn down the police commissioner's offer to act as an informer: 'It is the police world that is most threatened by the feminine because the feminine [...] does not live according to the rules of worldly authorities' (Hall 1980: 15). Miss Lunatic shows solidarity with the homeless, and is also friendly with those more financially better off. It seems appropriate that it should be the firemen whose company she particularly enjoys, as their role is to extinguish destructive fires, and Miss Lunatic tries to intervene in many situations where there are problems caused by symbolic fires, whether destructive ones between people or where the fire has gone out

13 In the short story, 'Lo que queda enterrado', when she continues beyond her station, María reacts with excitement to the experience of travelling illegally on the train (1984: 53–72).

and there is only despair.[14] However, she is not successful in her chosen role of mediator. Christ warned his disciples: 'Do not give dogs what is holy; and do not throw your pearls in front of pigs, or they may trample them and then turn on you and tear you to pieces' (Matthew 7. 6). This very same advice is given to Miss Lunatic for she seems to be unsuccessful in her endeavours, finding herself rejected as interfering and thrown out, but she seems to pay little attention:

> Lograba pocos resultados, pero no se desanimaba, y eso que la insultaron muchas veces por meterse donde nadie la había llamado, y llegaron a echarla a patadas de un local de Harlem [...].
>
> 'Lárguese de aquí, miss Lunatic [...] Después de todo, es echar margaritas a puercos.' (88–9)
>
> [She achieved few successes, but she didn't lose heart, in spite of the fact that she was often insulted for not minding her own business, and they even kicked her out of a place in Harlem [...].
>
> 'Get out of here, miss Lunatic [...] After all, it's like casting pearls before swine.']

There are a number of other parallels with the Christian story, such as the way Miss Lunatic frequents those areas inhabited by people on the margins of society just as Christ did, and her aversion to money, which she believes prevents human beings from really living.[15] Unlike the wealthy people depicted by Martín Gaite who rush through Central Park in their cars, Miss Lunatic enjoys people and also things, like the two champagne cocktails she has with Sara in a cafeteria. In her enjoyment of people she reveals her own wholeness: 'Cada persona es un mundo' [Each person is

14 This is another link between Miss Lunatic and St Francis, for the prayer attributed to him (though in fact from the early twentieth century) includes the lines 'where there is despair, [let us sow] hope; where there is darkness, light; where there is sadness, joy' (<http://www.franciscans.org/franciscan-praying/prayers-of-saint-francis>).

15 Also see Ribeiro de Menezes's 2014 article in which she argues that Martín Gaite's treatment of New York indicates an 'ambivalence towards materialism and progress' (55).

a whole world] and 'todos tenían alguna historia que contar' (87) [they all had a story to tell]. In *The Meno*, Plato has Socrates discuss shape: 'Let's try to tell you what shape is. [...] Let us define it as the only thing which always accompanies colour' (1956: 121). This image of the indivisible relationship between shape and colour seems to encapsulate this aspect of Martín Gaite's philosophy, with 'shape' and 'colour' being replaced by 'person' and 'story' respectively. This philosophy is the natural outcome of one of Martín Gaite's longstanding criticisms of collective social behaviour, namely the labelling of others as a result of projection or prejudice or laziness (1982: 19). It is not possible to label quickly and superficially someone to whom you are ready to listen, someone you believe has a story to tell simply by virtue of being a person.

Miss Lunatic's ability to see each person in his/her uniqueness (for their stories will not be the same), not only confirms her link with the highest form of the Feminine described earlier, but also indicates that, unlike almost all of us who live more or less in the illusory world of projection, she sees people clearly, as they are, without projecting aspects of herself into them. While projection is a part of life, insight into projections is necessary not only for personal growth and development, but also for the possibility of relatedness: 'Only when projections are taken back does relationship [...] become possible' (von Franz 1997a: 52). In her overall approach to others, as recognised by Cueto Veiga (2005: 117) and Pittarello (2009: 16), Miss Lunatic resembles the hunter in the Grimms' tale (who was also compared to Christ by one critic (Murphy 2000: 82)). However, her lack of effectiveness in more difficult situations and her admitted tiredness suggest that change is necessary.

The location of Miss Lunatic's encounter with Sara, the underground station, is significant as it suggests the unconscious. Each sees the other as the ideal response to their situation, for Sara is lost and cannot go on, while Miss Lunatic is tired and looking for someone younger with whom she can 'descargar [sus] fardos más secretos' [pour out [her] most secret burdens] (119). Miss Lunatic's impression of Sara, with her 'mirada tan transparente y candorosa' [open and candid gaze], seems to recognise the special nature of the child: 'sintió como si su viejo corazón se calentara ante las llamas de una inesperada hoguera' [she felt as if her old heart was warming itself in front of the flames of an unexpected bonfire] (121). This positive image of fire associates it with warmth, feeling and, as Miss Lunatic herself says, the heart – that neglected aspect of eros which urgently needs to be valued and developed. Joan Lipman Brown describes the effect Sara has on Miss Lunatic, who is prone to depression, as 'a felicitous twist [in which] Little Red Riding Hood comes to lead her progenitor out of the woods' (2017: 208). Sara shares Miss Lunatic's compassion for those on the margins of society and those who suffer. In this she resembles Altalé. Although Altalé's compassion was primarily for her father, a more personal relationship, she also responded positively to the proposal for his tenants to improve their lot. In addition, Sara responds to people in the street and on the underground with whom she has no personal relationship.

So, although Miss Lunatic is concerned with spirit – for which fire is a symbol – her spirit, which is a feminine spirit of reconciliation, seems not to be able to burn brightly in the darker places where it is most needed. Her explanation for her lack of effectiveness is of the kind often given by politicians when their message is not accepted: 'He debido explicarme mal' [I mustn't have explained what I meant properly] (89). As we saw in *Castillo*, this is typical for such symbols: 'The symbol of the Self [...] is especially threatened by the possibility of becoming a dead formula' and 'of needing the constant renewal of understanding and contact' (von Franz 1996: 54). Miss Lunatic, like Cambof Petapel in *Castillo*, seems to be a symbol of the Self which is wearing out and in need of renewal. Sara could represent either a new symbol of the Self or an ego: 'The child is [...] an apt symbol of the Self – of an inner future totality and, at the same time, of undeveloped facets of one's individuality' (von Franz 1996: 192).

The Mystery of Miss Lunatic

As Domenico Cusato recognises (1996: 496), some aspects of *Caperucita* recall episodes from the New Testament, the most important of which is the Transfiguration of Christ. In the Gospels Christ takes Peter and two other apostles up to a high mountain where they witness the transfiguration of Christ, Moses and Elijah, and hear the voice of God identifying Jesus as his Son. It is as if Christ wants them to know who he really is, to see the other (divine) aspect of himself: 'There in their presence he was transfigured: his face shone like the sun and his clothes became as dazzling as light' (Matthew 17. 2). Later they become afraid and fall on their faces but are told by Jesus, 'Stand up, do not be afraid' (Matthew 17. 6–7). Joseph Campbell, discussing the 'freedom to pass back and forth across the world division, from the perspective of the apparitions of time to that of the causal deep and back' (1968: 229), suggests that the Transfiguration of Christ is a rare example of a myth '[displaying] in a single image the mystery of the ready transit' (Ibid. 229). Campbell also argues that 'the transfiguration of Jesus was witnessed by devotees who had extinguished their personal wills, men who had long since liquidated "life," "personal fate," "destiny," by complete self-abnegation in the Master' (Ibid. 236). This description echoes von Franz's interpretation of those who will enter the Kingdom of Heaven, discussed in relation to Serena in *Castillo*, that is, persons who have made considerable progress on the path of individuation and have developed 'an unreflecting capacity for obeying the Self' (von Franz 1995b: 109). Campbell also reminds the reader of Jesus's instruction to his disciples: 'Whosoever will lose his life for my sake shall find it' (Matthew 16. 25). Losing one's life in individuation would mean letting go of ego motivations in order to respond to the Self which, paradoxically, would lead to living one's unique self. The three apostles who accompanied Jesus to the mountain were given insight into the other side of Campbell's 'world division'.

In contrast to the solitude of the mountain location of the Transfiguration of Christ, Miss Lunatic's 'transfiguration' occurs in a busy café in which filming is taking place. In the moment of transfiguration, Sara sees Miss Lunatic's face replaced by that of the Statue of Liberty and 'rodeado de un fogonazo resplandeciente' (140) [surrounded by a shining flash of light]. Sara's response to the transformation of Miss Lunatic is similar to that of the apostles as, blinded by the sight, she closes her eyes. This reaction is followed by her recognition of the true nature of Miss Lunatic, which also finds a parallel in the New Testament. Christ asks his apostles who they think he is and Peter replies: 'You are the Christ, the

Son of the living God.' The answer is well received for Jesus replies 'Simon son of Jonah, you are a blessed man! Because it was no human agency that revealed this to you but my Father in heaven' (Matthew 16. 16–17). When Sara recognises her, Miss Lunatic's first words echo the Gospel: 'Dios te bendiga, Sara Allen, por haberme reconocido [...]; por haber sido capaz de ver lo que otros nunca ven, lo que nadie hasta hoy había visto' [God bless you, Sara Allen, for having recognised me [...], for having been able to see what others never see, what until today no one has seen] (139). However, there is an important difference between Peter the apostle and Sara Allen, for the little girl's recognition of the true nature of her companion comes not only as the result of revelation, but of having pieced together all the information. When Miss Lunatic asks Sara: '¿No sería miedo a la Libertad?' (137) [Would it not be fear of Liberty?], and imitates the statue holding up the torch, the gesture and words set in train a series of thoughts through which Sara pieces together information she has read and observed.

First, with her lively interest and curiosity, Sara responded to the map of Manhattan she received from Aurelio by studying it, learning the street names and underground and bus lines. Her knowledge of the suburb enabled her to travel as far as she could before her courage failed her and Miss Lunatic stepped in like a fairy godmother. In addition, she had gleaned a lot of information from the book from her grandmother, *Construir la Libertad*, including the name of the muse of the sculptor, Madame Bartholdi. Seeing the changes in Miss Lunatic's hand, which has become younger and soft, as well as her ability to imitate very well the posture of the statue, is like a revelation. Unlike the apostles, Sara finds she has understood everything, although she explains this as being a special kind of understanding, 'como se entienden los milagros' [the way miracles are understood] (139). Miracles, she seems to be saying, are not understood in the same way as facts, marvellous occurrences have their own truth. Her dedication and interest, her habit of responding to whatever comes her way, have yielded a marvellous and unexpected reward. As the gifts came from Aurelio and her grandmother, they can be said to have anticipated the fairy godmother and facilitated Sara's experience, just as the gift of amber from *el señor* facilitated Sorpresa's first encounter with the Self in *Pastel*. As Teruel affirms with reference to Miss Lunatic's encounter with both Edgar Woolf and Sara Allen – and which is no less true of this scene: 'Lo que puede parecer [...] fruto del azar, es también – y sobre todo – obra del esfuerzo' [What might appear to be [...] due to fate, is also – and above all – the result of effort] (2006: 146).

Despite Martín Gaite's scene taking place in a crowded café, with many others present and filming going on around them, as Cusato observes, only Sara witnesses the transformation (1996: 498). In St John's Gospel, Jesus promised that 'the hour is coming when you will worship the Father neither on this mountain nor in Jerusalem. [...] the hour is coming [...] when true worshippers will worship the Father in spirit and truth' (John 4. 21–3). This new transfiguration has moved from the mountain, a traditional place of encounter with the Divinity, into the bustle of everyday life.

Sara is thus given the same kind of insight as the apostles, and Miss Lunatic's final words to Sara – 'aunque no me veas, yo no me voy, siempre estaré a tu lado' [even though you don't see me, I am not going away, I will always be by your side] (158) – resemble those of Christ to his apostles after the Resurrection and just before finally leaving them: 'And look, I am with you always; yes, to the end of time' (Matthew 28. 20). Because Sara has seen Miss Lunatic 'pass back and forth across the world division' (Campbell 1968: 229), she can accept the reassurance. On the other hand, Miss Lunatic's exhortation that 'quien no ama la vida no lo encuentra' [whoever does not love life will not find it] (158), appears to be the opposite to Christ's assurance that 'anyone who loves his life loses it; anyone who hates his life in this world will keep it for eternal life' (John 12. 25). However, Miss Lunatic seems to be using the word 'love' in relation to the essential Christian injunction to love God and all human beings as oneself, and not to the choice between the way of the ego or the Self to which Christ refers. Campbell connects the transfiguration of Christ with individual persons who have opted for the Self rather than the ego. He describes the experience as, paradoxically, one in which an individual 'no longer tries to live but willingly relaxes to whatever may come to pass in him; he becomes, that is to say, an anonymity. The Law lives in him with his unreserved content' (1968: 237). As already discussed, the paradox lies in the fact that this is the way to realise one's individuality, one's uniqueness.

Sara is like the typical heroine of fairy tales who responds at each step because it seems the right thing to do –like von Franz's tree image discussed in Chapter 1 – not because she is seeking a reward, and she is rewarded for that very reason. This attitude is illustrated in fairy tales such as *Mother Hulda*, where the good daughter falls into the well and, finding herself in a different world, responds by taking the bread out of the oven, shaking the apples from the tree, and carrying out all the work for Mother Hulda as well as she can. Her reward is a shower of gold. Her sister, wanting the same riches for herself, throws herself into the well and ignores the calls from the bread burning in the oven and the ripe apples. Making straight for Mother Hulda's house, she behaves in a lazy way and does not do the work. Expecting a shower of gold when she is about to leave, a kettle of pitch is tipped over her instead (Hall 1980: 207–13).

Nevertheless, the experience of witnessing Miss Lunatic's transformation – the sudden, blinding recognition – has the effect on Sara of a shock, making her heart pound. It is the kind of situation in which one is in danger of losing one's soul: 'Individual experiences of the first menstruation, childbirth, a nightmare, a crucial realization, or retirement leave facets of the self exposed' (Hall 1980: 168). At such times Hall believes that what is necessary is a mediator between consciousness and the unconscious (Ibid. 168). Of the four aspects identified by Toni Wolff as representing the feminine psyche – Mother, Hetaira, Amazon and Medial – it is the last which seems to be symbolised by Miss Lunatic/Madame Bartholdi. The medial feminine is the aspect most closely connected with the unconscious, mediating between the inner and outer worlds and, according to Hall, is characterised by figures such as the Wise Old Woman and the Sibyl. Like Christ reassuring the apostles immediately after the transfiguration, Madame Bartholdi utters the exhortation found frequently in the New Testament, 'no tiembles, no vuelvas a tener miedo jamás' [don't be afraid, don't ever be afraid again] (139), also confirming that this has been a life-changing experience for Sara.

Domenico Cusato also draws attention to Sara's eyes, their openness and innocence, drawing a parallel with Christ's reference in the New Testament to the pure in heart and the promise made in the Beatitudes(1996: 498) – the blessings declared as part of the Sermon on the Mount – that 'they shall see God' [Matthew 5: 8]. For the critic seeing God means 'assurgere alla sfera di un più alto intendimento' [attaining the level of higher understanding]

(Ibid. 498), which, in this case, means that Sara is able to recognise the true nature of Miss Lunatic (Ibid. 499). However, in what he regards as the final parallel between the stories – Miss Lunatic's parting words, which were discussed above – Cusato concludes that the values personified in Miss Lunatic mean that Martín Gaite's *acompañante mágico* can be compared to Christ (Ibid. 499). Earlier, I drew a link between Miss Lunatic and the hunter in the Grimms' version of LRRH, and also referred to the connection made by Murphy between the hunter and Christ. Jung and others have also linked Christ with the Self and Miss Lunatic can be regarded as a symbol of the Self, which would seem to confirm Cusato's conclusion. However, a distinction must be made between the Self and a symbol of the Self. It is not the Self that requires to be renewed, but the image or symbol of it, which Miss Lunatic represents.

The Encounter with the Wolf

Critics have seen Chapter 11, which shares part of its title (*Caperucita en Central Park*) with the title of the book, as a crucial point in the story (Moulin 1997: 148, Beckett 2002: 310, and Pérès 2004: 157). In contrast with Sara's mother and resembling the little girl's grandmother, Miss Lunatic encourages Sara to walk in Central Park where, instead of a real wolf, Sara meets Edgar Woolf, the millionaire *Rey de las Tartas* [King of Tarts]. Their encounter takes place in a clearing among the trees. This is a place where magical things can happen, as in *Pastel* where Sorpresa buried the piece of amber in the place where she was baptised. Sorpresa's action freed her from the clutches of the witch and opened the door to a glimpse of the Self and the understanding of her vocation. Sara's encounter in the clearing leads to love for her grandmother and Mr Woolf and the possibility of freedom for herself.

Aurelio was the *Rey de los Libros*, the intellectual and spiritual element, while Edgar Woolf seems to represent the material world. Rich, obsessive and lonely, having few friends, there are hints of Lucandro, and his wolfish appearance has been commented on by critics (Roger 1992: 330 & Llorente 2002: 11 n.5). However, unlike the friendless rich miser, Lucandro, Edgar Woolf has both a lifelong friend, Greg Monroe, and a positive mission – he is searching for the perfect strawberry tart, the only flavour which is not a success in his cake shop. The colour and shape of the strawberry link it to the heart and to eros and suggest that, unlike Lucandro, he is open to a new dimension in his life, as Couso recognises: 'A diferencia del lobo del cuento de Perrault, [Edgar Woolf] tiene sentimientos y se muestra deseoso de cambiar de vida' [Unlike the wolf in Perrault's fairy tale, [Edgar Woolf] has feelings and is anxious to change his life] (2010: 74). He also treats his employees much better than Lucandro his tenants, paying them well. He is associated with another positive symbol: the building in which he lives and has his highly successful cake business is octagonal, suggesting wholeness. However, as his search indicates, there is something missing and the lack of a good strawberry tart in his professional life may also reflect a lack of eros in his personal life. The tower in Lucandro's castle where Altalé and Cambof Petapel had their rooms was also octagonal but, in contrast to Edgar Woolf, Lucandro had no influence there. In this tale, Woolf's friend, Greg Monroe, also lives in the tower and it includes the workers in the business along with all those who shop and eat there, so it is a much more comprehensive symbol.

Mr Woolf wears a gold ring on his index finger. Cambof Petapel/ Amir's ring was blue; el *señor de la Casa Grande's* red. Gold is the colour of intuition and the metal is incorruptible, so this is a more powerful and complete symbol. As discussed earlier, the index finger indicates the way forward and has also been linked with the Holy Spirit, the development of the spiritual principle and of Christianity. Gold is also the colour associated in the story with the Statue of Liberty and, therefore, Miss Lunatic and the Self as Sara stuck a gold star on the map of Manhattan to mark the place of the Statue of Liberty. A silver star showed where her grandmother lived. Silver is associated with the moon and the feminine, but, unlike gold, it blackens, which emphasises Miss Lunatic's more significant role as a symbol of the Self.

In addition to his search for the perfect strawberry tart, Mr Woolf's lament that no woman has ever loved him confirms that eros is missing from his. The search for the strawberry tart has caused him to behave in unusual ways such as walking alone in Central Park.[16] The quest, therefore, makes him get out of his car and open himself to the possibility of changing from being one of the kind of people Martín Gaite criticised for rushing through the park in their limousines and being too wrapped up in making money, to someone who is open to other experiences. It is this openness which leads to his meeting first Miss Lunatic and then Sara. Disappointed that Miss Lunatic has not come to his apartment as she had promised, he found himself drawn towards the park and, crucially, acted on his instinct. The search for the strawberry tart, as hinted at in the symbolism of the ring, leads him into contact with his inner self.

The fact that Edgar Woolf meets Sara and not Miss Lunatic suggests that Sara could be the new symbol of the Self, that she has taken the place of Miss Lunatic as the latter desired. In his exaggerated emotion and dramatic gestures, his crying and begging for the recipe when he has tasted the strawberry tart in Sara's basket, Mr Woolf reveals his undeveloped feeling. Because Sara places little value on the recipe, she is more than willing to hand it over, and this willingness has been described as symbolising 'l'abandon des valeurs de la mère' [giving up her mother's values] (Pérès 2004: 158). Odartey-Wellington's view of the tart as representing 'el conjunto de los valores patriarcales que sostiene la madre de Sara y que es la fuente de su opresión' [the set of patriarcal values that Sara's mother supports and which are the source of her oppression] (2000: 551), also suggests that these values have been rejected. The outcome of handing over the recipe benefits all the main characters and is crucial for their development. Here, as is often the case, the treasure sought is in the possession of someone else.

16 Beckett proposes that 'an analogy is suggested between the serial killer who had haunted Morningside Park and Edgar Woolf who often has his chauffeur let him off in Central Park to walk' (2002: 325). However, as Beckett recognises, a complete contrast between the two seems to be indicated in Sara's seeing before her a pair of men's shoes and wondering if the vampire of the Bronx had moved to Central Park, then being enormously relieved to see 'un señor bien vestido, con sombrero gris y guantes de cabritillo, sin la menor pinta de asesino' [a well-dressed man, with a grey hat and kid gloves, not looking at all like a murderer] (158).

But whereas in traditional fairy tales it is usually guarded by an ogre or a monster or a witch – all shadow figures which can represent unconscious feeling manifesting itself in a desire for power – here it is in the possession of someone (Sara's grandmother, Rebeca) who does not share the seeker's perspective of its value. And far from needing to overcome the keeper of the treasure with power or magic or wiles, it is a question of relating, of eros. On the other hand, the recipe is valuable to Vivian, but it imprisons her in an empty ritual. Giving it up should, therefore, represent a liberation, a freeing from the compulsion to which a negative animus seems continually to drive her.

Once Edgar Woolf has found the treasure he sought, he also begins to discover another, for him unusual, kind of richness in the simplicity of enjoying eating strawberry tart with Sara in the park. The symbolism of the strawberry tart is also realised on another level with the discovery that the keeper of the secret recipe is the red-headed singer he loved from afar as a young man. Unusually for Martín Gaite, the *pelirroja* [redhead] here is a positive character. Edgar Woolf's desire to meet the singer who once seemed to sing her songs only for him – she had even thrown a carnation to him[17] – leads him to instruct his chauffeur to take his time bringing Sara to her grandmother's house so that he can get there first. This creates a parallel with the original fairy tale although in this re-telling it is the little girl not the wolf who requests the separate journeys.

17 Pérès suggests that the scene Edgar Woolf recalls, in which Rebeca (alias Gloria Star) threw a flower to him after their eyes met 'est la réécriture d'une scène d'un dessin animé de Tex Avery, *Red Hot Riding Hood*, daté de mai 1943' [is the rewriting of a scene from a cartoon by Tex Avery, *Red Hot Riding Hood*, dated May 1943] (2004: 159), although in Avery's version it is Red Riding Hood who is on stage and the setting is quite different. Pittarello considers that 'en particular, coincide la subversión de los caracteres principales' [in particular, the subversion of the main characters is the same] (2009: 14). However, any similarities between Avery's film – 'in which violence and sexuality are key ingredients' (Beckett 2008: 208) – and *Caperucita* seem quite superficial.

The Wolf and the Grandmother

Naturally, when Edgar Woolf reaches Sara's grandmother's house he does not eat Rebeca. Nor does he fulfil Zipes's interpretation of the eating which was discussed earlier. Instead, when Sara arrives later at the house she finds one of her wishes has been granted as her grandmother is wearing the green dress from happier days which Sara had longed to see her wearing again. Sara sees green as a symbol of hope. Jung would agree – 'green signifies hope and the future' (1963: 432) and adds that 'green is the colour of the Holy Ghost, of life, procreation and resurrection' (1963: 289), which links it to other aspects of Martín Gaite's story. Dancing together, Rebeca/Gloria seems to have responded positively to Edgar Woolf and it seems likely that she will be taken up into his world, which means that the missing eros element will be restored to him along with the strawberry tart. His life will be richer, less one-sided, influenced by a perspective which is more personal, original, and which celebrates life and story. As Carbayo-Abengózar concludes: 'Aunque en un primer momento [su intención] responde a un deseo de beneficiarse con la receta de la tarta, se desplaza tras su conversación con la niña, hacia un deseo de amor y comprensión' [Although at first [his intention] corresponded to his wish to profit from the recipe for the tart, following his conversation with the little girl it shifts towards a desire for love and understanding] (1998a: 141). Mr Woolf represents prevailing collective values, and the completion of these by the eros element is a very positive development.[18]

In his analysis of the traditional tale of *Little Red Riding Hood*, Ronald Murphy argues that the wolf 'drops dead by the heaviness of the material things which he seeks to have in his belly' (2000: 82). This is a similar fate to that suffered by Lucandro, who clung to his material wealth and the fear and suspicion it generated, in the end dropping into the moat and being transformed into an aquatic guard-fish. Murphy sees the traditional tale of

18 In a very different reading, one critic sees this development at the end of the story as one which 'perpetua valores patriarcales tradicionales' [perpetuates traditional patriarchal values] (Morales Ladrón 2002: 180).

LRRH as a struggle between good and evil. This is a new generation and, in Martín Gaite's re-telling, the wolf – Edgar Woolf – does not die. Instead he is reconciled with his opposite, Sara's grandmother, and as a result is no longer weighed down by material things.

Endings

At the beginning of the story, Sara rejected the endings of the books she had received from Aurelio. The new endings she proposed for *Robinson Crusoe* and *Alice in Wonderland* reflected a desire to remain in the fairy-tale world and not, as it were, leave the ball at midnight to return to the world of every day. This resembles the attitude of Matilde in *Balneario*, who wanted to hold onto the siesta dream, to stay there, as an escape from the dull routine of her life at the spa. A number of critics highlight Sara's desire to change the endings of her favourite stories, with Blejer seeing it as subversive 'porque reconfiguran el significado de toda la obra' [because they reshape the meaning of the whole work] (2007: 15). However, Sara's attitude to these stories and their endings changes in the course of the novel. This change in attitude can be seen, for example, when she wakes up after dreaming about Books Kingdom and feels as though she has fallen from the clouds, only to be immediately assailed by sensible questions concerned with the reality of the situation such as what Aurelio might look like. Thus she begins to find a way of managing the two worlds instead of trying to stay in one of them. Later, as she grows through her disappointments with the adult world, she realises that the fairy-tale ending states are necessarily only temporary places. She identifies with Robinson Crusoe on his island, but recognises it for what it should be, namely a place to stay only while she is developing her dreams. Finally, almost at the end of the book, when she wants to hide from Edgar Woolf's chauffeur, Peter, she is aware that she cannot change her size like Alice in Wonderland, but has to do the best she can crouching behind a wall. Thus, unlike Matilde in *Balneario*, she loses her desire to remain only in the fantasy world, and accepts the reality of the original endings.

Sara and Individuation

Sara's confidence during her encounter with Mr Woolf in Central Park results from her time with Miss Lunatic/Mme Bartholdi and the experiences and the new awareness she has attained. The impact of this experience is seen more clearly as the story reaches its conclusion. Initially in her ride in Edgar Woolf's limousine, Sara behaves just like any other ten-year-old, asking questions about the car and trying out all the gadgets. However, that the whole adventure represents progress in the individuation process seems to be confirmed when she wakes up from her sleep in the limousine and is talking with the chauffeur: 'Y podía elegir su propia respuesta, sin dejar de sentir, al mismo tiempo, una alegría interior que nunca iba a querer ni poder – lo sabía – compartir con nadie' [And she was able to choose her own response, without ceasing to feel, at the same time, an inner happiness that she knew she would never wish or be able to share with anyone else] (192). This corresponds to von Franz's description of how the individual relates to the four psychological functions following much progress in individuation: 'At that moment there are no longer four functions because one transmits one's feeling of life into an inner center, and the four functions remain only as instruments which can be used at will, taking them up and putting them down again' (von Franz, 1993b, 142).

Discussing the individuation process, von Franz also describes how there comes a moment when the individual must decide between returning to the collective and making a sacrifice of the secret they have learnt by talking about it, or accepting the loneliness but keeping secret all that has been discovered: 'These are two opposites in which the process of individuation culminates. When a new symbol of the divinity is built up during the process, the divinity is either sacrificed to strengthen a community or kept secret within the individual' (von Franz, 1995b: 130). Joseph Campbell makes a similar comment which Martín Gaite observes in her notes on *The Hero with a Thousand Faces*: 'Retener la sabiduría para sí mismo o comunicarla?' [Keep the learning to yourself or communicate it?] (2002a: 78). This is the same dilemma that faces Sara. When she wakes up she knows that the decision she has to make is a choice between the outer world and the inner. At the beginning, it was not clear whether Sara represented an ego or an immature symbol of the Self, and both interpretations are possible. If we understand Sara as representing the ego, and Miss Lunatic/Mme Bartholdi as symbolising the Self, it could also mean that Sara, having made considerable progress in the individuation process, had access to the deeper levels of the unconscious. However, as has already been indicated, the development of the story suggests that she could be the new symbol of the Self and has replaced Miss Lunatic. In light of the latter, the dream she has in Mr Woolf's limousine, in which she was very small and riding in Miss Lunatic's pram, would be appropriate in representing her lack of development. Soliño considers that 'Sara is [a] worthy heiress, and this legacy [from Miss Lunatic] is much more appropriate for the lively and intelligent girl than the recipe for a strawberry cake, no matter how delicious' (2002: 94).

Although Miss Lunatic has left Sara to go elsewhere in Manhattan, when the book ends Sara is on her way to the Statue of Liberty by means of an underwater tunnel. As soon as she puts in the coin Miss Lunatic gave her and says her magic word – '¡Miranfú!' – she finds herself sucked into a warm air current.[19] At the end of the tale, Sara could, therefore, be going to Liberty to take up her new role, having made her choice between the inner and the outer as a result of her adventure: 'Lo que ocurría en el exterior de Manhattan, al otro lado de la ventanilla, había dejado por completo de interesarle' [What was happening outside in Manhattan, on the other side of the car window, no longer interested her at all] (192). This is a significant change from the Sara at the start of the story who was so taken with the glamorous part of the city, and wanted to be an actress spending all day drinking champagne, eating oysters, and buying coats with ermine

19 Critics have identified a number of intertextual connections with Lewis Carroll's *Alice in Wonderland* in addition to the direct references in the novel (Bayó Belenguer 2002; Blejer 2007; Calvi 1992–3; Llorente 2002; and Odartey-Wellington 2004a) with this scene particularly being singled out (Calvi 1992–3: 69; Cueto Veiga 2005: 118; and Odartey-Wellington 2004a: 220). The underwater tunnel to the Statue of Liberty is also compared with the underground tunnel beneath the East River, which seems so magical to Sara (Pérès 2004: 157; Ribeiro de Menezes 2014: 53–4).

collars. Von Franz has pointed out that in psychological interpretations of myths often 'there is a constant shift between interpreting the hero as a symbol of the Self and as a symbol of the ego' (1996: 57). After exploring both roles she concludes that the hero can be described as 'an archetypal figure which presents a model of an ego functioning in accord with the Self' (Ibid. 62). This description seems to fit very well with Sara's role and the transformation which results in the shift in her focus of interest from the outer to the inner worlds would represent the effect of the encounter of an ego with the Self. This shift from the outer to the inner also connects Sara with the experience of Pentecost discussed in Chapter 1.

So, Sara does not go home to Brooklyn. Brown describes the ending as Sara '[embarking] on a magical trip to the Statue of Liberty' (2017: 203). A typical feature of fairy tales is what Marie-Louise von Franz calls the *rite de sortie* – a sentence with which the storyteller closes the tale in order to bring the listener/reader back to the real world 'because a fairy tale takes you far away into the childhood dream world of the collective unconscious, where you may not stay' (von Franz 1996: 41). Von Franz goes further and suggests that to be able to go about your everyday life you 'may not be absent-minded and puzzle about the story. We have to be switched out of the fairy tale world' (Ibid. 41). In *Caperucita* there is no *rite de sortie*. Because of this, everything stays on the level of the imagination. Again, as in *Castillo*, it appears that everything remains in the unconscious with no attempt to integrate it into everyday life. On the other hand, bearing in mind the recent loss of her daughter, Martín Gaite's ending can also be seen as 'un valiente acto de fe en la vida' ([a courageous act of faith in life] Pittarello 2009: 17).

The Importance of Story

A further aspect which Sara and Miss Lunatic have in common points the way to the renewal of eros –which in Vivian and in Miss Lunatic's failings at reconciliation has been shown to be necessary – namely that they both love stories. Just as the gifts from Aurelio were instrumental in allowing Sara to discover the older lady's secret, so her imaginings of his bookshop gave her the first inkling of a new way of living. And it is through the character of Miss Lunatic/Madame Bartholdi that Martín Gaite takes her philosophy of meaningful living to a new level. 'Nunca he encontrado un quehacer más importante que el de escuchar historias' [I have never come across a more important task than listening to stories] (125), Miss Lunatic tells Sara. From first writing stories, then telling them, Martín Gaite now makes a dramatic shift by having one of her most significant characters argue that what really matters is *listening* to stories. Most of the time we hear what others say, only rarely do we really listen. When we speak of dialogue, what we generally have in mind is people talking. In placing the emphasis on listening, Martín Gaite not only declares that the most important thing in life lies within the scope of everyone, but she also posits the means by which eros, relatedness, can be renewed. One could define listening in the way that von Franz has written about eros: 'It means genuine interest in the other person and in establishing relationship, being there for the other person' (von Franz 1993a: 211). It is impossible to really listen to someone's story and remain unrelated to them. The people depicted in the streets and on the underground of New York who talk to themselves or to imaginary listeners, are not being listened to. Martín Gaite would argue that many of us do not have the habit of listening, even asking questions without listening to the answer (2002a: 389).

Conclusion

Caperucita offers a kind of gospel, with a different message of living, one within reach of everyone, regardless of wealth. A gospel of love which is achieved through respect for the word, the story, and the stories of others which are necessarily different from our own. As Miss Lunatic says, 'todos tenían alguna historia que contar, algún paisaje de infancia que revivir, alguna persona querida a la que añorar, algún conflicto para el cual pedir consejo' [all of them had a story to tell, some childhood scene to relive, a beloved person to yearn for, some dilemma to seek advice about] (87). No longer writing, or even necessarily engaging in conversation, though that is still important, what matters is listening, which means relating, and signifies the birth of eros between two unique human beings. Unlike LRRH, Martín Gaite's heroine is committed to fulfilling her role and, instead of the battle between good and evil in the original tale, here the opposing elements are reconciled through the characters of Rebeca and Edgar Woolf. This re-telling, which sets out the way forward for the renewal of eros, can, therefore, be said to further develop the meaning of the original tale, in which the feminine principle was brought into consciousness through the rescuing of Little Red Riding Hood and her grandmother from the belly of the wolf.

CHAPTER 5

'A lo más oscuro amanece Dios': The Dawning of the Self in *La reina de las nieves*

Introduction

This novel, which Carmen Martín Gaite described as 'una novela tan complicada y "especial"' [such a complex and 'special' novel] (1994: 12), has nevertheless been criticised for 'infantilismo' [childishness] and because it 'oscila entre la realidad y la fantasía' [swings between reality and fantasy] (Salustiano Martín 1994: 33). Other critics are more positive, applauding Martín Gaite's subverting of the traditional quest tale in which a male hero seeks his father. Here a woman, Casilda, goes in search of her father and a young man, Leonardo, embarks (albeit unknowingly) on a search for his mother (Odartey Wellington 2000 & 2003). Contrasts persist in critics' responses to various aspects of the novel including the ending, which some have likened to the first Christmas and the birth of the Son (Bravo 1998: Lindström 2009) or as illustrating Leonardo's psychic wholeness (Cruz-Cámara 2008). In contrast, Martín considers that it '[sobra] enteramente' [is completely unnecessary] (1994: 33). Critics' attitudes to the main protagonists, Leonardo Villalba and Casilda Iriarte, are also striking in their contrasts. Annick Le Scouzec Masson finds an air of unreality about both (2003: 82), and José Jurado Morales describes them as 'dos seres descolocados en el mundo' [two beings out of place in the world] (2003: 320). Carlos Uxó (1998b) considers Leonardo to be an unreliable witness, while Kathleen Glenn (1996) regards him as immature and childish, concluding that, in contrast to other works by the writer, he is not a lifelike character who captures readers' imagination and interest.

The ambiguity of Leonardo's sexuality is noted by a number of critics (Carbayo-Abengozar 1998a; Cruz-Cámara 2008; Odartey-Wellington 2000 & 2003). Martín Gaite's depiction of Leonardo's sensitivity and creativity are in keeping with her insistence, as recorded in her notebooks in the 1960s, on the importance of women and men becoming whole by developing aspects traditionally associated with the opposite gender. Her own sympathy for her protagonist, which Salustiano Martín (1994) so deplores, is acknowledged by Paoli who explains Leonardo's strangeness as the result of having – like Kay in Andersen's fairy tale – a piece of glass in his eye (2002).

María Elena Soliño sees in Casilda a direct descendant of Serena, the protagonist of *Castillo*, both in 'her open expressions of a free sexuality' and in the 'strong and loving communication' between herself and her mother (2002: 156). Discussing *Castillo*, I offered an alternative perspective on Serena's behaviour, but there is no doubt that the bond between Casilda and the mother who died at her birth is profound. However, the freedom-loving Casilda is not universally well-regarded. Ingrid Lindström describes Casilda's perspective on freedom as 'una libertad sin responsabilidad' [a freedom without responsibility] (2009: 156), while Bravo considers her independence to be closer to 'the egotism of the traditional male model' as it 'seems oblivious of the needs of others' (1998: 227). These readings seem to be related to Casilda's giving up her son 'in order to be free and to continue to write' (Bravo 1998: 227). However, there is a suggestion in the novel that Casilda bore Leonardo as a generous act of surrogacy.

Reina clearly differs from *Castillo*, *Pastel*, and *Caperucita*, which can be read by adults or children, in that it is a full-length novel for adults and bears no resemblance to the language, style or form of the fairy tale. Furthermore, the main protagonist of *Reina* is a young man of thirty, whereas the heroes of the *cuentos* are all female and, with the exception of Serena, are young girls. There are differences, too, in the treatment of time and place. As advised by the author in her *nota preliminar* to *Reina*, the story is set in the late 1970s, and she began taking notes for it in the middle of that decade. The settings of Madrid and Galicia – which form the backdrop onto which the novel is woven (Paoli 1998) – are also recognisable to readers. Although in *Caperucita* familiar locations in New York are used as a contemporary setting for magical occurrences, the settings of the other two *cuentos* do not correspond in the same way to actual locations, and in none of the three tales is the time frame so clearly specified. The story 'se inicia a principios de setiembre, en que la señora de la Quinta Blanca da un paseo por la aldea, y se extiende hasta el veinticuatro de diciembre' [it starts in early September, when the owner of the Quinta Blanca takes a walk through the hamlet, and goes on till 24 December] (Jurado Morales 2003: 323).

Nevertheless, the novel bears the name of the well-known fairy tale by Hans Christian Andersen – *The Snow Queen*[1] – and, in the words of O'Leary and Ribeiro de Menezes, establishes an 'intertextual dialogue' (2008: 144) with the source tale. The fairy tale is closely woven into the story, as recognised by the author in her dedication of the book to Hans Christian Andersen. Martín Gaite also refers to Andersen and his story in a poem from the collection *Después de todo* (2001b). 'La última vez que entró Andersen en casa' [the last time Andersen came into the house] (95) depicts the Snow Queen not as a literary figure but as Death – 'pero esta vez no era literatura' [but this time it was not literature] – and refers to the death of her only daughter, Marta, in April 1985. In her *nota preliminar* Martín Gaite explains that it was this experience which, for a number of years, led to her abandoning this novel which she had begun in 1975. Paoli sees a parallel between Martín Gaite's abandoning her notes for the novel for seven years following the death of her daughter, and the journey of the protagonist of *Reina*, Leonardo Villalba who spends seven years wandering, 'd'exil de soi' [in exile from himself] (2004: 243).

There are also differences between this novel and the *cuentos* in the depiction of the individuation process. In *Reina* encounters with the anima predominate and there is an important development towards the end in respect of the relationship with the Self. Most of the figures encountered are female, both positive and negative, and they mirror the inner development of Leonardo. Finally, whereas *Castillo* and *Caperucita* drew on traditional fairy tales, in *Reina* Martín Gaite takes a literary tale as her inspiration and

1 The English translation takes a quite different title – *The Farewell Angel* – from the drawing which Mónica gives to Leonardo on the eve of her departure for Australia.

integrates it into her text, where it acts as a reference point and support to Leonardo Villalba.

Hans Christian Andersen's *The Snow Queen*

The protagonist of *Reina*, Leonardo Villalba, records parts of the source tale in some detail in his notebooks, makes regular reference to it, and interprets both the story and his changing reaction to it. Andersen's fairy tale is in seven parts and begins with a promise to the reader or listener: 'When we arrive at the end of it we shall, it is to be hoped, know more than we do now' (Andersen 1995: 70). At the end of Martín Gaite's novel, too, both the protagonist, Leonardo, and the reader also know a good deal more than they did at the start.

Andersen's child protagonists, Kay and Gerda, live next door to each other, and play and listen to Gerda's grandmother's stories together. From their respective houses they communicate by sitting under the rose-trees in the window boxes on the roof or through their frosted bedroom windows in winter. Their idyllic friendship is broken when a magic mirror, created by a wicked magician, is dropped and shattered. The mirror made 'everything good and beautiful, when reflected in it, [shrink] up to almost nothing, whilst those things that were ugly and useless were magnified, and made to appear ten times worse than before' (Andersen 1995: 70). The fragments of glass from the mirror are each as powerful as the whole mirror and they 'sometimes get into people's eyes, causing them to view everything the wrong way [...] Some people were so unfortunate as to receive a little splinter into their hearts – that was terrible! The heart became cold and hard, like a lump of ice' (1995: 71–2). The effect of the glass splinters resembles what happens as a result of projection – the means by which unconscious contents are made conscious. Other people – individuals or groups – act as hooks for the projection of such contents. Because what is perceived largely belongs to the perceiver, the image is distorted. Unlike Andersen's tale, however, the distortion can be positive as well as negative, as, for example, when a person falls in love. The working out of a mutual projection is, according to von Franz, 'part of a process of reciprocal individuation, of becoming conscious and whole in the encounter' (1980: 140). The Christian injunction concerning the need to attend to the log in one's own eye before trying to remove the splinter in someone else's reflects the psychological reality of projection. Discussing the effect of the 'blindness' produced by projection, Martín Gaite writes that

> ver la paja en el ojo ajeno y no ver la viga en el propio quiere decir, sobre todo, que la paja del ojo ajeno esté analizada, penetrada y elaborada a partir de la exasperación que produce la ceguera a que nos condena esa viga propia. (2002a: 274)
>
> [to see the splinter in the other's eye and not the log in one's own means, above all, that the splinter in the other's eye should be analysed, explored and developed starting from the exasperation produced by the blindness to which our own log condemns us.]

Kay is one such unfortunate person, as two of the glass splinters enter his eye and heart. The resulting change in Kay's behaviour, which causes him to mock and mimic, to tease Gerda and enjoy rougher games, is seen by some critics as being typical of adolescence (Lederer 1990: 27; Wullschläger 2000: 244). Kay's competitiveness and brashness lead him one day to tie his little sledge to the biggest sleigh he sees in the great square in the town. The sleigh belongs to the Snow Queen and results in his being carried off to her palace. During the journey he tries unsuccessfully to loosen his sledge and becomes very frightened. However, when he tries to pray the 'Our Father' – the prayer first taught by Christ to his apostles – he finds he has forgotten the words and can only recite the multiplication table. This is the first indication of the deeper problem which Andersen's tale is seen by critics to represent – a dependence on logic and the resulting coldness and lack of feeling. It also illustrates the importance of wholeness, a view which Christopher Booker supports, arguing that when the splinters enter Kay's eye and heart, 'he can no longer see straight and whole, and he can no longer feel for others' (2005: 198); he is 'both dead to the true feminine and stunted in his masculinity' (Ibid. 264).

Most of the rest of the story (four of the seven parts) recount Gerda's search for her friend Kay, beginning with the rejection of her beloved red shoes. During her quest she encounters a mischievous old woman who tries to distract her from her task; two ravens, a prince and princess; a robber-girl and her band; and the wise women of Lapland and Finland, all of whom try to assist Gerda in her search. There is an apparent reversal in this tale of the roles which feminist criticism claims for male and female fairy-tale characters. Here Gerda carries out all the action and Kay, imprisoned in the palace, is not even aware that he needs to be rescued. For Booker, Gerda is able to do this because she '[represents] in herself both of the qualities he lacks: the femininity of her feeling, and, in her courage and spirit, the masculine strength he needs as well' (2005: 265). There are, of course, many examples of fairy tales in which the female character is the active one, and Gerda is in a tradition which includes Gretel, who saves her brother Hansel, and Beauty, who redeems her Beast.

In psychological terms the story can be read in the same way as the embedded tale of 'Eros and Psyche' in Apuleius's *The Golden Ass*. Jungian psychologists have interpreted it variously as representing the psychological development of a man – in which the inner feminine, the anima, is active – or of a woman, in which the woman herself redeems a frozen animus figure. In Apuleius's embedded tale, 'Eros and Psyche' – which von Franz describes as a fairy tale – she identifies Psyche as an anima and describes her as 'the principle of a love that has no trace of egoistic motives and whose goal signifies the individuation of the man, with a liberation from all rationalistic one-sidedness' (1980: 133). This link between the anima and love also echoes Macmurray and reflects the role of Gerda in Andersen's fairy tale. Wolfgang Lederer, a psychiatrist who, with his colleagues, analysed *The Snow Queen* as if it were a psychiatric case (Lederer 1990), identifies Gerda as the personification of the inner feminine of Kay/Andersen. However, he refers to the anima only as a positive figure when, in fact, it is more complex, with both positive and negative aspects and various stages of development: 'We may as well [...] use Jung's terminology and call her an *anima* figure: that aspect of man which, if any, is inspired and creative' (1990: 174). In his fairy tale, Lederer argues, Andersen sends this anima figure 'on a long voyage through the night of the unconscious' (174). Booker agrees that the story ends with '[a] shift from the limited centre of [Kay's] personality in which he has spent most of the story, to that deeper centre which he consciously recognises to be his true self. [...] he is united with the 'other half' who has at last both set him free and made him whole' (2005: 227). On the other hand, in an essay in which she analyses *The Snow Queen* from a Jungian perspective, Marilyn Matthews considers that 'the triumvirate of the feminine goddess – the old one, the queen, and the maid – and the fact that it is the little girl who must make the heroic journey suggests that this tale is primarily about woman's individuation' (1992: 83).

All the time Gerda is searching for him, Kay is in the Snow Queen's palace, in the centre of which there is a frozen lake on which the Snow Queen sits when she is at home and which she calls 'The Mirror of Reason'. When the Snow Queen leaves the palace, Kay – 'quite blue, nay, almost black with cold, but he did not observe it' (Andersen 1995: 113) – is charged with trying to form the word 'Eternity' from the fragments of ice from the lake which 'was broken into a thousand pieces, [which] so exactly resembled each other' (Ibid. 113). The Snow Queen has promised him that, if he succeeds, 'thou shalt become thine own master and I will give thee the whole world and a new pair of skates besides' (Ibid. 113). There are differing responses to this promised reward, with Lederer seeing it as frivolous – 'Clearly she is mocking his childish and futile aspirations' (1990: 67). In a quite different interpretation, W. H. Auden argues that the promise 'has not only a surprise and subtlety of which the folk tale is incapable, but also a uniqueness by which one can identify its author' (in Wullschläger 2000: 246 n1). At the same time, this promise to give the whole world to Kay is not unlike the temptation of Christ in the New Testament in which the devil promised Him all the kingdoms of the world in return for Christ falling at his feet and doing him homage, which was discussed in connection with Lucandro in *Castillo*. As Lederer says, 'the expected "good" [from the re-assembling of the fragments of ice] is a good only in the sense of the Snow Queen (or the Devil)' (1990: 65). So although Kay tries to achieve the Snow Queen's promised reward and can 'form the most curious and complete figures [and] often formed whole words', the fact that the word 'Eternity' eludes him seems positive. Paradoxically, the puzzle may also be impossible for Kay because eternity embraces the supernatural, the unconscious and, therefore, wholeness. In the inner world the boy is frozen with only one part of the pair of opposites of thought and feeling available to him. Thus, wholeness eludes him.

In the final part of the fairy tale Gerda reaches the palace and weeps hot and bitter tears when she finds her friend sitting 'cold, silent, motionless', unresponsive to her embrace (Andersen 1995: 114). Her tears at 'his unkindness' melt the ice in Kay's heart, causing him to cry, releasing the splinter from his eye, and enabling him to recognise both Gerda and the nature of the place he is in: 'How cold it is here! how wide and empty!' (Ibid. 114). As a result of this change, 'the pieces of ice took part in their joy; they danced about merrily, and when they were wearied and lay down they formed of their own accord the mystical letters' (Ibid. 114), spelling out the word 'Eternity'. This formation of the word 'eternity' as a result of Gerda freeing Kay from his former state seems to confirm the importance of wholeness both within the individual personality – thought is not enough, there must also be a place for feeling, for the world of eros – and also between the conscious world and the supernatural, eternal dimension represented by the word formed by the pieces of ice. This is the key to rendering the Snow Queen powerless: '[She] might now come home as soon as she liked – it mattered not; Kay's charter of freedom stood written on the mirror in bright icy characters' (Ibid. 115). Had Kay formed the word himself, he may have gained the material rewards promised but, because he was first freed by Gerda and made whole through the release of his frozen feelings, his reward will be a spiritual one.

The friends retrace most of Gerda's journey, helped again by the wise women and the robber-maiden, and arrive home to Gerda's grandmother's house where they find they are now 'full-grown persons'. This is clarified by the grandmother, who reads to them from the Bible: 'Unless ye become as little children, ye shall not enter into the kingdom of heaven' (119). The two friends understand this to mean that they are 'grown up and yet children – children in heart' (119). María Elena Soliño is critical, seeing this as meaning that they are neither one thing nor the other: 'Kay and Gerda are neither adults nor children […], the image of being stuck is taken as a happy ending' (2000: 189). Lederer, too, sees the ending as the weakest part of the story: 'Even his best stories remained flawed, as *The Snow Queen* is flawed by its timorous, inconclusive ending' (1990: 177). However, to a committed Christian like Hans Christian Andersen, being able to enter the Kingdom of Heaven would represent the greatest achievement. The Kingdom of

Heaven (also called the Kingdom of God) is not described in the New Testament as a place or something to be achieved only after death, but as a way of living in the here and now: 'The coming of the kingdom of God does not admit of observation and there will be no one to say, "Look, it is here! Look, it is there!" For look, the kingdom of God is among you' (Luke 17. 20–1). In this interpretation, the depiction of Kay and Gerda at the end of *The Snow Queen* implies that their lives have a new dimension, which is also the effect of the individuation process. In connection with Serena's response to her dreams in *Castillo*, I discussed von Franz's interpretation of Christ's promise that only little children would enter the kingdom of heaven. She argues that it does not represent a regression but rather 'the restoration of an unreflecting capacity for obeying the Self' as a result of individuation (1995b: 109). Thus, at the end of his tale Andersen appears to be indicating that both protagonists have changed, that Gerda's quest has resulted in both of them developing that new relationship with the Self. Booker agrees that it is the attainment of wholeness which enables Kay to grow up (2005: 198 & 265). So, it is not only the reader/listener who knows more by the end of the story, but also the two young protagonists. This differs from the interpretations of both Wullschläger – who considers that 'Kai grows up, and Gerda doesn't, so saving him by her innocence' (2000: 245) – and Lederer, who argues that 'Gerda manages not to get trapped, but she also manages not to learn anything. She goes through all her adventures essentially untouched and unimpaired, but also unenriched. [...] She insists, in the last analysis, on getting along on the strength of her religious faith alone' (1990: 175–6).

In fact, Gerda's first step in the process of individuation takes place when she throws her red shoes into the river, an act on which critics have commented in some detail. Although she does it in exchange for information regarding the whereabouts of Kay, the effect is that of falling into the individuation process and into the hands of the Self. Critics generally point out that Gerda throws her red shoes into the water and the river throws them back. However, the tale suggests that the first time Gerda did not throw the shoes far enough and they stayed near the edge and were returned to her, as if she was not sufficiently willing to let go of them. Before throwing them a second time, Gerda gets into a little boat to ensure that the shoes are in the middle of the river. Her action in throwing the shoes causes the boat to move and carry her downstream. This is the unplanned and, to her, disturbing start of her adventure: 'The boat was not fastened, and her movements in it caused it to glide away from the shore. She saw this, and hastened to get out, but by the time she reached the other end of the boat it was more than a yard distant from the land; she could not escape, and the boat glided on. Little Gerda was much frightened and began to cry' (81). Gerda thus finds herself on the water, a symbol of the unconscious, and can be interpreted as the little girl being in the hands of the Self.

The shoes are an important symbol and Gerda's sacrifice of them is linked to the aim of individuation, namely the relationship with the Self. However, prevailing critical views differ considerably from this interpretation. Most critics see the shoes as symbolising a sexuality which Andersen feared and which, as a result, he forced Gerda to renounce in favour of purity: 'Gerda makes the crucial – and Christian – decision to remain pure' (Lederer 1990: 37). However, because we stand on our feet and, therefore, our shoes, they can be seen as representing the stand we take, our viewpoint: 'Shoes represent the standpoint' (von Franz 1990: 21). Earlier, in connection with Little Red Riding Hood's colourful garment, I cited claims that the colour 'red' could be interpreted as sin, sexuality, life, sacrifice, blood, freedom, and as being linked to the Christian feast of Pentecost. I also argued that red symbolises feeling and, therefore, includes love and eros, which are connected to the feminine. However, any interpretation must make sense within the context of the story, and as Gerda's whole search for her friend is driven by her friendship, it would not make sense to interpret her rejection of the shoes as renouncing love and feeling.

Lederer, despite concurring with the view that Gerda 'renounc[es] sexuality and choos[es] the path of virtue' (1990: 38), also asserts that on the final stage of Gerda's journey, when she is 'without shoes, without gloves, alone in that barren region, that terribly icy-cold Finland' (Andersen 1995: 110), 'having left her shoes behind and her gloves [...] she has left her ego behind altogether. Not just the red shoes but all shoes are now gone' (1990: 63). So, here Lederer links the shoes with the ego, which brings them closer to the interpretation above of the personal standpoint. In fact, it can be argued that the ego is left behind, not only when she is barefoot and gloveless near the end, but also at the start of her quest when she throws the shoes into the river. Therefore, the red shoes themselves can be seen to symbolise the ego, Gerda's ego, her own standpoint. By giving them up at the start of her journey she is putting herself in the hands of the Self. Thus the red colour would represent the *sacrifice* of the ego and her action in letting go of the shoes would mark an important step in the process of individuation for Gerda. This interpretation is also in keeping with Andersen's conclusion. Matthews considers that the red shoes can symbolise a number of aspects – 'courage, emotions, sexuality, and love' – and decides that 'Gerda's journey begins [...] with a willing loss of her emotional standpoint, a willingness to float down the river and be carried by the process' (1992: 85). It is a conscious sacrifice, but Gerda's frightened reaction when the boat begins to move and her cry for help when she sees the old woman's cottage, suggest that she had not fully anticipated the implications of giving up her standpoint.

The emphasis on Reason in the Snow Queen's palace has, not surprisingly, led critics to see the story as a struggle between Reason and Emotion, as one which contrasts 'cold reason and warm feelings' (Grønbech 1980: 102). Andersen is described as having a 'dislike of a reliance on reason and of the arid, intellectual life', believing that 'love conquers all [...] a reliance on reason and the intellect leads to barren misery' (Wullschläger 2000: 76). In his collection of essays *Reason and Emotion*, the Scottish philosopher John Macmurray argues that 'we associate reason with a state of mind which is cold, detached and unemotional. When our emotions are stirred we feel that reason is left behind and we enter another world' (1992: 5). This is exactly the division which critics see as the essence of Andersen's fairy tale. However, Macmurray argues that the real opposition is not between reason and emotion, but between emotion and thought, with reason present in both: 'Reason is the capacity to behave consciously in terms of the nature of what is not ourselves. [...] Reason is thus our capacity for objectivity' (1992: 7). Regarded superficially 'objectivity' sounds impersonal, but, as discussed in Chapter 1, Macmurray convincingly argues that objective love is characteristic of personal, rather than organic life (1992: 15). His definition of love is very similar to 'objective cognition', which Jung sees as the outcome of the individuation process and which was described in Chapter 1 as equivalent to love.

It can, therefore, be argued that Kay is not trapped by reason, but rather – as suggested by his reciting of the multiplication table rather than the prayer he wanted to say – by logic, thought and the intellect, with no access to emotion or feeling. Thinking and feeling are two opposing functions in Jung's polaric psychological structure. This interpretation is also reflected in Martín Gaite's novel. Leonardo Villalba, the protagonist, does not appear to be trapped by the intellect or by logic, even though, following the death of his grandmother, he describes himself in terms of the story, as being like Kay in the Snow Queen's palace. His feeling has been frozen as he recognises in his notebooks (175), rendering him incapable of love or objective cognition until, as Martín Gaite's story develops, the ice melts and he is freed. As Soliño recognises, both Kay's and Leonardo's hearts have been frozen, 'leaving them unable to form connections to others' (150).

This lack of relatedness can also be described as a lack of eros or feeling. Feeling into the individual situation of another requires much awareness and considerable progress in the process of individuation in order to withdraw projections and have sufficient insight into their recurrence. Relatedness is, therefore, the highest, most conscious level of eros between persons. A lack of relatedness is what Martín Gaite seems to be describing in a journal entry from the early 1960s when she says that

> la falta de distancia – la justa para ver más que su letrero y otras cuantas particularidades personales: sus piernas, su nariz – convierte también en cosa a esa persona. (2002a: 43)

> [the lack of distance – just the right amount so as to see more than their label and a few other personal features: their legs, their nose – also converts this person into a thing.]

Her description illustrates what she herself describes as a good mirror. The good mirror sees us and accepts us exactly as we are, and this attitude is close to both Macmurray's definition of love and Jung's objective cognition, as well as to the real message of Christianity, in which the focus is on the reality of the other person. There are examples of both good and bad mirrors in *Reina*.

Structure of the Novel

O'Leary and Ribeiro de Menezes compare Martín Gaite's book to detective fiction (2008: 144). Divided into three unequal parts, the four unrelated chapters of the first part sow the seeds for what is to follow and introduce the main characters: Leonardo Villalba; his father, Eugenio; Casilda Iriarte (the latter's childhood friend and, later, lover); and several characters from the Galician village which plays such an important role in Leonardo's memory and imagination. The fragmentary presentation of these characters means that the connection between them is only revealed much later in the course of the novel. Nevertheless, important information is provided about the main characters: Leonardo's love of story and storytelling and his rejection of the way of life which led to his arrest on drugs charges; his father, Eugenio's inability to reconnect with his past and the poor communication with both his son and his mother; and the outsider – *la señora de la Quinta Blanca* – who now lives in Eugenio's childhood home in Galicia and who is at ease scrambling over the rocks at the shore. The second, and much longer, part covers the period between late October and December as related by Leonardo in his notebooks. It is these, written in his parents' house in Madrid after he has left Carabanchel prison and learnt of their death in a car accident, which give rise to the differing responses from critics to this character. Mixing detailed recording of his present feelings and actions with the memories they trigger, the notebooks take the story forward to the final part of the book, which reverts to the third-person narrative and leads the story to its controversial conclusion in which Leonardo and Casilda, sitting by a lighthouse in Galicia, become reconciled as mother and son.

In Leonardo's notebooks the story of *The Snow Queen* is singled out through extracts and reflections on the tale – particularly the role of Gerda – at key points in his journey. Fairy tales are generally associated with the feminine, with female tellers and listeners/readers. Leonardo represents a challenge to this perspective and some critics are disparaging of Leonardo's fondness for fairy tales, seeing it as a sign of immaturity and weakness. However, the whole novel is about the discovery of meaning in the life of Leonardo, and recovering a sense of meaning is the result of taking the path of individuation and the way which is unique to him which will enable him to discover his unique identity, thus overcoming a sense of hopelessness and of having no significance in the world or in life. The path for Leonardo, as presented by Martín Gaite, requires a return to a fairy tale from his childhood and using it as a guide along the road he has to take. While the response of critics who mock this behaviour as childish is understandable, it nevertheless fails to recognise the individual nature of the individuation process and the courage needed to follow it consciously. Jung describes his own experience of having to take up childish activities in order to move forward when, at a difficult time in his life, he had to make a connection with his eleven-year-old self and the games he played then, building houses and castles with stones, mud and bottles: 'This moment was a turning point in my fate, but I gave in only after endless resistances and with a sense of recognition. For it was a painfully humiliating experience to realise that there was nothing to be done except play childish games' (1983: 198). It is not difficult to see how following accepted collective patterns of behaviour and renouncing the path of individuation could appear as a more attractive option.

Carabanchel and First Steps to Freedom

Leonardo's rediscovery of his love of story while he is in Madrid's Carabanchel prison for drug offences leads to his playing a similar role in relation to his cellmate as the young Sofía Montalvo plays to her school friend Mariana León in *Nubosidad*. Similarly, Martín Gaite's sister Ana María recalls how, as children, she would often ask her sister to tell her a story at night:

> A la hora de dormir, le decía: 'Anda, Carmiña, cuéntame un cuento'. Y se le ocurrían unas historias con tanta fantasía que, cuando llegaba mi turno, me sentía incapaz de superarlas y le ponía como excusa que tenía mucho sueño. (in Soriano 2007: 269)

> [At bedtime I would say to her: 'Come on, Carmiña, tell me a story'. And she thought up such imaginative stories that, when it was my turn, I knew I could never do better than that and I would make the excuse that I was very sleepy.]

Although Leonardo always related his dreams to one or other of his acquaintances, the condition of imprisonment seems to provide the opportunity to employ his imagination as a means of combating his situation by transforming his perspective of the cell. This is typical of Martín Gaite's approach to difficult situations, as was discussed in relation to *Pastel*. Most importantly, the experience of prison breaks his links with a previous circle of acquaintances and a rootless existence, as well as providing him with an undemanding and interested interlocutor in his cellmate, Julián Expósito. At the same time it enables him to begin the reconnection to his past, particularly his childhood, and the recollection of how much he enjoyed *The Snow Queen*. Carabanchel as the start of the journey to freedom is also illustrated in Leonardo's impression of it as white like the Snow Queen's palace (40).

The comparison of Carabanchel with the Snow Queen's palace reinforces the sense of this period of Leonardo's life as a new start. His reference to having died, in his description of the prison, can be interpreted as a death to a former way of life, as a detachment from his former 'friends'. In her *Cuadernos* Martín Gaite cites the poet Cavafy – whose poem 'Ítaca' will act as a guide and inspiration to Leonardo in his inner journey – on the importance of detachment: 'Si no puedes hacer de tu vida lo que quisieras, trata al menos de no envilecerla con demasiados contactos con el mundo' [If you can't make of your life what you would like, try at least not to degrade it with too much contact with the world] (2002a: 395). When Leonardo tells Julián Expósito in their prison cell, 'si te limitas a estar aquí, sin preguntarte qué es esto ni porqué has venido, entonces es todo mentira, absurdo, y empiezas a estar bien, no se te clava' [if you confine yourself just to being here, without asking yourself what it's all about or why you have come here, then it's all a lie, absurd, and you begin to be all right, it doesn't get to you] (39). In part this reflects Martín Gaite's regard for not struggling against what you cannot change, as discussed in Chapter 1 in connection with her favourite joke. It also recalls a story she told in her notebooks about an experience a few months following her daughter's untimely death.[2] She turned once again to Simone Weil's *Gravity and Grace*, a book which she took everywhere:

> Siempre que abro al azar este libro tan gastado, tan subrayado, *La pesanteur et la grâce*, que desde hace años viaja conmigo a todas partes, me encuentro exactamente con la frase que más a cuento viene, que más estaba necesitando. (2002a: 611)
>
> [Whenever I open at random this book, *Gravity and Grace*, which is so worn and underlined and which for years has gone everywhere with me, I find exactly the words which are most relevant, the ones I most needed.]

On this occasion, only a few months after Marta's death, she read:

> Si nos consideramos en un momento determinado – el instante presente, desligado del pasado y del futuro – somos inocentes. En ese instante no podemos ser más de lo que somos. Aislar así un instante implica el perdón. (2002a: 611)
>
> [If we consider ourselves at a determined moment – the present moment, disconnected from past and future – we are innocent. At that moment we cannot be more than we are. Isolating a moment in this way implies forgiveness.]

The present moment, free of both memory and fear, is also free of pain. Inhabiting the present moment seems to have been Martín Gaite's general aim, given the value she placed on attentiveness, which is only attainable by letting go of both past and future.

A further link between Carabanchel and the palace of the Snow Queen – and between Leonardo and Kay – is suggested by one of Leonardo's former acquaintances, Ángela, who visited him in prison. During the car journey back to her flat following his release she recalls how he did not respond positively to her visits (60), and her description of his reactions to her resembles Kay's response to Gerda's appearance in the Snow Queen's palace when Kay does not recognise her (62). However, whereas Gerda weeps in sorrow at the state of her friend and thus frees him, Ángela is more preoccupied

2 This story is also related by Teruel (2006) and Brown (2017).

with Leonardo's behaviour towards her and with the contrast between this and the way she expected or wanted him to behave. Gerda's focus is ultimately on Kay while Ángela's is on herself and, thus, she is unable to free Leonardo from his frozen state.

The dream Leonardo has while he is imprisoned also marks an important step in his journey of individuation. It occurs during the siesta, while his cellmate, Julián, is betraying him to one of the more unpleasant prison guards in an attempt to protect himself, aware that his action will result in Leonardo being transferred to the psychiatric unit on suspicion of homosexuality. In Leonardo's dream an unknown woman comes to visit him in prison and Julián appears to be trying to help him by telling him not to go to the visiting room (34). At the time, the importance of the motifs in the dream – the portrait hanging above the piano in the Quinta Blanca and the house itself – are not clear and initially it appears as if Julián is trying to keep Leonardo away from threatening prison guards. Only with the development of the story can Julián's action in the dream be seen to be trying to prevent something important to Leonardo. Thus the dream appears to reflect a negative aspect of Julián, of which Leonardo is not consciously aware. This is typical of dreams, which often compensate the conscious perspective. The dream also affords a first glimpse of a mysterious feminine figure dressed in grey and with her face partly covered by a veil, which recalls in part the vision described by Sorpresa at the end of the story she invented (35). Emma Jung points out that figures of women that cannot be identified with actual persons often occur in dreams. They appear usually as the 'stranger', the 'unknown' or the 'veiled woman' (1981 82). Feminine figures in the dreams of men would usually represent the anima, which was identified by Jung as the contrasexual element, the soul of all men, and an archetype of great value. For Emma Jung the anima 'is predominantly conditioned by eros, that is, by the principle of union, of relationship' (Ibid. 59). From Ángela we learn that a woman, whose identity is not clear, has appeared in Leonardo's dreams over a period of some years, someone whose identity, like that of the anima, could have been a mother or a lover, and who Leonardo recognised as the Snow Queen (62). The Carabanchel dream, set in Galicia, opens a door to other positive images which appear later in the evening as Leonardo and Julián discuss the siesta dream and smoke cannabis, and include the memory of a place which evokes a feeling he describes as like returning to paradise (41).

Risk of Regression

Lederer argues that in Andersen's fairy tale 'Gerda [is] constantly in danger of accepting too much hospitality, of getting stuck in the wonderland of the (inner) world in which she travels' (1990: 175). Although Gerda appears to be in the hands of the Self when she steps into the boat and is carried down the river, hers is not a passive role and, therefore, she has to use her wits in her quest as she faces temptation and danger. This reflects the positive relationship between the ego and the Self. The first stop Gerda makes is at 'a large cherry orchard, wherein stood a little cottage with thatched roof and curious red and blue windows' (1995: 81). Although Gerda calls out to the wooden soldiers at the door, it is the stream – not the soldiers or the little girl herself – which 'drifted the boat to the land' (Ibid. 82) and enabled her to meet the old lady who lives there. The old lady 'wished very much to keep little Gerda to live with her' (Ibid. 83) and, as she is an enchantress, she causes Gerda to forget the quest she has embarked upon by hiding all the roses in the garden. She is successful until the little girl sees a painted rose on the old lady's hat and, remembering Kay, 'with bare feet, ran out into the wide world. Three times she looked back, there was no one following her; she ran till she could run no longer' (Ibid. 89). 'For Jung, the rose was a wholeness symbol of the Self, the balance between the conscious and the unconscious' (Matthews 1992: 83). This would mean that Gerda had been in danger of abandoning the path to wholeness, the individuation process, in exchange for a comfortable but less meaningful life. Thus the Self, in the form of the symbolism of the rose, whose realisation in Gerda the old woman tries to prevent, finds a way to remind Gerda of her task.

Ángela's apparent kindness in meeting Leonardo at the gates of the prison to take him back to her flat, represents a similar danger of slipping back into his previous way of life following the initial steps towards change made in Carabanchel. That the prison has marked the beginning of change for Leonardo is confirmed in conversation with Ángela in the car:

> – No tengo ganas de pensar. Si no me haces preguntas en un rato, te estaré muy agradecido.
> La chica pelirroja se echó a reír. Era la suya una risa que desafinaba, que no daba calor. [...]
> – ¿Agradecido tú? ¡Qué novedad! No sabía que los médicos de la cárcel hicieran milagros. (59)
>
> ['I don't feel like thinking. If you could not ask me questions for a while, I'd be very grateful.'
> The redheaded girl burst out laughing. Hers was a laugh that jarred, that had no warmth in it. [...]
> 'You grateful? What a novelty! I didn't know the prison doctors could perform miracles.']

Here Ángela resembles one of Martín Gaite's bad mirrors, reminding Leonardo of an earlier pattern of behaviour. Leonardo, having just been freed physically from prison, also needs psychological and emotional freedom to be able to build on the initial changes, and clearly will not find it in the company of his former group of friends. The way in which he manages to get away from them is the result of his paying attention, something which was impressed by Cambof Petapel on the young Altalé in *Castillo* (Martín Gaite 1992a: 50), and which McCully sees as an essential characteristic of fairy-tale heroes (1991: 54). The irritation Leo feels at the chatter and questions of Ángela extends to a physical irritation in his foot (64) to which he turns his attention. Had Leonardo let himself be distracted by Ángela – who, among other things, is telling him she believes he is the father of the child she is carrying – and not paid attention to himself, he seems unlikely to have focused on the old newspaper on the floor of the car, beneath his foot. Seeing the news item about the sudden death of his parents provides an unexpected link to his earlier life and the opportunity to reject Ángela, her car and his old life and to go back immediately to his parents' house.

Nevertheless, Ángela's chatter and questions also help to create memories for Leonardo, including a trip to Tangier and an important wish to have a child he could bring up alone and teach to be free (61). The effect of her chatter is, therefore, the opposite to the Snow Queen, who caused Kay to lose his memory completely, as Ángela contributes to the start of an important process which leads to Leonardo's recording memories in his notebooks and recovering a sense of himself. Ángela is also an anima figure, and, therefore, Leonardo's coldness towards her when she visited him in prison also reflects the lack of inner relatedness and communication within himself, represented symbolically by the glass partition between them during the prison visits.

Leonardo's Notebooks

Covering the period between his return to his parents' house and his first communication with the woman who lives in the Quinta Blanca, Casilda Iriarte, Leonardo's notebooks record the search for, and discovery of, family secrets. This long second section, like the novel itself, can also be divided into three parts. In the first Leonardo confines himself to the family house and begins the process of discovery of memories and secrets in his father's study.[3] The second takes place in a number of locations outside the house: his lawyer's office; the Puerta de Alcalá; a nightclub; and the flat of a young woman he meets at the nightclub. The final part, mirroring Leonardo's own inner journey, includes spaces both inside and outside the house, culminating in a telephone conversation with Casilda in which she invites him to spend Christmas in the Quinta Blanca.

These shifts between the inner and outer worlds and between dream and reality, reveal the development through individuation which, from the psychological development of the unique person, leads to a new relatedness

3 Lindström notes the importance of the dining-room in Leonardo's family home (2009), while Ollé (2004) discusses the role of a number of spaces in the same house. Martín Gaite's attitude to spaces is explored by Ribeiro de Menezes, who concludes that 'the true space of liberation in [the] novel is the space of writing' (2011: 155).

to others – to loving others as oneself. In this the novel resembles the source tale as interpreted by a critic of Andersen's work: 'That love is the meaning of life, and that the soul is immortal, is a theme running through Andersen's *oeuvre*, but [...] *The Snow Queen* [...] is one of a small number of tales whose action turns on this fundamental belief' (Wullschläger 2000: 355). The immortality of the soul comes up near the end of the novel in Casilda's reaction, on the day of the funeral of the retired village schoolteacher, Antonio Moura, to the news that he believed in life after death: 'No lo sabía. Y me consuela mucho saberlo, de verdad' [I didn't know that. And it comforts me very much to hear it, it really does] (268). Later, in the course of her long night-time conversation with her *criado* [servant] Mauricio Brito, she describes her own view of death as another beginning (305).

Dreams and Stories

The dreams in *Reina*, as in other works by Martín Gaite, often mark the beginning of a new stage in the dreamer's life, and its successful development depends on the dreamer's response to the dream. In addition to the dream Leonardo had in Carabanchel, about a mysterious woman, there are a number of other dreams in the novel which act to raise his awareness of potentially dangerous situations and indicate the way forward. The first, occuring during a nap shortly after leaving Ángela and arriving at his parents' home, involves Leonardo being with his father's wife, Trud,[4] and at the same time he is Kay following the Snow Queen (85). In the dream Trud/the Snow Queen puts her arm around him, freezing him and causing him to turn to ice. Still asleep, Leonardo realises that the only solution is to remember the story and tell it to someone, as if the story holds the key to his problems and to their solution. His relief when he wakens at

4 Trud is the woman Leonardo grows up believing to be his mother. To avoid confusion between Trud and Leonardo's natural mother, Casilda Iriarte, I will refer to both of them by name rather than their relationship to Leonardo.

remembering the start of the fairy tale confirms the importance he gives to dreams. However, rather than tell it to someone else, Leonardo tells it to himself in his notebooks, reflecting Martín Gaite's emphasis on the need to tell a story to yourself first before you can tell it well and convincingly to anyone else.

With the memory of how *The Snow Queen* begins comes the recollection of Leonardo's arrival in Galicia to spend summer holidays with his grandmother, which fills him with 'un estallido de resplandor' [a burst of brilliant light] which is like 'el brillo de una joya largo tiempo enterrada' [the sparkling of a jewel which had been buried for a long time] (96). This image of a jewel or precious stone is meaningful to Leonardo for he uses it again later in connection with Casilda. According to von Franz 'the image of a stone, jewel, or crystal appears with special frequency as a representation of the Self' (1997a: 335). This suggests that the experiences which Leonardo associates with jewels or precious stones will have a potentially meaningful role in the process of individuation which he is following. Thus, Leonardo's response to the memories and dreams so far suggest that he is already recovering the ability to recognise and hold on to what is meaningful for him. The way in which he seizes and holds on to the fairy tale and does not let go of it recalls the image used by Jesus to describe the Kingdom of Heaven: 'The kingdom of Heaven is like treasure hidden in a field which someone has found; he hides it again, goes off in his joy, sells everything he owns and buys the field' (Matthew 13: 44). The memories, connections and understanding which follow the first dream in the Madrid house include reconsideration of his perception of Trud and her link with the Snow Queen.

Trud and the Snow Queen

In Leonardo's dream Trud turns into Andersen's fairy-tale protagonist, an image which would be approved by Rosa Figueroa, the former servant of Leonardo's grandmother, who describes the American as icy and from a cold northern place, which recalls the original fairy tale: 'Her strong castle is very far off, near the North Pole' (108). This comparison is further strengthened by Leonardo's new understanding of an experience following his grandmother's death. Recalling the morning when he was given a letter from his grandmother, who had died some months before, he remembers that it was snowing, something which is invariably meaningful and magical to him (157). The letter, which he had expected would bring him the healing and answers that he had long hoped for from his grandmother, was given to him by Trud dressed in a white velvet dressing gown. Her physical appearance together with the snow enable him to see that Trud is the Snow Queen (160).

The implication of this is that his father, Eugenio, is married to the Snow Queen, and, therefore, in the symbolism of the story, is like a Kay who was never rescued by Gerda and who has never left the ice palace. In Andersen's story, Kay was afraid of the Snow Queen on the journey to her palace, although her first kiss froze all his feeling. In Eugenio's relationship with his wife there is also fear in, for example, the way he and his son felt they had to speak more quietly so as not to disturb her or the impact of her sudden arrival on any warm communication between father and son. Fear is the opposite of love and friendship, something that was testified by Julián Expósito's description of the uniquely positive impact of Leonardo's presence on his feelings of fear. Trud's resentment of any intimacy between father and son and the consequent creation of reactions and feelings which are filled with unreason, not only support Leonardo's assessment of her icy qualities and her likeness to the Snow Queen, but also illustrate the effect of being imprisoned in her palace as being prevented from feeling and relating, from eros and love, rather than being locked in a game of reason. Eugenio was prevented from carrying out his decision to leave Trud/the Snow Queen's palace by the car accident in which they both died. Leonardo is more fortunate, and the insight he gains brings a clarity of perception which allows him to find distance from Trud without guilt.

The Quinta Blanca and the Snow Queen's Palace

Not surprisingly, critics support Leonardo's interpretation of Trud as the Snow Queen. Several have also connected the Quinta Blanca with the Snow Queen's palace, albeit transformed. Jurado Morales considers that 'la Quinta Blanca es una inversión del Palacio de Hielo de Andersen, es decir, los sentimientos sustituyen al vacío afectivo' [the Quinta Blanca is a reversal of Andersen's Ice Palace, that is, feelings replace the emotional vacuum] (2003: 310). As well as the transformation resulting from the new inhabitant Casilda Iriarte, Leonardo's natural mother, offering him love, there is a further contrast with the fairy-tale location in her emphasis, at the start of her telephone conversation with Leonardo, that she is only interested in things which lie outside the field of logic (251). For Turpín,

> la Quinta Blanca se erige en parangón del castillo de *la Reina de las Nieves*, donde deambulan los recuerdos, el pasado, la memoria que quiere conquistar Leonardo Villalba. (1994: 53)
>
> [the Quinta Blanca is set up in contrast to the castle in *The Snow Queen* where memories, the past, and the memory which Leonardo Villalba wants to recover, all roam.]

As le Scouzec Masson argues, 'la Quinta Blanca, comme le château des contes, materialise bien le paradis de l'origine auquel [...] il será posible de revenir, et ce pour toujours' [the Quinta Blanca, like the castle in fairy tales, clearly depicts the Garden of Eden to which [...] it will be possible to return, and forever] (2003: 86). However, Leonardo cannot return until he has attained much greater consciousness; until, like Hans Christian Andersen's protagonists, he is in a position to confirm that he knows much more than he did at the start.

In contrast, Ingrid Lindström, disagrees that the Quinta Blanca and the Snow Queen's palace are related, arguing instead that

> si consideramos en qué morada Leonardo emprendió su labor de puzle [...], [el] chalet lujoso en un barrio madrileño de alta categoría sustituye en nuestra opinión al Palacio de Hielo mientras que la Quinta Blanca equivale a las buhardillas de las casas contiguas del cuento. (2009: 158)

> [if we consider in which dwelling Leonardo began his work on the jigsaw [...], the luxurious house in a high-class Madrid suburb, in our opinion, replaces the Ice Palace while the Quinta Blanca is equivalent to the attic rooms of the adjacent houses in the fairy tale.]

The argument is well-founded and more compelling than the direct links made between the Quinta Blanca and the ice palace. Nevertheless, there is also a connection between Inés Guitián and the Snow Queen and, therefore, another sense in which the Quinta can be said to play the role of the Snow Queen's palace.

The source of Leonardo's father, Eugenio's difficulties in relationships is his mother, of whom he was afraid – the same grandmother who iss such a figure of caring and support to Leonardo. For example, the letters from Sila/Casilda, which Leonardo finds in his father's safe, indicate that, although five years older than the eight-year-old freedom-loving lighthouse-keeper's daughter, Eugenio's fear of his mother made him more reluctant than the young Sila to stay out late. It was Inés who tried to keep him away from Sila, whom he loved, resulting in his going to Chicago to study and to his marrying the infertile Trud. There was also a certain coldness in her request, along with her son, that Casilda provide a son to the childless couple, an heir to the Quinta Blanca. Some critics describe Leonardo's birth as the result of an affair between Casilda and Eugenio, but Eugenio's recollection of what happened could also suggest something more akin to surrogacy: 'Cuando volviste de Inglaterra y yo te busqué, cuando te pedí aquello [...] algo que nadie más que tú podía concederme, cuando te lo pidió también mi madre' [When you came back from England and I sought you out, when I asked you that [...], something that only you could grant me, when my mother asked you the same thing] (300). Furthermore, despite the connection Leonardo makes between Trud and the Snow Queen in the scene with the letter, the little piece of distorting mirror which entered Leonardo's heart came not from Trud but from the letter from his grandmother, which failed to provide the answers he sought. Leonardo had hoped for so much from the letter and was left disappointed, just as he had been whenever he had asked her for information about his family and background. Described by Leonardo as a *monserga* [sermon], the posthumous letter was the opposite of what he had expected, containing only practical advice and other things such as information about the house she had left him and details of accounts, which recalls Kay trying to pray the Our Father and only being able to think of his multiplication tables. Far from reaching out to her grandson and explaining the secret of his origins or even expressing any real feeling, it is objective and practical, and identifies Inés, not only as symbolic of the Snow Queen, but also as someone else who has been kissed by the Snow Queen and who remains unredeemed.

Inés enjoys puzzles and word games and when Leonardo returns to the family home in Madrid, he imagines her and speaks to her, but she speaks in riddles which he cannot understand. The resolution of riddles requires cleverness, the use of the mind, unlike the fairy tales which she used to tell him as a child, which also appeal to the heart. So while she resembles the grandmother in Andersen's tale who 'stroked [Kay's] hair and told him some stories' (1995: 74), she has other aspects which are more cerebral and secretive, particularly about the family, and she admits to Leonardo that she may have got a piece of glass in her eye years before, even before his father was born (101). It is Leonardo's reaction to his grandmother's letter that leads to his identification with Kay becoming complete and with it a sense that the state is permanent and that, unlike Kay, there is no possibility of his being rescued by someone like Gerda (159). However, whereas Kay lost his memory involuntarily at the second kiss of the Snow Queen, Leonardo seems determined to wipe out his own past by selling the Quinta Blanca and all its contents, with the sole exception of his grandmother's bed, which was brought to the house in Madrid. The years of travelling, wandering, mainly superficial relationships and drug-taking which follow, correspond to his time in the Snow Queen's palace.

The Anima

The story of *The Snow Queen* is concerned with wholeness, completeness, whether Gerda is interpreted as a woman rescuing her cold, imprisoned animus, freeing herself to create and giving her 'a capacity for reflection, deliberation, and self-knowledge' (Jung 1959: 16); or as an anima '[giving] relationship and relatedness to a man's consciousness' (Ibid. 16). This connects the story with individuation which, as Jung emphasised, 'seems to tend not toward perfection but toward completeness' (in von Franz 1993b: 59). The Snow Queen herself appears to be a prime example of an anima figure. Through her power and magnificence, she is archetypal, containing little that is personal. She is also an ambiguous figure, creating beauty through the Northern Lights, while at the same time holding captive and preventing feeling and relatedness. In the case of Leonardo the story appears to be the development of relatedness to the inner feminine, the anima, which results in the corresponding development of his relationships with women. There are five female characters in Martín Gaite's novel who reflect Leonardo's relationship with his inner self: Ángela, the *pelirroja* who visits him in Carabanchel; Clara, whom he met in Verona when he was travelling and working; Almu and Mónica, whom he encounters following his meeting with the lawyer, don Octavio; and Sila/Casilda, the love of his father's life and Leonardo's natural mother.

As in the case of the animus, Jung also identified four stages of development in the anima which, broadly speaking, move from physical to spiritual and can be both positive and negative. Von Franz describes them as moving from biological relationship, through romantic eros, to spiritualised eros and finally wisdom (1997a: 317). The doctrine of the Catholic Church concerning the Assumption of the Virgin Mary into Heaven, proclaimed by Pope Pius XII in 1950, is often identified in Jungian writings as a very significant psychological event because of the dignity and respect it affords a collective image of woman, by taking her up into a heavenly realm previously reserved to a masculine Godhead. In Christianity the figure of Mary has traditionally been regarded as a mediator between God and human beings, which places her in a positive collective anima role. The highest development of the anima is seen as wisdom and, according to von Franz, 'in the psychic development of modern man this stage is rarely reached' (1964: 185). The overall structure is helpful only if interpreted broadly and not reduced to a process to which all individual psychological development must be made to correspond.

Because the anima – like its counterpart the animus – contains collective as well as personal aspects, it cannot be integrated into consciousness but only related to. As with all unconscious contents, the anima is first encountered in projected form, either onto another human being or appearing as a figure in a dream. With all of these experiences of the unconscious the ultimate aim seems to be relatedness – Jung's 'objective cognition' – and this implies, in the conscious world, the recognition of the personhood of all human beings. In turn, this demands the presence of eros, not power, in relationships – hence the link between 'objective cognition' and 'love'. According to Jung 'the anima becomes, through integration, the Eros of consciousness' (Jung 1959: 16).

As already discussed in earlier chapters, like the animus, the anima contains both positive and negative aspects and, as with the unconscious in general, it is often the face we turn towards it which determines its response to us. The unconscious seeks to become conscious and it can only do so where human beings take an attitude of respect towards it. Where it is resisted it can break through in a way which is uncontrolled, unconscious, and which cannot be integrated into the personality.

Von Franz records that Jung 'found that a beneficial effect arises from attempting to objectivize contents of the unconscious in the awake state and relate to them consciously. This can be done through painting or sculpting – or, more rarely, through dancing – but principally through writing down inwardly observed phenomena' (1993b: 146). This was the practice Jung called Active Imagination. As a child, Leonardo drew his own versions of the characters that peopled his favourite childhood stories with the exception of the Snow Queen, despite the fascination she held for him. Nor was she depicted in his book. Consequently, he was haunted by her. Had he been able to draw her he may have felt free. He often drew Gerda and Kay but, when he rejected the ending of Andersen's tale, his drawings of Gerda changed into an ugly little girl in rags (154). The anima figure of Gerda turns ugly because she reflects Leonardo's rejection and lack of trust towards her. In respect of the women he meets and remembers in his notebooks, here too he begins with fear and coldness.

Anima Figures in *Reina*: Ángela and Clara

Ángela, the redhead who visited Leonardo in prison, is an example of an elemental anima figure who is also ambiguous. Red-headedness is not a positive characteristic for Martín Gaite. In *Nubosidad* a *pelirroja* is having an affair with Sofía's husband, Eduardo. And, on her deathbed, Martín Gaite advised her sister Ana María, who recalls the conversation in an interview:

> '¿Sabes con quién hay que tener cuidado?' '¿Con quién?' 'Con el pelirrojo de Ohio.' Y comprendí lo que quería decirme. Hay que guardarse de esos hispanistas que vienen después y agarran todo lo que encuentran, para publicar cosas que incluso el autor ha dicho que no se publiquen. (in Soriano 2007: 277)
>
> ['You know who you need to be careful of?' 'Who?' 'The redhead from Ohio.' And I understood what she meant. You need to watch out for those hispanists who will come afterwards and grab everything they find, in order to publish things that even the author has said should not be published.]

Although Leonardo related his dreams to her, he does not see Ángela as a friend or interlocutor, for when she comes to meet him on the day of his release from prison he cannot even remember her name.

The anima figure is sometimes portrayed as keeping a man from his duty, in the manner of the eponymous heroine of Bizet's opera *Carmen* who keeps Don José from returning to his regiment. Similarly Ángela, too, distracts Leonardo at an important point, preventing him from taking a step out of his directionless lifestyle just when he has resolved to leave his aimless life behind. When Ángela came up behind him, Leonardo recalls he was scribbling quotes from a number of books – as Martín Gaite often did in her own notebooks – and invoking the sea (91–2). The sea is a well-known symbol of the unconscious, and thus it appears that the real impetus in this scene comes from there, for the scene takes place shortly before he is arrested which, although at the time would have seemed very negative, nevertheless represents a new opportunity for Leonardo. His perception of the impact of this scene with Ángela on the direction of his life and his general hostility to his former companions means that this is one of two scenes which require to be exorcised through more positive anima experiences. Both scenes involve Ángela, the negative anima figure.

Ángela remains sufficiently aware of Leonardo's movements to be waiting for him on his release and she represents someone who would try to hold him in her world, suggesting – without being certain and despite living with someone else – that Leonardo may be the father of her unborn child (60). In this light, Leonardo's coolness towards her seems to represent to him the best means of safeguarding himself. Martín Gaite ties up this part of the story rather neatly by having Ángela's child stillborn some weeks later. The waiter who gives him the news also relates that Ángela is still in hospital, and provides a more balanced view of the young woman whose own life had been at risk, describing her as nice and intelligent (192–3).

Leonardo's unresponsiveness to the news and general lack of interest in the young woman along with his self-protecting coldness continue until he is safely in Galicia at the end of the novel, and has just met Casilda Iriarte. Casilda's utterance outside the railway station of similar words to those Ángela said the day she met him outside Carabanchel – 'Tengo el coche allí' [The car's over there] and then asking him why he does not get in (322) – take Leonardo back to the day of his release two months earlier (58). However, the changes he has undergone enable him to feel compassion for Ángela – 'Pobre chica, no parecía muy feliz, y él no se había enterado bien de por qué sufría' [Poor thing, she didn't seem very happy and he hadn't really understood why] (322) – without obscuring the clarity of vision which enabled him to recognise that she would only have led him back to a dangerous situation for his personal development.

This compassion for Ángela, seeing her as a person, represents a move away from projection and towards the objectivity and reason described by Macmurray as characterising personal life. It is achieved only after meeting Mónica and making contact with Casilda, and, most importantly, following weeks of detailed writing in his notebooks which helps restore a sense of his real identity. Like Sofía in *Nubosidad* – 'Desde que me he puesto a escribir, mi vida ha dado un giro copernicano' [Since I started writing, my life has done a u-turn] (1992: 71) – Leonardo also experiences a transformation in the development of an inner relatedness to himself which is reflected in the shift in his perspective on Ángela. The effect of writing which Leonardo experiences corresponds to the outcome promised by Martín Gaite to anyone who tells their story and believes it: 'Contar alivia de ese peso insoportable con que nos abruma lo meramente padecido, nos convierte en protagonistas' [Telling your story lightens that unbearable heaviness with which what we only suffer weighs us down, it changes us into protagonists] (1988a: 122). What effects the change seems to be the growing consciousness of the experience. Helen Luke, in an essay on suffering, identifies two types of experience. The first is 'totally unproductive, the neurotic state of meaningless depression' and she links this with 'images of weight bearing *down*' (1995: 56). This is a passive and very common state which she illustrates as 'simply lying down under the weight of outer circumstances or inner mood' (Ibid. 56). The second experience, which she regards as 'the essential condition of every step on the way to what C. G. Jung has called individuation', she also regards as carrying a weight but doing so 'in full consciousness' by accepting it (Ibid. 56) which is also what writing or telling your story is attempting to do.[5]

Regarding Leonardo's telling his story in his notebooks, Odartey-Wellington argues that 'aunque estas notas apunten a hechos verdaderos, vividos por él en el pasado' [although these notes may point to real events, which he lived in the past] (1997: 81), the problem lies in that 'sin reelaborar, son meros datos personales sobre las andanzas de un joven decadente y no tienen ninguna transcendencia' [without reworking, they are no more than personal details of the adventures of a decadent young man and they have no significance] (Ibid. 81). In 'El Gato con Botas' Martín Gaite argued that 'Lo realmente importante es la elaboración solitaria de esa versión ficticia y la credibilidad que él mismo consigue prestarla' [What really matters is

5 Luke emphasises that acceptance does not mean not seeking release from suffering: 'In fact the two attitudes are one, and real acceptance will lead us to seek the appropriate help' (1995: 58). As in the discussion in Chapter 1 about the impact of consciousness on projection, she considers that the impact of consciousness and acceptance of suffering has a much wider impact than the individual concerned: 'Every time a person exchanges neurotic depression for real suffering, he or she is sharing to some small degree in the carrying of the suffering of mankind, in bearing a tiny part of the darkness of the world. Such a one is released from his small personal concern into a sense of *meaning*' (Ibid. 59).

the development on his [the Cat's] own of that made-up version and the credibility which he himself manages to give it] (1988a: 148). Leonardo's version appears to reflect real events as Odartey-Wellington points out, and, in the same essay, Martín Gaite promises that 'el narrador entusiasmado, el que está convencido de aquello que cuenta, no pierde nunca las riendas de su destino' [the enthusiastic storyteller, the one who is convinced by what he's telling, never loses control of his destiny] (1988a: 123). What Leonardo draws on, as he increasingly takes control of his life as a result of telling his story in his notebooks, are the spiritual qualities of the character of Gerda: courage, love, determination, loyalty and selflessness.

The lack of meaningful relationships with women seems to be typical of Leonardo's years of wandering. A young Italian woman, Clara, who, in retrospect, can be seen as a potential interlocutor was nevertheless unable to free Leonardo from his prison of the fear of relatedness. Clara shines subsequently in Leonardo's memory as a positive anima figure during the first phase of writing his notebooks in his father's study when he wishes to imitate the relationship between his father and Sila. However, trying to create a parallel in his imagination through Clara fails to work as he realises when he tries to re-imagine their last meeting in Verona with a different ending. Nevertheless, his perspective on the emptiness of other relationships at that time and his recognition of his own fear of real intimacy reveal the effects of the writing on his self-knowledge and acceptance of himself, including less attractive aspects. The thread which the memory of Clara enables him to recover can also be developed further through encounters with other women.

Angels

Christopher Booker identifies typical helpers in stories as 'a benevolent, usually wise old man, and a beautiful young [...] woman' (2005: 77). The first of these figures corresponds to the lawyer, don Octavio Andrade, who Leonardo meets at the start of the second phase of his notebooks. The solicitor, like the wise old man in fairy tales assists in Leonardo's recovery of his memory by reminding him of his plans to go to Morocco and of his previous determination to rid himself of the Quinta Blanca (161). The information he provides about the woman who bought the Quinta Blanca – including her name – and that she has recently published a book of essays – confirms the importance of his role in Leonardo's journey.

The dangers of slipping back into a familiar, less conscious, state was something faced by both Gerda (in the old woman's cottage) and Leonardo (in Ángela's car). Again Leonardo, after leaving the lawyer's office and heading for a familiar nightclub, is threatened by regression to a previous pattern of living. However, in general, if Martín Gaite's characters are sufficiently attentive to information from within themselves as well as without, the characters are neither destroyed nor abandoned, but find the path to new ways of living. In the case of Leonardo, he is also protected by angels.[6]

There are three angels in *Reina*. The first is on Leonardo's grandmother's bed, on the headboard – an angel playing a trumpet. A bed is the place where, asleep, we are closest to the unconscious and also to death. It is appropriate that, just as sleeping in this bed at the time of Inés Guitián's funeral marked the end of an important period in Leonardo's life, the new phase, following his release from prison, should begin with his putting the same bed together in his parents' house in Madrid. Between these two phases, it figured in many of his dreams. The bed is also the means by which he first goes into his father's study when, after cutting his hand putting it together, he needs to find painkillers. Angels are often seen as messengers of God and as guardian spirits. The angel on the bedhead is a proclaiming, announcing angel, which could be a messenger of the Self, symbolising the need to wake from sleep or unconsciousness, and thus would be related to the new discoveries Leonardo makes.

The angel with the mirror atop the Puerta de Alcalá, where he shelters after leaving don Octavio, reminds Leonardo of the shattered magic mirror in *The Snow Queen* except that he imagines that this mirror reflects all the good in the world. This image gives rise to an important fantasy

6 Le Scouzec Masson lists all the references to angels in the novel, and includes Mauricio Brito as 'l'ange gardien' (2003: 88).

which parallels Andersen's fairy tale and involves getting a piece of good mirror in his eye which can fight the piece already there and get rid of it, thus freeing his soul and letting him cry. In this passage, Leonardo likens himself to Kay in a more detailed fashion, spelling out his problem clearly, along with the necessary solution. The positive image assists him simply by 'posándose sobre [las ideas negras] ingrávido y silencioso' [perching on [the gloomy ideas], heavy and silent] (176). Leonardo clearly sees this as sufficient for the light to dispel the darkness without the need for a struggle. Martín Gaite's imagery is more concerned with the reconciliation of opposites than their polarisation, as was discussed in relation to *Pastel*. Thus Leonardo's invented story is a powerful image which represents a means of overcoming the effects of the splinters of glass from the mirror in Andersen's tale.

The third angel resembles one of those on the balcony of the *Casa Grande* invented by Sorpresa – the angel reading a book, with which the former *novia* of *el Señor* had been identified. Mónica draws a similar angel for Leonardo as a gift, entitling it 'The farewell's angel' (213), which also provides the title of the English translation. The farewell follows only a very short meeting between the two, but the impact, image and memory of the young woman indicate that she quickly comes to represent a positive anima figure. The reading angel is significant because of their shared love of books.

Anima Figures in *Reina*: Almu and Mónica

The spiral staircase down into the Madrid nightclub resembles both Sorpresa's descent into the wine cellar in search of champagne in *Pastel* and Martín Gaite's own references to the *neverending* (2002a: 394). Sorpresa's descent to bring back a bottle of champagne was seen on the one hand as artificial and likely to have only a temporary effect on *el señor's* dark moods and depressions, and on the other as being more positive because of its associations, its special nature, and the symbolism of wine as spirit.

Martín Gaite's oft-recorded need to make contact with a deeper part of herself is also linked with awareness and spirit, more developed, less unconscious than in the case of Sorpresa. Leonardo also makes the descent of the spiral staircase in search of contact with the unconscious, as he goes there in search of drugs.

Martín Gaite mentions the use of drugs several times in her *Cuadernos*, as in 1974 when she writes: 'Droga = anestesia. Quien la toma es porque no se atreve a soñar con posturas extremas ni a inventar nada' [Drug = anaesthetic. Whoever takes it does so because they daren't dream about taking an extreme stance or of inventing anything] (2002a: 185). The desire expressed by Leonardo as he left the Puerta de Alcalá was for *posturas extremas* [extreme positions] but, in Martín Gaite's eyes, he would lack the courage to carry the desire forward by himself. In a commentary from 1975 on a novel by Pierre Drieu la Rochelle on the theme of drug addiction, Martín Gaite praises the way it highlights 'la soledad esencial del hombre que es incapaz de hacer nada suyo ni de dejar huella en nadie' [the essential loneliness of the man who is incapable of doing anything of his own or of leaving his mark on anyone] (2002a: 363–4). The implication of her attitude is that drug-taking is incompatible with individuation.

For his part, Jung did not support the use of drugs because of the impossibility of integrating all the contents of the unconscious released during the experience. Without such integration, contact with the unconscious is rendered meaningless. He, therefore, saw no need for the insights provided by drugs because 'there is no point in wishing to know more of the collective unconscious than one gets through dreams and intuitions. The more you know of it, the greater and heavier becomes your moral burden, because unconscious contents are transformed into your individual tasks and duties as soon as they become conscious' (Jaffé 1986: 72–3). For both Martín Gaite and Jung, therefore, drugs are a means of escaping from life, either because of a lack of courage or the absence of an ethical dimension which recognises the responsibility of integrating into the day-to-day reality of life what has been learnt during the experience of drugs. Despite Leonardo's increasing awareness and inner strength, the habit of recreational drug-taking continues. However, Jung's emphasis on integration implies a living contact with the unconscious and also some form of expressing the experiences, for example in words or music. The habit developed over the previous weeks of writing in his notebooks, keeping the connection to the inner journey, noting down ideas and associations remains strong as shown by his writing on whatever he has to hand wherever he is, including on a paper napkin in the nightclub.

The shift from depending on his ego as the source of all action and his growing consciousness mean that Leonardo responds to the advice of a familiar waiter, who warns him, in response to his confident assertion of having left the past behind, that something always remains (193). The earlier memory of Clara, his rejection of her, and his subsequent more superficial liaison, also enable him, despite the effect of drugs and alcohol, to recognise the potential emptiness which is likely to follow a similar response to Almu, a young woman who gives clear indications of being attracted to him. The detailed recollection in the notebooks of the shifts in his perceptions and his responses to the music and movements around him, the thoughts and feelings he experienced, recall von Franz's description of the only way for a man to relate to the anima: 'If a man has really learned to contact his anima [...] he will try constantly to follow his feeling, his Eros side, without considering any other elements, and in that way walk through seemingly incompatible worlds on the razor's edge' (1996: 94). Uxó argues that where there's sexual desire there's no possibility of communication: 'Almudena queda descalificada casi de inmediato como posible interlocutora al revelarnos Leonardo el deseo sexual que ella le provoca' [Almudena is almost immediately disqualified as a potential interlocutor when Leonardo reveals to us the sexual desire that she arouses in him] (1999a: 66). This is similar to Leo's comparison of his and his father's relation with Sila – 'él te besaba. Yo te entiendo mejor porque no te he besado' [He kissed you. I understand you better because I haven't kissed you] (125) – and is also true of his relationship with Ángela.

Martín Gaite peppers her stories with information that really does come from all over, confirming that paying attention is the way to be able to bind again what has become loose. The angel on the Puerta de Alcalá is an example as is the newspaper on the floor of Ángela's car. Another example is a song by Patsy Cline from the sixties that Leonardo hears in the nightclub, which is about a broken relationship. Not only does it lead

Leonardo to muse on his own behaviour towards the women he has known, but he recalls that he first heard the singer on the last day he spoke to his grandmother before she died and before getting the splinter in his eye. At crucial points in the novel, the fairy-tale reference is never far away as when, having resisted the temptation to return to his old patterns of behaviour with Almu and slipped out of the nightclub without saying goodbye, Leonardo vividly recalls Gerda. Because of the progress he has made in his own personal development, he recognises for the first time the meaning in her search for Kay, which he had previously rejected and, along with this, the possibility of being rescued by Gerda. This represents a complete transformation of his attitude towards the development and outcome of Andersen's tale. Changing the endings of stories is a familiar theme in Martín Gaite's work. In *Caperucita* Sara initially changed the endings – saving the wolf in *LRRH*, leaving Robinson Crusoe on his island, and complaining because Alice in Wonderland regarded all her experience as a dream. Both Leonardo and Sara initially seek to freeze the stories in the unconscious, so that there is no wholeness, no integration of consciousness and unconsciousness. However, Sara changed her attitude to these endings. In *Pastel* Sorpresa refuses to accept the ending her mother and the women in the village want for her (marriage and children) and thus changes her own ending, which is also a refusal of the collective projection onto her.

Having first resisted the *canto de sirena* of Ángela, and now of Almu, Leonardo can thus appreciate the parallel experience in the fairy tale. However, his conclusion that Gerda's quest represents an act of rebellion against fate does not accord with the interpretation that it represents an aspect of the individuation process, described as the effort to 'make what fate intends to do with us entirely our own intention' (Jaffé 1986: 79). This is another way of describing the development of a capacity for unreflecting obedience to the Self, or becoming like little children, or, in old-fashioned language, obeying the will of God, something which Jung saw as essential. Gerda has rebelled against inertia, against the temptation to regress, against getting stuck. Leonardo seems to be more concerned with not being passive in the face of events. Individuation involves an active relationship between ego and Self, as the writer Bergengruen asserts: 'Basically, individuation consists of constantly renewed, constantly needed attempts to amalgamate the inner images with outer experience' (in Jaffé 1986: 79).

In *Pastel* Sorpresa repeatedly emphasises the dangers of looking back, and recalls the fate of Lot's wife in the Old Testament, who was turned into a pillar of salt when she looked back at Sodom, despite being warned not to. However, when Leonardo discovers that, on this cold winter's night, he has left his coat in the nightclub next to Almu, his concern is less clear cut than Sorpresa's, allowing for the possibility that going back or looking back might be the right thing to do. What matters, like the heroes of the stories Sorpresa was keen to emulate, is that he decides for himself. However, because Leonardo has already rejected on an inner level the possibility of returning to an old pattern of behaviour, his physical return to collect his coat brings no apparent temptations, with the nightclub even appearing more harmless than when he had entered earlier (202). On the other hand, Almu's decision, on seeing him, to leave at the same time, and his acceptance of her offer of a lift on her scooter, suggest that he may have to face further temptations. However, Almu resembles the Robber Maiden in Andersen's tale, who appears dangerous but provides Gerda with food and the means to travel to Lapland, for she is the means by which Leonardo has one of the most important encounters in the novel.[7]

Almu's chatter in the nightclub and praise of her friend included a claim that 'Mónica atiende' [Mónica pays attention] (186), which for Martín Gaite is the most important attitude to take. In contrast, Almu is depicted as the kind of person criticised by Martín Gaite as a bad mirror, labelling people she meets too quickly and superficially. For Soliño, Mónica is like one of those 'magical helpers' who assist lost fairy-tale characters (2002: 150). Don Andrade corresponded to Booker's wise old man. Mónica represents Booker's second helper, the beautiful young woman. Although we do not learn much about Mónica's physical appearance, there is much beauty in the brief encounter between her and Leonardo.

7 The contrasts between the nightclub and Almu's flat are highlighted by Uxó (1999a), while Dravet-Barbusse chooses the Puerta de Alcalá as the counterpart for the nightclub (2003).

Leonardo's meeting with Mónica reflects and confirms the positive development of Leonardo's relationship with the inner feminine. Agitated, distraught over the amount of sorting and packing still do to before she leaves to join her boyfriend in Australia, Leonardo brings solace to the young woman and their encounter represents the kind of meeting between two people described by Castillejo as seeming to include another dimension: 'For there to be a meeting, it seems as though a third, a something else, is always present. You may call it Love, or the Holy Spirit. Jungians would say that it is the presence of the Self' (1990: 12). Again there is the link between these three themes discussed in Chapter 1. Leonardo's conclusion, as he looks around the untidy bedroom where Mónica lies sleeping peacefully as a result of his support, is that he felt 'totalmente seguro [...] de estar después de mucho tiempo en el sitio que me correspondía y haber dicho lo que tenía que decir' [utterly sure [...] after a long time of being in the right place and of having said what I had to say] (218–19). This confirms not only the magic of Castillejo's 'meeting' but also how much Leonardo has evolved over the preceding weeks. Mónica affords Leonardo the opportunity to care for her without being afraid, as he recognises after she has fallen asleep: 'A mí mismo me extrañaba haber sido capaz de inyectar consuelo y dulzura a un ser desesperanzado, y más aún que me hubiera salido de forma tan natural' [I surprised myself at being capable of injecting comfort and gentleness into a human being in despair, and even more so that it should have emerged in such a natural way] (219) One of Monica's books is *The Sacred and the Profane* by Mircea Eliade, which Leonardo had previously been given in Italian by Clara, which suggests that Mónica replaces and develops the role played by Clara. Leonardo's surprise at his behaviour with Mónica indicates how unaware he was of the role he played for his cellmate in Carabanchel, Julián Expósito, who also found him a source of comfort. From not being aware, not really being interested in others, Leonardo is able to recognise his reactions and assess their value as in his relation to Almu, and to go out naturally, to respond without effort to Mónica. The positive development of Leonardo's relationship with the inner feminine is thus strengthened through his meeting with Mónica. Nevertheless, as Mónica is preparing for her departure for Australia later in the day she would present no lasting constraint to Leonardo's freedom, no challenge to his fear of *amores románticos* [romantic love affairs].

Mónica plays two other crucial roles in Leonardo's story. First, his efforts to reassure her result in his recalling lines from Cavafy's poem 'Ítaca' which, from that moment, will act as a support and guide, particularly the last line about not forcing the pace of the journey (218). Secondly, among the books being left behind from which she urges him to take what he wants, he finds the book of essays written by Casilda Iriarte which don Octavio had mentioned. The cover of the book is one of his favourite paintings by Caspar David Friedrich (219) – which creates another meaningful connection between himself and the enigmatic Casilda. When Leonardo first glimpses the book, he sees it surrounded by tongues of fire (219). The tongues of fire are reminiscent of Pentecost, suggesting the creative power and meaning it holds for Leonardo and the important role the book will play for 'meaning makes a great many things endurable – perhaps everything' (Jung 1983: 373). The description of this discovery as 'el diamante para abrochar [el collar de la noche]' [the diamond clasp to fasten [the necklace of the night]] (219) is a further example of jewels referring to experiences which are charged with meaning for the young man. In this case it closes a whole night of important and contrasting experiences for his earlier description of the evening before meeting Mónica was that it was like 'la cáscara amarilla [...] del limón exprimido' [the yellow peel [...] of a squeezed lemon] (195). Earlier I discussed the symbolism of a precious stone. Von Franz comments further on the symbolism of the crystal as 'the union of the most extreme opposites' (1997a: 336)

Mónica also takes Leonardo forward in his journey by, again unwittingly, facilitating his encounter with the final, complex anima figure of Casilda when, some days later, he finds himself again outside the same block of flats. His delight at recovering a connection with Mónica which will enable him to write to her through Almu, strengthens his spirit and, with it, his resolve to telephone Casilda Iriarte. Mónica also assists in his re-creating, much more positively, the scene with Ángela which detained Leonardo in the house where he was arrested. Imagining Mónica coming up behind him, as she had done in Almu's flat only to put her hands on his shoulders and watch him taking notes and speak to him, he is able to overlay the emptiness of the earlier, actual experience with Ángela. The timing of the fantasy puts Mónica in the role of 'the Gerda who will initiate the journey towards his rescue' (Soliño 2002: 150).

Vertigo

The title of Casilda's book of essays, *Vértigo*, also describes Leonardo's experience in the days following his meeting with Mónica, when he has read the book and connected it to the papers in his father's safe: 'El mar se me estaba metiendo en casa, y de nada iba a servirle poner diques de cartón piedra' [the sea was flowing into the house and it was going to be no good putting up papier mâché barriers] (234). This is a clear reference to invasion by the unconscious, which is what causes the vertigo: 'The sea is a symbol of the collective unconscious, because unfathomed depths lie concealed beneath its reflecting surface' (Jung 1953: 48). As discussed in connection with Sara's discovery of the true identity of Miss Lunatic in *Caperucita*, Nor Hall describes the effect on the soul of a crucial realisation, namely that it is left exposed through the freeing of energy from the unconscious. Leonardo's connection is between what he has read from the papers in his father's safe – letters from Sila and the first draft of a novel with a heroine called Silveria – and the book of essays by Casilda Iriarte. The realisation that all three are the same person and the inrush of that glimpse of new awareness results in dizziness as consciousness tries to grasp its meaning.

Leonardo is sufficiently aware to realise the force of what is happening and his powerlessness to stop it. It seems like an experience of madness, as he describes it 'Ante síntomas graves de amenaza, era yo el primero en escuchar la señal de alarma y acudir a vacunarme contra la locura' [In the face of serious threatening signs, I was the first to heed the alarm signal and to go to forearm myself against the madness] (235). The only successful way to relate to it is through the word: 'Conseguí que no me fuera mal. En mis cuadernos queda constancia de ello' [I managed to get myself through it. It's on record in my notebooks] (235). This is not a defence, there is none in this case, but rather an attitude of respect, a listening, a partnership, as he records in detail his experience in words and drawings of nightmarish scenes reflecting his psychological experience of the sea invading everything. And this acceptance, recognition and respect, this sense that, overwhelming as it is, there is meaning in the experience, is what saves Leonardo and leads to the significant increase in awareness and development displayed at the end of the novel.[8] Drawing and expressing the invasive images is a means of relating to them and avoiding being overwhelmed by them, as is writing. He is also supported by the many notes which Mónica has written in the margins as it gives him a real sense of her presence.

The successful outcome of these experiences is reflected in the purchase of new clothes and immediately discarding the old ones in a rubbish bin in the street (242). Thus, he rejects the collective image of himself retained by those who knew him previously. This is in sharp contrast with the writer's novella, *Balneario*, in which the protagonist, Matilde, has a long and detailed dream depicting a process of individuation. However, the only change is very minor, very superficial, when she puts on a dress she has not worn before (246). This is an example of a change of clothes which does not reflect an inner change, but is intended only to impress others.

Casilda Iriarte

While Leonardo longs to meet the woman who has meant so much to his father, who seems so spirited, and who lives in the house he would like to buy back, unlike Casilda, he is unaware of their real relationship. So the fear they both feel at the prospect of meeting has a different source (307). For Leonardo, fear gives rise to a sense of insecurity to which his response is a desire for power. Fantasising about gaining power over Casilda by using his

8 This idea of meaning in apparent madness reflects Martín Gaite's criticisms of what she perceives as psychiatrists' determination to cure, as discussed in Chapter 1.

perceived attractiveness to women, the pre-eminence of relating to himself and others particularly in recent days, and the habit of openness and honesty he has developed through his writing mean that the self-deception is short-lived and, again, he recognises and admits his fear. The force of the image of Mónica in all this is striking – the way in which the prospect of being able to make contact with her spurs him to also make contact with Casilda and even to hope that the three of them could be together, none of which contain an impulse to power. Thus, Mónica reflects a positive image of the inner feminine, supporting him as he moves to make other relationships.

In contrast to Mónica and the impulse towards relatedness which she inspires, the language Leonardo uses to describe Casilda is typical of the kind of language which conveys the anima as a more impersonal being – he calls her 'ella' [she] like the *novelas rosas* of his childhood. The vagueness of the term and the fear he admits indicates the anima and projection but it is a distancing, collective view, suggesting awe and fear. Later, Leonardo's more biographical description of her, based on the information he gleans from the book and papers, imply a person who is, as the lawyer put it, *especial*, contributing to his reaction.

Casilda is also the woman who is comforted by the thought of life after death and who, according to Mauricio Brito, insists that 'a lo más oscuro amanece Dios, con tal de que lo dejemos amanecer' [God will dawn in the deepest darkness, provided we let him] (93). Rosa Penna identifies differences between Martín Gaite's and Andersen's stories, such as 'la importancia que en aquél [cuento de Andersen] tiene la oración como auxilio en momentos de peligro, y como clave final de todo el cuento' [the importance that prayer has in [Andersen's story] both as help in times of danger and as the final key to the whole fairy tale] (1995: 258).[9] However, Casilda's expression runs like a theme through the book. It reflects what takes place at the end of the novel and is recalled by Leonardo on two earlier occasions. First, during the difficult period following his reading of Casilda's book and discovering more of her identity, although at this stage

9 Andersen's ending, in which he claims that Gerda and Kay have become like little children, also has a connection with Martín Gaite's novel.

he is still unaware of her connection with Mauricio Brito. At that time, to Leonardo the phrase is a 'buena entradilla para un cuento de hadas' [good opening for a fairy tale] (222), which indicates the level – of mystery – at which he experiences the words. The second occasion is when he telephones the Quinta Blanca, Mauricio answers and it is the first association Leonardo makes. The character Casilda has never known her mother, has lost a husband, lived most of her life without the man she loved, and given up her child. She also left a beloved grandfather. Discussing the meaning to be found in suffering in a lecture to the Guild of Pastoral Psychology,[10] Robert Mercurio, a lecturer in psychotherapy, argues that this 'rests in the symbolic experience and in our ability to question the suffering, to seek the hidden and apparently unknown and unknowable face of God that is hidden in it all' (2011: 17). This recalls not only Casilda's assertion but also Martín Gaite's response to the tailor's murder of his children in Madrid in the 1960s which was discussed in Chapters 1 and 4.

Mauricio Brito

One character to whom critics respond positively is Mauricio Brito, the Brazilian who works for Casilda and who spent some time working for Leonardo's father in Madrid. I have already mentioned the depiction of Mauricio Brito as an 'ange gardien' (Le Scouzec Masson 2003: 88). Paoli also regards him highly, referring to him as the most mysterious and fascinating character (2002: 10). Mauricio has worked for Casilda for twenty years and a close relationship has developed between them, yet it is not equal, for Mauricio is paid and, in this case, paid to listen. What transforms the relationship is Mauricio's love for his *señora*, revealed in both his concern for her physical, emotional and psychological well-being, his

10 The Guild was founded in London in 1937 with Jung as its patron. In 1939 he gave a talk on 'The Symbolic Life', in which he discussed religion and the possible development of Christianity, and which is included in Volume 18 of his Collected Works, *The Symbolic Life* (1977).

acceptance of her mood swings, and his delight in seeing her relaxed and hearing her speak. In addition, his role in relation to Casilda is not passive, even as listener: 'El que escucha no pertenece al reino de las sombras ni de los muertos' [The one who listens does not belong to the kingdom of the shades nor of the dead] (282). In Casilda's relationship with Mauricio, despite her reference to *amigo*, there is also dependence, as she recognises (330). Anne Paoli argues that, far from being a servant, 'il est surtout le confidant, l'allié de Casilda' [he is above all the confidant, the ally of Casilda] (2002: 13). He also shares with Miss Lunatic a predilection for listening and responding. This includes listening and responding to himself as when Leonardo arrives at the house in Madrid and Mauricio explains that he has stayed there, despite having packed and locked up and being ready to get the train, because he was expecting Leonardo (88).

Leonardo's astonishment that Trud could have put up with anyone so mysterious for three years when he was on loan, as it were, from Casilda to the home of Leonardo's father indicates the special nature of Mauricio, who is the most compassionate character in the novel. He is the only one to express sympathy for Trud: 'Es que ella estaba enferma. Hay que tenerlo en cuenta. Muy enferma' [It's because she was ill. You need to bear that in mind. Very ill] (90). One of the most vivid images of Mauricio early in the novel is of his standing in the doorway of the house in Madrid 'en el umbral que separa lo de dentro de lo de fuera' [on the threshold that separates inner and outer things] (81). From being a threshold guardian in a literal sense, his role extends to the symbolic level, which makes him, along with Mónica and Andersen's heroine, Gerda, one of the most helpful characters in Leonardo's journey, as the young man acknowledges, for his determination to write stems from his conversation with Mauricio in Madrid (222).

Gerda

Following his recognition that Gerda did make efforts to rescue Kay and that she was right to do so, Leonardo refers to Gerda and her journey at a number of other key points towards the end of the journey depicted in the novel. Initially, his interpretation is literal, as a journey in the world rather than a symbolic experience and results from the fear and insecurity he feels in the face of the daunting image of Casilda. However, in his comparisons between himself and Gerda he tends to regard himself negatively, mocking himself for thinking he has undergone a miraculous change 'simplemente por tomar unas píldoras, comprarte ropa nueva y disfrazarte de chico sano y normal' [simply by taking a few pills, buying some new clothes and disguising yourself as a healthy, normal guy] (250). Gerda, on the other hand, worked hard, and had faith. Martín Gaite's heroes generally work to achieve their development but often that work is interior. On the other hand, Leonardo underestimates the value of the journey he has made.

Secondly, after being initially put off by the winter weather in the north of Spain, the recollection of Gerda's difficult journey in lands covered in snow and ice spurs him to accept Casilda's invitation to spend Christmas at the Quinta Blanca. The memory of Andersen's heroine enables him to see his excuse for what it really is, namely fear (310). However, when Leonardo arrives in Galicia at the end of the novel, he is finally able to loosen his grip on a story which played such an important role in his childhood and intensely so in the short period covered by the novel, because he is reaching a new stage in his life and his personal development. It is typical for Martín Gaite's protagonists to have a dream at this stage in their journey. In *Nubosidad* Sofía has a reconciling dream about her mother while sleeping on her children's sofa after leaving home and before going to meet Mariana. Martín Gaite's *Caperucita*, Sara, sleeps in the limousine and dreams of Miss Lunatic before deciding to go to the Statue of Liberty. Altalé's dream, the night before her fifteenth birthday, affords the final guidance before she leaves the three-walled castle. Her mother's big dream comes earlier in her journey, but it is also the start of a new phase in her life, which eventually leads to her leaving the castle. Leonardo's dream is more akin to a nightmare but it, too, precedes a new stage.

The Ego or the Self

The dream Leonardo has on the sleeper to Galicia represents a significant challenge. Dreaming that he is on board a steamroller which is out of control, destroying everything in its path and heading for the Quinta Blanca, he notices that it is getting colder (309). In some ways this dream recalls the young Kay on his sledge heading for the market square where he meets the Snow Queen and cannot get away from her. Thus it represents a dangerous moment for Leonardo, confirmed by the reference to the cold and to his apparent powerlessness to stop the destructiveness of the steamroller. Leonardo likened that journey of Kay (and, in Martín Gaite's imagination, Gerda[11]) to the short journey from the church to the cemetery following his grandmother's funeral and recalls that sleet began to fall then and he cried for the last time. After the funeral, Leonardo remembers sitting in the rain in the garden of the Quinta Blanca next to a statue of Minerva. As the goddess of wisdom, Minerva would appear to represent a positive step but, as the goddess who sprang from the head of Zeus, she could also be seen to confirm Leonardo on the path of Kay and things of the head rather than the heart. This second experience of the journey suggests that it might present a new opportunity to escape the Snow Queen.

The Spanish artist Óscar Domínguez (1906–57) created two paintings in 1937 involving a steamroller and a rose, 'La machine infernale' and 'La apisonadora y la rosa'. In both paintings a huge steamroller breaks up when it comes into contact with a tiny rose. Domínguez was championing creativity in the face of destructive machinery. In Leonardo's dream the steamroller can be interpreted as representing the ego, while the rose, as discussed earlier in this chapter, was for Jung 'a wholeness symbol of the Self' (Matthews 1992: 83).

The steamroller representing an ego driving its way forward without regard for things and people and experiences in its path, is in keeping with

11 As Calvi points out, the episode in which both Kay and Gerda go down to the square was invented by Martín Gaite and does not form part of Andersen's tale (1996: 514).

Martín Gaite's assessment of the impact of the ego in her notebooks: 'El "yo" deja su marca en el mundo destruyendo' [The 'ego' leaves its mark on the world by wrecking it] (2002a: 175). The nightmare, in which the apparently unstoppable steamroller is moving towards the Quinta Blanca, where a woman stands in the garden waving her arms, suggests that Leonardo is set on a course which will ultimately destroy what he loves most. The fact that he wakes up just before reaching the gate to the Quinta Blanca suggests that it will be possible for him to choose an alternative course.

The inner struggle which ensues, in which he recalls both Mónica and Cavafy, is between, on the one hand, the poet's advice not to rush the journey and, on the other, looking back at his meeting with Mónica with 'la nostalgia por lo no alcanzado' [nostalgia for what was not achieved]. It is, therefore, a struggle between reality and unreality. His longing for Mónica is based only on fantasy, on images of scenes which did not occur and may never happen, despite the success of their first meeting. In contrast to this, Cavafy's advice not to force the pace of the journey would mean letting go of an ego-driven approach to life in favour of a readiness to respond to both life and to the Self. This was the approach discussed in Chapter 1 in connection with the tree and the man at the racecourse in Martín Gaite's favourite funny story. The decision is not an easy one for Leonardo for he refers to having complicated arguments with himself. His depiction of what opting for the ego would really mean – 'Forzar la travesía era [...] sumirse en la parálisis que espanta el milagro' [Forcing the pace meant [...] being seized by the paralysis which scares away the miraculous] (311–12) – leads him to choose reality over unreality, the Self over the ego. Thus the culmination of this stage of Leonardo's inner journey comes when he decides to stop planning and rehearsing and insisting on controlling and simply accept the possibility that each moment might bring and respond to it more fully:

> Tenía que olvidar el texto de todas las conversaciones que había ensayado y rectificado a solas, de todas las preguntas imaginarias, pensar simplemente que iba de viaje en un tren cómodo y no a bordo de ningún apisonadora infernal, que había escapado de

> espacios donde el aire empezaba a oler a muerto, que tenía treinta años y que había amanecido un día sin nubes. (312)[12]
>
> [I had to forget the text of all the conversations that I had rehearsed and corrected on my own, all the imaginary questions, think only that I was travelling in a comfortable train and not on some infernal steamroller, that I had escaped from places where the air had begun to smell of death, that I was thirty and the day had dawned without a cloud.]

This is further evidence that it all began in Carabanchel where he tried to advise Julián Expósito to do the same. Leonardo then had to go through a long journey of meetings and discoveries, of writing and reflection, before it could become a more lasting reality.

A New Relatedness

As discussed at the start of the chapter, critics have noted that the reconciliation and freeing of emotions takes place on Christmas Eve,[13] and have even drawn parallels with 'the birth of the son' (Bravo 1998; Lindström 2009). Christmas is about the birth of Love and Leonardo's words before he cries recall that it is a long time since someone loved him. The freedom to cry confirms the absence of power, the presence of eros, love, and the acceptance of the present moment. This is in sharp contrast to Trud, the woman Leonardo thought was his mother, who, according to Rosa Figueroa, loved no one (18).

12 In Chapter 3 Sorpresa took hold of her situation by asserting a number of basic facts about herself, which also recalled Jung's own attempts to cope with the inner forces which assailed him at a difficult period in his life (1983: 215).

13 Andersen's story *The Snow Queen* was first published on 21 December (Wullschläger 2000: 243). Some see this day – the shortest and, therefore, darkest of the year – as the start of the coming of the light, which Christmas symbolises.

Christmas is also the birth of the Light and the transition from darkness to light is encapsulated in Leonardo's request to Casilda as they journey from the station to the Quinta Blanca:

> A mí, te lo confieso, me suele importar poco que me entiendan o no [...] prescindo mucho de los demás. Por eso también lo que me está pasando hoy es francamente raro; me refiero a que pensar yo para mis adentros no me baste. En una palabra, Casilda [...], que quiero saber lo que piensas tú, necesito saberlo. (325)

> [I have to admit I don't usually care whether anyone understands me [...] I don't have much time for other people. That's also why what is happening to me today is really strange; what I mean is that it's not enough for me to think things to myself. In a word, Casilda [...], I want to know what you're thinking, I need to know.]

From compassion for Ángela and feeling for Clara and Mónica, Leonardo has moved further to wanting to listen and to relate to another human being. By relating and listening first to himself, he finds he spontaneously wants to listen to Casilda, not as a result of a sense of duty or obligation. This seems to represent a shift from the lower level of eros with its 'relations based merely on projection [and] characterized by fascination and magical dependence' (von Franz 1980: 177) which he initially felt towards Casilda, to real interest in the other. This new experience could only emerge following a turning towards and loving himself. The aim of the individuation process is wholeness or, as Jung put it, completion (in contrast to perfection), which also seems to be the meaning behind *The Snow Queen*. With development in the individuation process comes insight into, and withdrawal of, projections onto other individuals and groups, and a corresponding increase in real relatedness. Leonardo's development is also marked by a shift from fear or a desire to be in a position of power to one in which eros prevails.

Conclusion

At several points in the story, the presence of the unconscious has been represented by the sea so beloved of both Leo and Casilda. It is fitting, therefore, that the piece of glass should be washed from Leonardo's eye when he and Casilda have stopped on the way to the Quinta Blanca, just by the lighthouse where Casilda grew up and the rocks over which both of them scrambled in their respective childhoods and which Leonardo recognised in the inspirational photo of the young Sila 'flying' over the rocks. There is, however, a difference between the two stories in that Gerda weeps over Kay, whereas Leonardo is freed to weep in the presence of Casilda. As I mentioned at the start of the chapter, Salustiano Marín criticised this final paragraph as being entirely superfluous and representing 'una conclusión que acaba tiñendo de irrealidad el entero conjunto de la novela' [a conclusion which ends up tingeing the whole of the novel with unreality] (1994: 33). In contrast, O'Leary and Ribeiro de Menezes see 'an echo of *Sleeping Beauty*' in this final scene (2008: 157) as the splinter of glass which falls from Leonardo's tears pricks Casilda's hand. I discussed the fairy tale of *Sleeping Beauty* in relation to both Altalé in *Castillo* and Sorpresa in *Pastel*. Both protagonists, far from falling asleep, developed a higher level of consciousness, just like Leonardo. In addition, the original tale of *Sleeping Beauty* was also described as an awakening, a resurrection to wholeness, to the restoration of the whole feminine which had previously been neglected in the palace and the kingdom. It is this kind of openness and refusal to impose the individual will and prejudge which demonstrate the possibility of achieving that unreflecting capacity for obeying the Self discussed in Chapter 2. This also brings the end of this stage of Leonardo's story into line with Kay and Gerda as this responsiveness to the Self was earlier interpreted as the meaning of the ending to Andersen's fairy tale.

Concluding Thoughts

This work has brought together Carmen Martín Gaite's fairy tales and the Jungian process of individuation with the aim of showing how the Spanish writer's stories depict aspects of the process. Despite Martín Gaite's professed lack of sympathy for psychiatrists, it can be seen that Jung represents a challenge to her perspective on his profession and that the two have much in common: the focus on the individual person, the religious outlook, and the importance of awareness and wholeness. Jung and other Jungians have seen in the process of individuation a correspondence to a new phase of Christianity – the Age of the Holy Spirit – and connections between the stories explored here and the symbolism of the Holy Spirit have been identified in the analysis. The aim of individuation was identified by Jung as objective cognition and this has been interpreted as love. The feminine principle of eros, relatedness, also linked with the Holy Spirit and individuation, has been identified as a key aspect of the development of all these stories.

As in the traditional fairy tales, aspects of the Jungian process of individuation are depicted in Martín Gaite's four fairy-tale works. The animus appears in its negative form in *Castillo* and in *Caperucita* Sara's mother Vivian is seen as being in the grip of a negative animus. The creative animus is depicted in *Pastel* and *Caperucita* through the characters of *el señor de la Casa Grande* and Aurelio Roncali respectively. In *Reina* it is the anima which predominates, in both its negative and positive aspects. Personifications of the Self can be seen in the wise man Cambof Petapel in *Castillo* and in Miss Lunatic in *Caperucita*. There is a glimpse of the Self at the end of Sorpresa's story in *Pastel*, while at the end of *Reina*, Leonardo chooses reliance on the Self over the ego. Fairy tales are generally associated with girls, so the decision to have a male hero in *Reina* who not only likes fairy tales but, at the age of thirty, finds himself compelled to re-engage with a favourite fairy tale, *The Snow Queen*, in order to reconnect with himself, to rediscover his identity and values, has exposed *Reina* and its protagonist to criticism. However, Leonardo Villalba's experience illustrates the loneliness of the individuation process and the way in which responding to it requires a turning away from collective patterns of behaviour. The outcome of *Reina* also suggests the benefits of taking the path of individuation when Leonardo, having spent weeks recovering and discovering himself, is able to stop planning and express spontaneous interest in another human being.

The theme of listening runs through all of the works – from Serena and Altalé listening to their dreams; through Sorpresa listening to other people's stories, to her own inner world and her intuition; to Leonardo and his shift from listening to himself and his own stories to wanting to listen to others. The embedded stories, too, illustrate the importance of listening – Altalé to Cambof in *Castillo*, Mauricio Brito to Casilda in *Reina*. However, it is in *Caperucita* that the importance of listening is presented most clearly. Miss Lunatic is a wonderful creation by Martín Gaite with a glorious message – that everyone has a story to tell and each person is a whole world – which recognises the individual nature of each person and, at the same time, what they all have in common. Socrates' definition in *The Meno* of shape as 'the only thing which always accompanies colour' (1956: 121), encapsulates this philosophy, with 'shape' and 'colour' being replaced by 'person' and 'story' respectively. Miss Lunatic and Sara's declaration that there is nothing they like doing more than listening to stories (more even than telling them), puts the focus on the other, on all others, which is the basis of community and reminds us of Marie-Louise von Franz's definition of eros: 'It means genuine interest in the other person and in establishing relationship, being there for the other person' (von Franz 1993a: 211). Real relatedness can only take place between persons as Jung and John Macmurray have argued. And personhood is discovered and developed through individuation, by attention to the information that comes from all over, including from dreams, and by relating to and accepting both oneself and other persons through listening, as Martín Gaite has shown.

Bibliography

Acinas, Blanca. 2004. 'Littérature et psychanalyse: une cure réussie', in *La littérature pour enfants*, ed. Michel Moner and Christine Pérès (Paris: L'Harmattan), 275–8.

Alemany Bay, Carmen. 1990. *La novelística de Carmen Martín Gaite: Aproximación crítica* (Salamanca: Ediciones de la Diputación de Salamanca).

Allenby, Amy. 1956. *Jung's Contribution to the Religious Problem of Our Time (Guild Lecture No. 91)* (London: The Guild of Pastoral Psychology).

Álvarez Vara, Ignacio. 2005. 'CMG con NYC de fondo', in *Visión de Nueva York*, by Carmen Martín Gaite (Madrid: Siruela, Círculo de Lectores), 125–30.

Andersen, Hans Christian. 1995. *Hans Anderson's Fairy Tales* (London: The Folio Society).

Armstrong, Karen. 2005. *A Short History of Myth* (Edinburgh: Canongate).

Asper, Kathrin. 1994. *Being-in-Oneself – Being-in-the-World (Guild Lecture No. 246)* (London: The Guild of Pastoral Psychology).

Bair, Deirdre. 2004. *Jung: A Biography* (London: Little, Brown).

Baring, Anne, and Jules Cashford. 1993. *The Myth of the Goddess: Evolution of an Image* (London: Penguin, Arkana).

Bartolomé, Esther. 1982. 'El castillo de las tres murallas', *Quimera* 20: 55–6.

Bayley, Harold. 2006. *The Lost Language of Symbolism* (Mineola, NY: Dover). One-volume republication of Volumes I and II of the original 1912 edn published by Williams & Norgate, London as *The Lost Language of Symbolism: An Inquiry into the Origins of Certain Letters, Words, Names, Fairy-Tales, Folklore, and Mythologies*.

Bayó Belenguer, Susana. 2002. 'Unpopular Culture: The Fairy Story and Carmen Martín Gaite's *Caperucita en Manhattan*', in *Spanish Popular Texts* by Anne White and Shelley Godsland (New York: Peter Lang), 191–207.

Beckett, Sandra L. 2002. *Recycling Red Riding Hood* (New York: Routledge).

——2008. *Red Riding Hood for All Ages: A Fairy-Tale Icon in Cross-Cultural Contexts* (Detroit, MI: Wayne State University Press).

——2009. *Crossover Fiction: Global and Historical Perspectives* (New York & London: Routledge).

Bessière, Bernard. 2004. 'Brèves réflexions sur quelques référents iconographiques de *La Reina de las Nieves*', in *La littérature pour enfants*, ed. Moner and Pérès, 271–3.

Bettelheim, Bruno. 1978. *The Uses of Enchantment: the Meaning and Importance of Fairy Tales* (London: Penguin).

Blanco López de Lerma, María-José. 2009. 'The feminism of an antifeminist in Carmen Martín Gaite's *Cuadernos de todo*', *Journal of Romance Studies* 9/1: 47–57.

——2013. *Life-Writing in Carmen Martín Gaite's 'Cuadernos de Todo' and her Novels of the 1990s* (Woodbridge: Tamesis), 244.

Blejer Eder, Daniella Bettina. 2007. 'De la madriguera a la libertad: Intertextualidad como subversión en *Caperucita en Manhattan*', *Anuario de investigación en literatura infantil y juvenil* 5: 9–23.

Bloom, Harold (ed.). 2005. *Hans Christian Andersen* (Philadelphia, PA: Chelsea House).

Boa, Fraser. 1994. *The Way of the Dream – Conversations on Jungian Dream Interpretation with Marie-Louise von Franz* (Boston & London: Shambhala).

Bonaventure, Leon. 1976. *The Contribution of Analytical Psychology to a Christian Psychology (Guild Lecture No. 183)* (London: The Guild of Pastoral Psychology).

Booker, Christopher. 2005. *The Seven Basic Plots: Why we tell stories* (London: Continuum).

Borau, José Luis. 1997. 'Presencia del cine en la obra de Martín Gaite', in *Al encuentro de Carmen Martín Gaite*, ed. Emma Martinell (Barcelona: Gráficas Alsina), 48–51.

——2007. 'Al día siguiente', *Turia: Revista Cultural* 83: 249–60.

Bravo, María Elena. 1998. 'Literature as Mother and Lover. Some Reflections on Carmen Martín Gaite's *La reina de las nieves*', in *Estudios en honor de Janet Pérez: El sujeto femenino en escritoras hispánicas*, ed. Susana Cavallo, Luis A. Jiménez and Oralia Preble-Niemi (Potomac: Scripta Humanistica), 215–30.

Brown, Joan Lipman. 1987. *Secrets from the Back Room: The Fiction of Carmen Martín Gaite* (Mississippi: University of Mississippi Press – Romance Monographs).

——1988. 'The Challenge of Martín Gaite's Woman Hero', in *Feminine Concerns in Contemporary Spanish Fiction by Women*, ed. Roberto C. Manteiga, Carolyn Galerstein and Kathleen McNerney, 86–98.

——1993. 'Carmen Martín Gaite', in *Spanish Women Writers: a Bio-Bibliographical source book*, ed. L. G. Levine et al. (Westport, CT: Greenwood Press), 286–95.

——(ed.). 2013. *Approaches to Teaching the Works of Carmen Martín Gaite* (New York: The Modern Language Association of America).

——(ed.). 2015. 'Carmen Martín Gaite in the Twenty-First Century: What Defines Her Legacy?', *Hispania* 98/4: 662–78.

——2017. 'Rescuing Red Riding Hood: Carmen Martín Gaite's *Caperucita en Manhattan*', *Hispania* 100, 2: 202–12.

Bryant, Christopher. 1979. 'Escape from the Labyrinth', in *The Search for Meaning, Guild Spring Conference 1979 (Guild Lecture No. 196)* (London: The Guild of Pastoral Psychology), 1–22.

Calvi, Maria Vittoria. 1990. *Dialogo e conversazione nella narrativa di Carmen Martín Gaite* (Milano: Arcipelago).

—— 1992–3. '*Caperucita en Manhattan* o la magia della parola', *Quaderni del Dipartimento di Lingue e Letterature Neolatine* 7: 65–78.

—— 1996. 'La Regina della Neve di Carmen Martín Gaite', in *Tradizione, innovazione, modelli. Scrittura femminile del mondo iberico e americano*, ed. E. Perassi (Roma: Bulzoni), 501–17.

—— 2001. 'Reanudar el hilo', *Espéculo: Revista de Estudios Literarios* <http://pendientedemigracion.ucm.es/info/especulo/cmgaite/hilo.html> accessed 22 July 2017.

—— 2002. 'La scrittura dell'io in Carmen Martín Gaite', *Culture* XX: 1–9 <http://www.club.it/culture/culture2002/maria.vittoria.calvi/corpo.tx.calvi.html> [accessed 22 July 2017].

—— 2007. 'Introducción', in *El libro de la fiebre*, by Carmen Martín Gaite (Madrid: Cátedra).

—— 2012. 'Un cuento autobiográfico de Carmen Martín Gaite: "El otoño de Poughkeepsie"', in *En breve: cuentos de escritoras españolas (1975–2010), estudios y antología*, ed. Ángeles Encinar and Carmen Valcárcel (Madrid: Biblioteca Nueva), 73–89.

Campbell, Federico. 2004. 'Carmen Martín Gaite', in *Conversaciones con escritores* (México: Consejo Nacional para la Cultura y las Artes, Fondo Editorial Tierra Adentro), 231–40.

Campbell, Joseph. 1968. *The Hero with a Thousand Faces* (Princeton, NJ: Princeton University Press).

Cantavella, Juan. 1995. 'Carmen Martín Gaite: Contemplar la vida con una pluma en la mano', in *Semblanzas entrevistas: Carmen Martín Gaite, Narciso Yepes y Manuel Gutiérrez Mellado* (Madrid: PPC), 11–90.

Carbayo Abengózar, Mercedes. 1998a. *Buscando un lugar entre mujeres: buceo en la España de Carmen Martín Gaite* (Málaga: Universidad de Málaga).

—— 1998b. 'A manera de subversión: Carmen Martín Gaite', *Espéculo: Revista de Estudios Literarios* <http://pendientedemigracion.ucm.es/info/especulo/cmgaite/carbayo.htm> [accessed 22 July 2017].

—— 2000. 'Los sueños y los recuerdos en la literatura de Carmen Martín Gaite: Un camino de ida y vuelta', in *IV Congreso Internacional de Caminería Hispánica*, ed. M. Criado del Val (Madrid: Ministerio de Fomento), 1127–40.

—— 2004. 'Lo raro no es sólo vivir, lo raro es también hablar', in *Carmen Martín Gaite*, ed. Alicia Redondo Goicoechea, 19–32.

Carrillo Romero, María Coronada. 2010. *La visión de lo real en la obra de Carmen Martín Gaite* (Cáceres: Universidad de Extremadura, Servicio de Publicaciones).

Catechism of the Catholic Church. 1994 (London: Geoffrey Chapman).

Celaya, Beatriz. 2007. 'El amor es una tara: *Cuadernos de todo*, de Carmen Martín Gaite', *Neophilologus* 91: 221–41.

Cervantes, Miguel de. 2009. *Novelas ejemplares II* (Madrid: Espasa Calpe).

Chauchadis, Claude. 2004. 'Jeux sur le nom des personnages et jeux de lettres dans *La Reina de las Nieves*', in *La littérature pour enfants*, ed. Moner and Pérès, 259–63.

Chodorow, Joan. 2006. 'Active Imagination', in *The Handbook of Jungian Psychology: Theory, Practice and Applications*, ed. Renos K. Papadopoulos (London & New York: Routledge), 215–43, 246.

Chown, Linda E. 1983. 'American Critics and Spanish Women Novelists, 1942–1980', *Signs* 9/1: 91–107.

Ciplijauskaité, Biruté. 2000. *Carmen Martín Gaite (1925–2000)* (Madrid: Ediciones del Orto).

Claremont de Castillejo, Irene. 1990. *Knowing Woman: A Feminine Psychology* (Boston & Shaftesbury: Shambhala). Reprint of original 1973 edn published by Putnam, New York for the C. G. Jung Foundation for Analytical Psychology.

Collins Dictionary of the English Language. 1979, ed. Patrick Hanks (London & Glasgow: Collins).

Contadini, Luigi. 2000. 'Esperienza e scrittura nella narrativa di Carmen Martín Gaite (a proposito di *La reina de las nieves, Lo raro es vivir, Irse de casa)*', *Rassegna Iberistica* 70: 13–21.

Cox, David. 1960. *God and the Self (Guild Lecture No. 112)* (London: The Guild of Pastoral Psychology).

—— 1975. *The Devil (Guild Lecture No. 182)* (London: The Guild of Pastoral Psychology).

Cremades García, Raúl. 2011. *La dama de los cuadernos* (Alcalá de Guadaíra, Sevilla: Paréntesis).

Crowther, Brenda. 2013. *The Remora: An Interpretation of 'Sleeping Beauty' (Guild Lecture No. 314)* (London: The Guild of Pastoral Psychology).

Cruz-Cámara, Nuria. 2008. *El laberinto intertextual de Carmen Martín Gaite: Un estudio de sus novelas de los noventa* (Newark, DE: Juan de la Cuesta – Hispanic Monographs).

Cueto Veiga, Margarita. 2005. '*Caperucita en Manhattan* de Carmen Martín Gaite o el secreto de los cuentos', in *Literatura actual en Castilla y Leon: Actas del II Congreso de Literatura Contemporánea*, ed. José Ma Balcells, 115–21.

Cuevas García, Cristóbal, and Enrique Baena (eds). 2000. *Escribir Mujer. Narradoras Españolas Hoy* (Málaga: Publicaciones del Congreso de literatura española contemporánea).

Curran, Ronald T. 1992. '"*Snow White*", "*Cinderella*", and *Dracula*: When the Ferris Wheel Stops', in *Psyche's Stories* Vol. 2, ed. Murray Stein and Lionel Corbett (Wilmette, IL: Chiron Publications), 93–110.

Cusato, Domenico Antonio. 1996. 'Su Alcune Fonti di *Caperucita en Manhattan* de Carmen Martín Gaite', in *Tradizione, innovazione, modelli*, ed. Perassi, 481–500.

Davies, Catherine. 1998. 'Writing from Within, with her Own Voice: Carmen Martín Gaite', in *Spanish Women's Writing 1849–1996* (London: The Athlone Press).

Débax, Michelle. 2004. 'Le jeu des devinettes ou "Los acertijos de la abuela"', in *La littérature pour enfants*, ed. Moner and Pérès, 249–57.

Diéguez, María Luz. 1989. 'Entrevista con Esther Tusquets', *Letras Femeninas* 15/1–2: 131–40.

Doyle, Kathleen A. 2000. 'Mapping Future Paths: Fantasy and Self Discovery in Carmen Martín Gaite's Books for Children', in *La mujer hispana en el mundo: sus triunfos y sus retos*, ed. Jorge H. Valdivieso, L. Teresa Valdivieso and Enrique Ruíz-Fornells (Phoenix, AZ: Orbis Press), 212–17.

Dravet-Barbusse, Catherine. 2003. 'La ville, lieux et limites: la représentation de deux espaces du centre de Madrid dans *La Reina de las Nieves*, de Carmen Martín Gaite', *Cahiers d'études romanes* 8: 131–9.

Dundes, Alan (ed.). 1989. *Little Red Riding Hood: A Casebook* (Madison: University of Wisconsin Press), 247.

El Saffar, Ruth. 1982. 'Carmen Martín Gaite and *El castillo de las tres murallas*', *Letras Femeninas* 8/2: 46–53.

—— 1983. 'Liberation and the Labyrinth: A Study of the Works of Carmen Martín Gaite', in *From Fiction to Metafiction*, ed. Mirella Servodidio and Marcia L. Welles (Lincoln, NE: Society of Spanish & Spanish-American Studies), 185–95.

Estés, Clarissa Pinkola. 1992. *Women who Run with the Wolves* (London: Rider). Page numbers refer to 1998 edn.

Ferber, Michael. 1999. *A Dictionary of Literary Symbols* (Cambridge: Cambridge University Press).

Fernández, Celia. 1979. 'Entrevista con Carmen Martín Gaite', *Anales de la narrativa española contemporánea* 4: 165–72.

Fernández Hoyos, Sonia. 2004. 'El viaje y la aventura en *El pastel del diablo* de Carmen Martín Gaite: una propuesta de lectura', in *Actas del VII Congreso Internacional de la Sociedad Española de Didáctica de la Lengua y la Literatura*, ed. Aurora Marco, Pilar Couto Cantero, Elva Aradas Carollo and Fernando Vieito Liñares (A Coruña: Deputación da Coruña), 569–78.

Fernández-Lamarque, María. 2013. 'The Voice of Zarathustra's Nietzsche in Carmen Martín Gaite's *Caperucita en Manhattan*', *International Research in Children's Literature* 6/1: 76–89.

Fernández Rodríguez, Carolina. 2001. 'El cuento de hadas como germen de la novela finisecular: *Red Shoes* (1998) y *La reina de las nieves* (1994)', in *El cuento en la década de los noventa: Actas del X Seminario Internacional del Instituto de Semiótica Literaria, Teatral y Nuevas Tecnologías*, ed. F. Gutiérrez Carbajo and J. Romera Castillo (Madrid: Visor Libros, UNED), 207–17.
Fordham, Michael. 1958. *The Objective Psyche* (London: Routledge & Kegan Paul).
Franz, Marie-Louise von. 1964. 'The process of individuation', in *Man and his Symbols*, ed. C. G. Jung, 158–229.
—— 1980. *Projection and Re-collection in Jungian Psychology: Reflections of the Soul* (La Salle & London: Open Court).
—— 1990. *Individuation in Fairy Tales* (Boston & London: Shambhala).
—— 1992. *The Golden Ass of Apuleius: The Liberation of the Feminine in Man* (Boston & London: Shambhala).
—— 1993a. *The Feminine in Fairy Tales* (Boston & London: Shambhala).
—— 1993b. *Psychotherapy* (Boston & London: Shambhala).
—— 1995a. *Creation Myths* (Boston & London: Shambhala).
—— 1995b. *Shadow and Evil in Fairy Tales* (Boston & London: Shambhala).
—— 1996. *The Interpretation of Fairy Tales* (Boston & London: Shambhala), 248.
—— 1997a. *Archetypal Dimensions of the Psyche* (Boston & London: Shambhala).
—— 1997b. *Archetypal Patterns in Fairy Tales* (Toronto: Inner City Books).
—— 1999. *The Cat: A Tale of Feminine Redemption* (Toronto: Inner City Books).
—— 2002. *Animus and Anima in Fairy Tales* (Toronto: Inner City Books).
Freixas, Laura. 2011. *Entre escritoras: Carmen Martín Gaite* <https://www.sas.ac.uk/videos-and-podcasts/culture-language-and-literature/entre-escritoras-carmen-martin-gaite> [accessed 22 July 2017].
Fromm, Erich. 1951. *The Forgotten Language* (New York: Holt, Rinehart and Winston).
Gardner, W. H., and N. H. MacKenzie (eds). 1970. *The Poems of Gerard Manley Hopkins* (Oxford: Oxford University Press).
Gazarián Gautier, Marie-Lise. 1983. 'Conversación con Carmen Martín Gaite en Nueva York', in *From Fiction to Metafiction*, ed. Servodidio and Welles, 25–33.
Glenn, Kathleen M. 1996. '*La Reina de las Nieves* by Carmen Martín Gaite', *Anales de la literatura española contemporánea* 21/1–2: 177–9.
Glenn, Kathleen M., and Lissette Rolón Collazo (eds). 2003. *Carmen Martín Gaite: Cuento de nunca acabar/Never-ending Story* (Boulder, CO: Society of Spanish & Spanish-American Studies).
González Couso, David. 2008a. 'Alas de libélula: *El pastel del diablo* de Carmen Martín Gaite', *Moenia – Revista lucense de lingüística & literatura* 14: 391–403.
—— 2008b. *Una propuesta de lectura para 'Caperucita en Manhattan'* (Almería: Asociación Procompal).

—— 2008c. *Los perfiles gallegos de Carmen Martín Gaite* (Almería: Asociación Procompal).

—— 2009. 'Carmen Martín Gaite y su geografía literaria', *Espéculo: Revista de Estudios Literarios* 41 <https://pendientedemigracion.ucm.es/info/especulo/numero41/cmggeoli.html> [accessed 22 July 2017].

—— 2010. *Caperucita en Manhattan de Carmen Martín Gaite* (Berriozar, Navarra: Cénlit).

—— 2014. 'El tiempo de la incertidumbre: Notas para la lectura de *El pastel del diablo*, de Carmen Martín Gaite', *Espéculo: Revista de Estudios Literarios* 52: 36–47 <https://pendientedemigracion.ucm.es/info/especulo/Carmen_Martin_Gaite_Especulo_52_2014_UCM.pdf> [accessed 28 June 2017].

Gould, Joan. 2006. *Spinning Straw into Gold: What Fairy Tales Reveal about the Transformations in a Woman's Life* (New York: Random House).

Gracia, Jordi. 2000. *Historia y crítica de la literatura española – 9/1 Los nuevos nombres: 1975–2000. Primer suplemento* (Barcelona: Crítica), 249.

Gracia, Jordi, and Domingo Ródenas. 2011. *Historia de la literatura española 7. Derrota y restitución de la modernidad 1939–2010* (Barcelona: Crítica).

Grimm, Jacob and Wilhelm. 1996. *Grimm's Fairy Tales* (London: The Folio Society).

Grønbech, Bo. 1980. *Hans Christian Andersen* (Boston: Twayne).

Guerrero Solier, Eloísa. 1992. 'El interlocutor en la obra de Carmen Martín Gaite', *Analecta Malacitana* XV/1–2: 319–31.

Hall, Nor. 1980. *The Moon and the Virgin: Reflections on the Archetypal Feminine* (London: The Women's Press).

Hannah, Barbara. 1977. *Jung: His Life and Work – A Biographical Memoir* (London: Michael Joseph).

Harding, M. Esther. 1982. *Woman's Mysteries Ancient and Modern: A Psychological Interpretation of the Feminine Principle as portrayed in Myth, Story and Dreams* [1955] (London: Rider), 2nd edn.

—— 1983. *The Way of All Women: A Psychological Interpretation* [1933] (London: Rider).

Hart, David L. 1992. '"*The Water of Life*" – A Story of Healing and the Transformation of Consciousness', in *Psyche's Stories* Vol. 2, ed. Stein and Corbett, 141–56.

Hart, Stephen M. 1993. *White Ink: Essays on Twentieth-Century Feminine Fiction in Spain and Latin America* (London: Tamesis).

Hauke, Christopher. 2006. 'The unconscious: personal and collective', in *The Handbook of Jungian Psychology*, ed. Papadopoulos, 54–73.

Hernández Álvarez, María Vicenta. 2005. 'La primera frase ... y el final del cuento: Dos cuentos maravillosos de Carmen Martín Gaite', *CAUCE* 28: 145–67.

Herralde, Jorge. 1997. 'Mi experiencia de editor de Carmen Martín Gaite', in *Al encuentro de Carmen Martín Gaite*, ed. Martinell, 57–8.
Howse, Christopher. 2011. *A Pilgrim in Spain* (London: Continuum).
Howes, Elizabeth B. 1960. *Son of Man – Image of the Self (Guild Lecture No. 109)* (London: The Guild of Pastoral Psychology).
Hughes, Gerard. 2008. *God of Surprises* (London: Darton, Longman & Todd), 3rd rev. edn.
Jacoby, Mario. 1975. *Love Your Enemies (Guild Lecture No. 180)* (London: The Guild of Pastoral Psychology).
Jaffé, Aniela. 1986. *The Myth of Meaning in the Work of C. G. Jung* (Zürich: Daimon), 2nd edn.
Jäger, Hans-Wolf. 1989. 'Is Little Red Riding Hood Wearing a Liberty Cap? On Presumable Connotations in Tieck and in Grimm', in *Little Red Riding Hood: A Casebook*, ed. Dundes, 89–120.
Jarrett, James L. 1995. *Jung and Kinds of Love (Guild Lecture No. 251)* (London: The Guild of Pastoral Psychology).
Jiménez González, Mercedes. 1992. '*El pastel del diablo*: un juego alegórico sobre la iniciación literaria de Carmen Martín Gaite', *Letras Femeninas* 18/1–2: 83–90.
Jung, C. G. 1953. *Psychology & Alchemy* (London: Routledge & Kegan Paul).
—— 1954. *The Symbolic Life (Guild Lecture No. 80)* (London: The Guild of Pastoral Psychology).
—— 1956. *Symbols of Transformation* (London: Routledge & Kegan Paul).
—— 1959. *Archetypes and the Collective Unconscious* (London: Routledge & Kegan Paul).
—— 1960. *The Structure and Dynamics of the Psyche* (London: Routledge & Kegan Paul).
—— 1963. *Mysterium Coniunctionis* (London: Routledge & Kegan Paul).
—— 1964a. *Civilization in Transition* (London: Routledge & Kegan Paul).
—— (ed.) 1964b. *Man and His Symbols* (London: Aldus Books).
—— 1970. *Psychology and Religion* (London: Routledge & Kegan Paul).
—— 1977. *The Symbolic Life* (London: Routledge & Kegan Paul).
—— 1983. *Memories, Dreams, Reflections* (London: Fontana).
—— 1991. *Archetypes and the Collective Unconscious* (London: Routledge & Kegan Paul).
Jung, Emma. 1981. *Animus and Anima* (Dallas, TX: Spring Publications).
Jung, Emma, and Marie-Louise von Franz. 1971. *The Grail Legend* (London: Hodder & Stoughton).
Jurado Morales, José. 2001. *Del testimonio al intimismo: los cuentos de Carmen Martín Gaite* (Cádiz: Servicio de Publicaciones de la Universidad).

—— 2003. *La trayectoria narrativa de Carmen Martín Gaite (1925–2000)* (Madrid: Gredos).

—— 2004. 'La mirada ajena: medio siglo de bibliografía sobre la obra de Carmen Martín Gaite', *Anales de la literatura española contemporánea* 29/1: 135–65.

Kapacinskas, T. J., and Judith A. Robert. 1992. '"*Rapunzel*" – Barrenness and Bounty, Differentiation and Reconciliation', in *Psyche's Stories* Vol. 2, ed. Stein and Corbett, 59–78.

Kast, Verena. 2006. 'Anima/animus', in *The Handbook of Jungian Psychology*, by Renos K. Papadopoulis, 113–29.

Kesey, Ken. 1962. *One Flew over the Cuckoo's Nest* (New York: Viking Press).

Knapp, Bettina. 2003. *French Fairy Tales: A Jungian Approach* (Albany, NY: State University of New York Press).

Lacruz Pardo, Javier. 1978. 'Carmen Martín Gaite: "En *El cuarto de atrás* se va viendo mi concepción del amor"', *Nueva* 6: 16.

LaLonde, Suzanne. 2010. 'Una perspectiva psicoanalítica de *Nubosidad variable* de Carmen Martín Gaite', *Espéculo: Revista de Estudios Literarios* 45 <https://pendientedemigracion.ucm.es/info/especulo/numero45/nubocmg.html> [accessed 22 July 2017].

Lang, Andrew. 1975. *Blue Fairy Book* (London: Penguin). Revised edn of 1889 publication by Longmans, Green Co. Ltd.

Le Scoezec Masson, Annick. 2003. '*La reina de las nieves*: Carmen Martín Gaite au confluent des imaginaires littéraires nordique et hispanique', *Les Langues Néo-latines: Bulletin Trimestriel de la Société des Langues Néo-latines* 324: 79–95.

Lederer, Wolfgang. 1990. *The Kiss of the Snow Queen: Hans Christian Andersen and Man's Redemption by Woman* (Berkeley: University of California Press).

Lindström Leo, Ingrid. 2009. *Scribo ergo sum: Aspectos existenciales en tres novelas tardías de Carmen Martín Gaite*, unpublished doctoral dissertation (Stockholm: University of Stockholm).

Llorente, Lucía I. 2002. '*Caperucita en Manhattan*: Caperucita en el país de las maravillas', *Espéculo: Revista de Estudios Literarios* 22 <https://pendientedemigracion.ucm.es/info/especulo/numero22/caperuci.htm> [accessed 22 July 2017].

Lluch Villalba, María de los Ángeles. 2000. *Los cuentos de Carmen Martín Gaite: Temas y técnicas de una escritora de los años cincuenta* (Pamplona: EUNSA (Ediciones Universidad de Navarra)).

Longford, Frank. 1978. *Francis of Assisi: a life for all seasons* (London: Weidenfeld & Nicolson).

López Guil, Itzíar. 2008. 'Escuchar por los ojos: a propósito de un cuento de Carmen Martín Gaite', *Versants – Revista suiza de literaturas románicas* 55/3: 87–98.

Luke, Helen M. 1981. *Woman: Earth and Spirit – The Feminine in Symbol and Myth* (New York: Crossroad).

—— 1995. *The Way of Woman: Awakening the Perennial Feminine* (Dublin: Gill & Macmillan).

Lüthi, Max. 1976. *Once Upon a Time – On the Nature of Fairy Tales* (Bloomington & London: Indiana University Press).

McCully, Robert S. 1991. *The Enigma of Symbols in Fairy Tales: Zimmer's Dialogue Renewed* (Lewiston, NY: The Edwin Mellen Press).

Macmurray, John. 1962. *Reason and Emotion* (New Jersey & London: Humanities Press). Page numbers refer to 1992 edn.

—— 1968. *Freedom in the Modern World* (London: Faber & Faber).

Mainer, José-Carlos. 2008. 'Prólogo', in *Carmen Martín Gaite: Obras completas I*, ed. José Teruel (Barcelona: Galaxia Gutenberg, Círculo de Lectores), 55–89.

March, Kathleen. 1995. '*La Reina de las Nieves* by Carmen Martín Gaite', *World Literature Today* 69/3: 557–8.

Márquez, A. B. 2005. 'Gotas de hada', in *Visión de Nueva York*, by Carmen Martín Gaite, 131–3.

Martín, Salustiano. 1991. '*Caperucita en Manhattan*: Huir de la realidad', in *Reseña de literatura, arte y espectáculos* 215: 33.

—— 1994. '*La reina de las nieves*: los peligros del infantilismo', in *Reseña de literatura, arte y espectáculos* 254: 33, 252.

Martín Gaite, Carmen. 1958. *Entre visillos* (Barcelona: Destino).

—— 1974. *Retahílas* (Barcelona: Destino).

—— 1975. *Ritmo lento* [1963] (Barcelona: Destino).

—— 1978. *El cuarto de atrás* (Barcelona: Destino).

—— (trans.) 1980a. *Bruno Bettelheim presenta los Cuentos de Perrault: seguidos de los cuentos de Madame d'Aulnoye y de Madame Leprince de Beaumont* (Barcelona: Crítica).

—— 1980b. *Fragmentos de interior* [1976] (Barcelona: Destino).

—— 1982. *La búsqueda de interlocutor y otras búsquedas* [1973] (Barcelona: Destino).

—— 1983. 'Retahíla con nieve en Nueva York (Para mi madre, *in memoriam*)', in *From Fiction to Metafiction*, ed. Servodidio and Welles, 19–24.

—— 1984. *Cuentos completos* (Madrid: Alianza), 4th edn.

—— 1987a. *Desde la ventana* (Madrid: Espasa Calpe).

—— 1987b. *Usos amorosos de la postguerra española* (Barcelona: Anagrama).

—— 1988a. *El cuento de nunca acabar* [1983] (Barcelona: Anagrama).

—— 1988b. *Las ataduras* (Barcelona: Destino), 2nd edn.

—— 1991a. 'Entrevista: Carmen Martín Gaite', *CLIJ (Cuadernos de literatura infantil y juvenil)* 26: 7–12.

——1991b. 'Introducción – El triunfo de la excepción', in *Cuentos españoles de antaño*, by Felipe Alfau (Madrid: Siruela), XI–XXVII.
——1992a. *Dos cuentos maravillosos* (Madrid: Siruela).
——1992b. *Nubosidad variable* (Barcelona: Anagrama).
——1992c. *Caperucita en Manhattan* [1990] (Madrid: Siruela), 10th edn.
——1993a. 'Entrevistamos a ... Carmen Martín Gaite', *Peonza – Boletín Trimestral de Literatura Infantil* 24: 24–30.
——1993b. 'Comentado por ... Carmen Martín Gaite', *Peonza – Boletín Trimestral de Literatura Infantil* 26: 55–6.
——1993c. *Agua pasada* (Barcelona: Anagrama).
——1994a. *La reina de las nieves* (Barcelona: Anagrama).
——1994b. 'Reflexiones sobre mi obra', in *Arba 4: Acta Romanica Basiliensia: La novela española moderna*, ed. Germán Colón, Tobias Brandenberger and Marco Kunz (Basel: Universität Basel), 105–19.
——1994c. *Esperando el porvenir: Homenaje a Ignacio Aldecoa* (Madrid: Siruela), 253.
——1994d. 'Estudio preliminar', in *Peter Pan y Wendy: La historia del niño que no quiso crecer*, by J. M. Barrie (Barcelona: Editorial Juventud), 7–33.
——1995. 'Estudio preliminar: Siguiendo el hilo', in *La princesa y los trasgos*, by George MacDonald (Madrid: Siruela), 11–43.
——1996. *Lo raro es vivir* (Barcelona: Anagrama).
——1998. *Irse de casa* (Barcelona: Anagrama).
——1999a. 'La verdad es que no me gustaría nada morir', *El Mundo*, 10 October 1999 <http://www.oocities.org/carmenmartingaite/entrevistas/entrevista08.html> [accessed 10 June 2017].
——1999b. *La hermana pequeña* (Barcelona: Anagrama).
——2001a. *Los parentescos* (Barcelona: Anagrama).
——2001b. *Después de todo, Poesía a rachas* (Madrid: Hiperión).
——2002a. *Cuadernos de todo* (Barcelona: Areté).
——2002b. *Pido la palabra* (Barcelona: Anagrama).
——2005. *Visión de Nueva York* (Madrid: Siruela, Círculo de Lectores).
——2006. *Tirando del hilo (articulos 1949–2000)* (Madrid: Siruela).
——2007. *El libro de la fiebre* (Madrid: Cátedra).
Martinell Gifre, Emma (ed.). 1993. *La Semana de Autor: Carmen Martín Gaite* (Madrid: Ediciones de Cultura Hispánica).
——(ed.). 1995. *Hilo a la cometa: La visión, la memoria y el sueño* (Madrid: Espasa Calpe).
——1996. *El mundo de los objetos en la obra de Carmen Martín Gaite* (Cáceres: Universidad de Extremadura, Servicio de Publicaciones).

—— (ed.). 1997. *Al encuentro de Carmen Martín Gaite: Homenajes y bibliografía* (Barcelona: Gráficas Alsina).

—— 1998. 'Entrevista con Carmen Martín Gaite', *Espéculo: Revista de Estudios Literarios* <http://pendientedemigracion.ucm.es/info/especulo/cmgaite/entr_cmg.htm> [accessed 22 July 2017].

Martini, Carlo-Maria. 2000. *Saving Beauty* (London: St Pauls).

Matthews, Marilyn L. 1992. '"The Snow Queen": An Interpretation', in *Psyche's Stories* Vol. 2, ed. Stein and Corbett, 79–92.

Medina, Héctor. 1983. 'Conversación con Carmen Martín Gaite', *Anales de la literatura española contemporánea* 8: 183–94, 254.

Menéndez y Pelayo, Marcelino. 1961. *Orígenes de la Novela III* (Madrid: Consejo Superior de Investigaciones Científicas).

Mercurio, Robert M. 2011. *The Unknown God and the Inferior Function (Guild Lecture No. 308)* (London: The Guild of Pastoral Psychology).

Merlo Morat, Philippe. 2004a. 'Un cuento, reque ... te cuento (réflexions sur le conte chez Carmen Martín Gaite)', in *La littérature pour enfants*, ed. Moner and Pérès, 177–95.

—— 2004b. 'De l'oralité à l'écriture en passant par l'image chez Carmen Martín Gaite', in *La littérature pour enfants*, ed. Moner and Pérès, 265–70.

—— 2008. *'La reina de las nieves' de Carmen Martín Gaite* (Berriozar, Navarra: Cénlit).

Moner, Michel, and Christine Pérès. 2004. *La littérature pour enfants dans les textes hispaniques* (Paris: L'Harmattan).

Morales Ladrón, Marisol. 2002. 'Caperucita reescrita: *The Bloody Chamber* de Angela Carter y *Caperucita en Manhattan* de Carmen Martín Gaite', *Revista canaria de estudios ingleses* 45: 169–83.

Moulin, Dorothée. 1997. '*Caperucita en Manhattan* de Carmen Martín Gaite: "It était une fois l'aventure de la lecture ..."', *IRIS* (published by the Centre de recherches sur les littératures ibériques et ibero-américains modernes, Université Paul Valéry, Montpellier), 145–57.

Murphy, G. Ronald. 2000. *The Owl, the Raven, and the Dove: The Religious Meaning of the Grimms' Magic Fairy Tales* (New York: Oxford University Press).

Myers, Eunice D. 1984. 'Four Female Novelists and Spanish Children's Fiction', *Letras Femeninas* 10/2: 40–9.

—— 2003–4. 'Carmen Martín Gaite's *El pastel del diablo*: The Hero's Initiation', *Letras Peninsulares* (Autumn/Winter): 409–30.

Navarro-Daniels, Vilma. 2006. 'La invención interminable de la historia deseada en *Lo raro es vivir* de Carmen Martín Gaite', in *Leading Ladies: Mujeres en la literatura hispana y en las artes*, ed. Yvonne Fuentes and Margaret R. Parker (Louisiana: Louisiana State University Press).

Neumann, Erich. 1963. *The Great Mother: An Analysis of the Archetype* (Princeton, NJ: Princeton University Press).
——1971. *Amor and Psyche: The Psychic Development of the Feminine* (Princeton, NJ: Princeton University Press).
Ochoa, Debra. 2009. 'New York as a Site of Female Transgression in Martín Gaite's *Caperucita en Manhattan* (1990)', *Romanitas, lenguas y literaturas romances*, 4.
Odartey-Wellington, Dorothy. 1997. 'Martín Gaite y el triunfo de la imaginación en *La reina de las nieves*', *Hispanic Journal* 18/1: 79–87.
——2000. 'De las madres perversas y las hadas buenas: una nueva visión sobre la imagen esencial de la mujer en las novelas de Carmen Martín Gaite y Esther Tusquets', *Anales de la literatura española contemporánea* 25/2: 255, 529–55.
——2003. '*La reina de las nieves*: El caso de un hombre en busca de su madre', in *Sexo(s) e identidad(es) en la cultura hispánica*, ed. R. de la Fuente Ballesteros and J. Pérez Magallón (Valladolid: Universitas Castellae), 113–20.
——2004a. '*Caperucita en Manhattan*: abriendo "brechas en la costumbre"', *Letras Peninsulares* 17/1: 211–21.
——2004b. 'The Reworking of Tales of Enchantment in Two Novels by Carmen Martín Gaite and Esther Tusquets', in *Reading the Popular in Contemporary Spanish Texts* by Shelley Godsland and Nickianne Moody (Newark, DE: University of Delaware Press), 121–35.
O'Leary, Catherine, and Alison Ribeiro de Menezes. 2008. *A Companion to Carmen Martín Gaite* (Woodbridge: Tamesis).
Ollé, Marie-Louise. 2004. 'À la recherche du corps perdu dans *La Reina de las Nieves*', in *La littérature pour enfants*, ed. Moner and Pérès, 279–91.
Orenstein, Catherine. 2002. *Little Red Riding Hood Uncloaked: Sex, Morality and the Evolution of a Fairy Tale* (New York: Basic Books).
Pacheco Oropeza, Bettina. 2004. 'La niña rara: *Caperucita en Manhattan*', in *Carmen Martín Gaite*, ed. Goicoechea, 115–21.
Palley, Julian. 1983. 'Dreams in Two Novels of Carmen Martín Gaite', in *From Fiction to Metafiction*, ed. Servodidio and Welles, 107–16.
Paoli, Anne. 1998. 'Mirada sobre la relación entre espejo y personaje en algunas obras de Carmen Martín Gaite', *Espéculo: Revista de Estudios Literarios* <https://pendientedemigracion.ucm.es/info/especulo/cmgaite/apaoli2.htm> [accessed 22 July 2017].
——2002. 'Approche de l'évolution narrative de Carmen Martín Gaite dans *La Reina de las Nieves*', *Espéculo: Revista de Estudios Literarios* 20 <https://pendientedemigracion.ucm.es/info/especulo/numero20/reinacmg.html> [accessed 22 July 2017].

——2004. 'Brève présentation de *La reina de las nieves*, de Carmen Martín Gaite', in *La littérature pour enfants*, ed. Moner and Pérès (Paris: L'Harmattan), 243–7.

——2007. 'Tradition et originalité dans *El castillo de las tres murallas*, de Carmen Martín Gaite', in *Savoirs, Pouvoirs et Apprentissages dans la Littérature de Jeunesse en Langue Espagnole*, ed. Michel Moner and Christine Pérès (Paris: L'Harmattan), 195–216.

Papadopoulos, Renos K. (ed.). 2006. *The Handbook of Jungian Psychology: Theory, Practice and Applications* (London & New York: Routledge).

Parks, Frances M. '"Maid Maleen" – An Image of Feminine Wholeness', in *Psyche's Stories* Vol. 2, ed. Stein and Corbett, 1–13.

Penna, Rosa. 1995. '*La reina de las nieves*: de Hans Christian Andersen a Carmen Martín Gaite', in *II Coloquio Internacional de Literatura Comparada: Cuento, El*, ed. Martha Vanbiesem de Burbridge (Buenos Aires: Fundación María Teresa Maiorana), 254–9.

Pérès, Christine. 2004. 'Parcours féminins dans deux récits pour enfants: Carmen Martín Gaite, *Caperucita en Manhattan* et Ana María Matute, *El verdadero final de la Bella Durmiente*', in *La littérature pour enfants*, ed. Moner and Pérès (Paris: L'Harmattan), 153–75.

Perrault, Charles. 1998. *The Fairy Tales of Charles Perrault* (London: The Folio Society).

Perriam, C., M. Thompson, S. Frenk and V. Knights. 2000. *A New History of Spanish Writing – 1939 to the 1990s* (Oxford: Oxford University Press).

Pittarello, Elide. 2004. 'Lo lúdico y lo sagrado en *La reina de las nieves de Carmen Martín Gaite*', in *Síntomas en la prosa hispana contemporánea 1990–2001*, ed. C. Cifuentes Aldunate (Odense: University Press of Southern Denmark), 131–50.

——2009. 'Prólogo: Las últimas novelas de Carmen Martín Gaite', in *Carmen Martín Gaite: Obras Completas II*, ed. José Teruel (Barcelona: Galaxia Gutenberg, Círculo de Lectores), 9–45.

Plato. 1956. *Protagoras and Meno* (Harmondsworth, Middlesex: Penguin).

Post, Laurens van der. 1978. *Jung and the Story of Our Time* (London: Penguin).

Pozuelo Yvancos, José Ma. 2009. 'Habitaciones propias: Obras Completas. Novelas I (1955–1978) y Novelas II (1979–2000) de Carmen Martín Gaite', in *Revista de Libros de la Fundación Caja Madrid* 155: 47.

Prince, Gerald. 2003. *A Dictionary of Narratology* (Lincoln: University of Nebraska Press), rev. edn.

Ramos, Alicia. 1980. 'Conversación con Carmen Martín Gaite', *Hispanic Journal* 1/2: 117–24.

Redondo Goicoechea, Alicia (ed.). 2004. *Carmen Martín Gaite* (Madrid: Ediciones del Orto).

——2009. *Mujeres y Narrativa: Otra Historia de la Literatura* (Madrid: Siglo XXI).

Ribeiro de Menezes, Alison. 2011. 'Gender and Space in Carmen Martín Gaite's *Nubosidad variable* and *La reina de las nieves*', in *Beyond the Back Room: New Perspectives on Carmen Martín Gaite*, ed. Marian Womack and Jennifer Wood (Bern: Peter Lang), 135–57.

——2014. 'New York as "Pórtico" in Martín Gaite's Late Works', *Espéculo: Revista de Estudios Literarios* 52: 48–56 <https://pendientedemigracion.ucm.es/info/especulo/Carmen_Martin_Gaite_Especulo_52_2014_UCM.pdf> [accessed 28 June 2017].

Robinson, Wendy. 1979. 'The Twentieth-Century Labyrinth', in *The Search for Meaning, Guild Spring Conference 1979 (Guild Lecture No. 196)* (London: The Guild of Pastoral Psychology), 23–39.

Rodríguez, Joe. 2006. 'The Search for Meaning in Carmen Martín Gaite's *El cuarto de atrás*', *Journal of Iberian and Latin American Studies* 12/1: 39–51.

Roger, Isabel M. 1988. 'Perspectivas críticas: horizontes infinitos – Carmen Martín Gaite: una trayectoria novelística y su bibliografía', *Anales de la literatura española contemporánea* 13: 257, 293–317.

——1992. '*Caperucita en Manhattan*', *Revista Hispánica Moderna* 45/2: 328–31.

Rolón-Collazo, Lissette. 2002. *Figuraciones: Mujeres en Carmen Martín Gaite, revistas feministas y ¡Hola!* (Madrid: Iberoamericana).

Saintyves, P. 1989. 'Little Red Riding Hood or the Little May Queen', in *Little Red Riding Hood: A Casebook*, ed. Dundes, 71–88.

Saiz Álvarez, José Manuel, and Eustasio Herrero Herrero (eds). 2007. *Luz en la quietud: Libro-homenaje a Carmen Martín Gaite* (Madrid: Ediciones FIEC).

Samuels, Andrew. 2008. 'New developments in the post-Jungian field', in *The Cambridge Companion to Jung*, 1–15.

Sánchez, Marjorie. 1991. 'Racionalidad e irracionalidad en un relato de Carmen Martín Gaite', *Quaderni di letterature iberiche e iberoamericane* 14/15: 47–70.

Sarmati, Elisabetta. 2014. 'Visiones de Nueva York en *Caperucita en Manhattan* de Carmen Martín Gaite', in *Espéculo* (*Revista de Estudios Literarios*) 52: 57–69 <https://pendientedemigracion.ucm.es/info/especulo/Carmen_Martin_Gaite_Especulo_52_2014_UCM.pdf> [accessed 28 June 2017].

Servodidio, Mirella, and Marcia L. Welles. 1983. *From Fiction to Metafiction: Studies in Honor of Carmen Martín Gaite* (Lincoln, NE: Society of Spanish and Spanish-American Studies).

Siurana, Elvira. 1989. 'Carmen Martín Gaite: "En el amor hay de todo"', *Poder y libertad: revista teórica del Partido Feminista de España* 10: 42–5.

Smith, C. Colin. 1964. *Spanish Ballads* (Oxford: Pergamon).

Sobejano-Morán, Antonio. 2003. 'Funciones textuales del espejo en la narrativa de Carmen Martín Gaite', in *Carmen Martín Gaite: Cuento de nunca acabar/ Never-ending Story*, ed. Glenn and Rolón Collazo, 183–95.

Soliño, María Elena. 2000. 'Colorín, Colorado, este cuento todavía no se ha acabado: Martín Gaite, Matute, y Tusquets ante los cuentos de hadas', in *Mujeres Novelistas en el Panorama Literario del Siglo XX: I Congreso de narrativa española (en lengua castellana)*, ed. Marina Villalba Álvarez (Cuenca: Ediciones de la Universidad de Castilla-La Mancha), 189–99.

——2002. *Women and Children First: Spanish Women Writers and the Fairy Tale Tradition* (Potomac: Scripta Humanistica).

——2003. 'Los cuentos de hadas de Carmen Martín Gaite: la voz feminina domina al lobo de la tradición', in *Carmen Martín Gaite: Cuento de nunca acabar/Never-ending Story*, ed. Glenn and Rolón Collazo, 197–213.

Soriano, Juan Carlos. 2007. 'Ana María Martín Gaite: "Nadie, ni siquiera yo, conoció del todo a Carmiña"', *Turia: Revista Cultural* 83: 267–79.

Stein, Murray. 1998. *Transformation: Emergence of the Self* (Texas: Texas A&M University Press), 258.

——2006a. *The Principle of Individuation: Toward the Development of Human Consciousness* (Wilmette, IL: Chiron Publications).

——2006b. 'Individuation', in *The Handbook of Jungian Psychology*, ed. Papadopoulos, 196–214.

——and Lionel Corbett (eds). 1991. *Psyche's Stories: Modern Jungian Interpretations of Fairy Tales, Volume 1* (Wilmette, IL: Chiron Publications).

——1992. *Psyche's Stories: Modern Jungian Interpretations of Fairy Tales, Volume 2* (Wilmette, IL: Chiron Publications).

——1995. *Psyche's Stories: Modern Jungian Interpretations of Fairy Tales, Volume 3* (Wilmette, IL: Chiron Publications).

Swann Jones, Steven. 2002. *The Fairy Tale: The Magic Mirror of the Imagination* (New York & London: Routledge).

Tatar, Maria. 1992. *Off With Their Heads! Fairy Tales and the Culture of Childhood* (Princeton, NJ: Princeton University Press).

Teruel, José. 2006. 'Un contexto biográfico para *Caperucita en Manhattan* de Carmen Martín Gaite', in *Género y géneros: Escritura y escritoras iberoamericanas*, ed. A. Encinar, E. Lofquist and C. Valcárcel (Madrid: Ediciones de la Universidad Autónoma), 143–51.

——2008. 'Introducción', in *Carmen Martín Gaite: Obras completas I*, ed. José Teruel (Barcelona: Galaxia Gutenberg, Círculo de Lectores), 9–54.

——(ed.). 2011. *Carmen Martín Gaite, Juan Benet: Correspondencia* (Barcelona: Galaxia Gutenberg, Círculo de Lectores).

——2014. 'Prólogo: Un lugar llamado Carmen Martín Gaite', in *Un lugar llamado Carmen Martín Gaite*, ed. José Teruel and Carmen Valcárcel (Madrid: Siruela), 9–18.

——and Carmen Valcárcel (eds). 2014. *Un lugar llamado Carmen Martín Gaite* (Madrid: Siruela).

Tuby, Molly. 1977. *Holding the Opposites (Guild Lecture No. 185)* (London: The Guild of Pastoral Psychology).

——1992. *Psychological Aspects of Eros (Guild Lecture No. 242)* (London: The Guild of Pastoral Psychology).

Turpín, Enrique. 1994. '*La reina de las nieves*: Carmen Martín Gaite y la lírica aplicada', *Quimera* 128: 50–6.

Uxó González, Carlos. 1998a. 'Carmen Martín Gaite: Revisión crítica de los estudios sobre su obra', *Espéculo: Revista de Estudios Literarios* <https://pendientedemigracion.ucm.es/info/especulo/cmgaite/c_uxo1.htm> [accessed 22 July 2017].

——1998b. 'El lector y la información narrativa en *La reina de las nieves* de Carmen Martín Gaite', *Anuario de Estudios Filológicos* XXI: 425–40.

——1999a. 'El interlocutor en *La reina de las nieves* de Carmen Martín Gaite', *Journal of Iberian and Latin American Studies* 5/1: 59–71.

——1999b. 'La Recuperación de la Memoria en *La Reina de las Nieves* de Carmen Martín Gaite', *Donaire* 13: 1–12, 259 <http://www.oocities.org/carmenmartingaite/estudios/estudio07.html> [accessed 22 July 2017].

Valcárcel, Carmen. 2010. 'Prólogo', in *Carmen Martín Gaite: Obras Completas III: Narrativa breve, poesía y teatro*, ed. José Teruel (Barcelona: Galaxia Gutenberg, Círculo de Lectores), 9–44.

Vassileva Kojouharova, Stefka. 2004. 'Las obras para niños de Carmen Martín Gaite', in *Carmen Martín Gaite*, ed. Redondo Goicoechea, 103–14.

Warner, Marina. 1994. *From the Beast to the Blonde – On Fairy Tales and their Tellers* (London: Chatto & Windus).

Weil, Simone. 2002. *Gravity and Grace* (London & New York: Routledge).

Welles, Marcia L. 1992. '*Dialogo e conversazione nella narrativa di Carmen Martín Gaite* by Maria Vittoria Calvi', *Revista Hispánica Moderna* 45/1: 154–6.

Wilson, Caroline. 2012. 'The Restoration of the Maternal Order. A Circle of Infinite? The Mother-Daughter Relationship in Carmen Martín Gaite's *Lo raro es vivir*', *Bulletin of Hispanic Studies* 89: 711–20.

Wolff, Toni. 1956. *Structural Forms of the Feminine Psyche* (Zürich: Students Association C. G. Jung Institute).

Womack, Marian. 2011. '*La reina de las nieves*: Retelling Andersen as a Parable of the Spanish Republic and *desmemoria*', in *Beyond the Back Room*, ed. Womack and Wood, 189–218.

Womack, Marian, and Jennifer Wood (eds). 2011. *Beyond the Back Room: New Perspectives on Carmen Martín Gaite* (Bern: Peter Lang).

Wullschläger, Jackie. 2000. *Hans Christian Andersen: The Life of a Storyteller* (London: Allen Lane).

Zahner-Roloff, Lee. 1992. '"*Snow White and Rose Red*" – Contained Oppositions', in *Psyche's Stories* Vol. 2, ed. Stein and Corbett, 111–22.

Zapata Ruíz, Teresa. 2007. *El cuento de hadas, el cuento maravilloso o el cuento de encantamiento: Un recorrido teórico sobre sus características literarias* (Cuenca: Ediciones de la Universidad de Castilla-La Mancha).

Zatlin Boring, Phyllis. 1977. 'Carmen Martín Gaite, Feminist Author', *Revista de Estudios Hispánicos* 11: 323–38.

Zecchi, Barbara. 1991. 'El cobijo de la infancia en la obra de Carmen Martín Gaite', *Mester* 20/2: 77–88.

Zipes, Jack. 1989. 'Little Red Riding Hood as Male Creation and Projection', in *Little Red Riding Hood: A Casebook*, ed. Dundes, 121–8.

—— (ed.). 1993. *The Trials and Tribulations of Little Red Riding Hood* (New York: Routledge), 260.

—— (ed.). 2000. *The Oxford Companion to Fairy Tales – The Western fairy tale tradition from medieval to modern* (Oxford: Oxford University Press).

Index

Hispanic Studies: Culture and Ideas

Edited by
Claudio Canaparo

This series aims to publish studies in the arts, humanities and social sciences, the main focus of which is the Hispanic World. The series invites proposals with interdisciplinary approaches to Hispanic culture in fields such as the history of concepts and ideas, the sociology of culture, the evolution of visual arts, the critique of literature, and the uses of historiography. It is not confined to a particular historical period.

Monographs as well as collected papers are welcome in English or Spanish.

Those interested in contributing to the series are invited to write with either the synopsis of a subject already in typescript or with a detailed project outline to either Professor Claudio Canaparo, Department of Iberian and Latin American Studies, School of Arts, Birkbeck College, 43 Gordon Square, London WC1H 0PD, UK, c.canaparo@sllc.bbk.ac.uk, or Peter Lang Ltd, oxford@peterlang.com.

Vol. 1 Antonio Sánchez
Postmodern Spain. A Cultural Analysis of 1980s–1990s Spanish Culture. 220 pages. 2007.
ISBN 978-3-03910-914-2

Vol. 2 Geneviève Fabry y Claudio Canaparo (eds.)
El enigma de lo real. Las fronteras del realismo en la narrativa del siglo XX. 275 pages. 2007.
ISBN 978-3-03910-893-0

Vol. 3 William Rowlandson
Reading Lezama's *Paradiso.* 290 pages. 2007.
ISBN 978-3-03910-751-3

Vol. 4 Fernanda Peñaloza, Jason Wilson and Claudio Canaparo (eds)
Patagonia. Myths and Realities. 277 pages. 2010.
ISBN 978-3-03910-917-3

Vol. 5 Xon de Ros
Primitivismo y Modernismo. El legado de María Blanchard.
238 pages. 2007.
ISBN 978-3-03910-937-1

Vol. 6 Sergio Plata
Visions of Applied Mathematics. Strategy and Knowledge.
284 pages. 2007.
ISBN 978-3-03910-923-4

Vol. 7 Annick Louis
Borges ante el fascismo. 374 pages. 2007.
ISBN 978-3-03911-005-6

Vol. 8 Helen Oakley
From Revolution to Migration. A Study of Contemporary Cuban and Cuban-American Crime Fiction. 200 pages. 2012.
ISBN 978-3-03911-021-6

Vol. 9 Thea Pitman
Mexican Travel Writing. 209 pages. 2008.
ISBN 978-3-03911-020-9

Vol. 10 Francisco J. Borge
A New World for a New Nation. The Promotion of America in Early Modern England. 240 pages. 2007.
ISBN 978-3-03911-070-4

Vol. 11 Helena Buffery, Stuart Davis and Kirsty Hooper (eds)
Reading Iberia. Theory/History/Identity. 229 pages. 2007.
ISBN 978-3-03911-109-1

Vol. 12 Matías Bruera
Mapping the Tasteland. Explorations in Food and Wine in Argentinean and European Culture. 240 pages. 2014.
ISBN 978-3-03911-345-3

Vol. 13 Angela Romero-Astvaldsson
La obra narrativa de David Viñas. La nueva inflexión de *Prontuario* y *Claudia Conversa*. 300 pages. 2007.
ISBN 978-3-03911-100-8

Vol. 14 Aaron Kahn
The Ambivalence of Imperial Discourse. Cervantes's *La Numancia* within the 'Lost Generation' of Spanish Drama (1570–90).
243 pages. 2008.
ISBN 978-3-03911-098-8

Vol. 15 Turid Hagene
Negotiating Love in Post-Revolutionary Nicaragua. The role of love in the reproduction of gender asymmetry. 341 pages. 2008.
ISBN 978-3-03911-011-7

Vol. 16 Yolanda Rodríguez Pérez
The Dutch Revolt through Spanish Eyes. Self and Other in historical and literary texts of Golden Age Spain (c. 1548–1673). 346 pages. 2008.
ISBN 978-3-03911-136-7

Vol. 17 Stanley Black (ed.)
Juan Goytisolo. Territories of Life and Writing. 202 pages. 2007.
ISBN 978-3-03911-324-8

Vol. 18 María T. Sánchez
The Problems of Literary Translation. A Study of the Theory and Practice of Translation from English into Spanish. 269 pages. 2009.
ISBN 978-3-03911-326-2

Vol. 19 Aino Linda Rinhaug
Fernando Pessoa. A Ludicrous Self. *Forthcoming.*
ISBN 978-3-03911-909-7

Vol. 20 Ana Cruz García
Re(de-)generando identidades. Locura, feminidad y liberalización en Elena Garro, Susana Pagano, Ana Castillo y María Amparo Escandón.
259 pages. 2009.
ISBN 978-3-03911-524-2

Vol. 21 Idoya Puig (ed.)
Tradition and Modernity. Cervantes's Presence in Spanish Contemporary Literature. 221 pages. 2009.
ISBN 978-3-03911-526-6

Vol. 22 Charlotte Lange
Modos de parodia. Guillermo Cabrera Infante, Reinaldo Arenas, Jorge Ibargüengoitia y José Agustín. 252 pages. 2008.
ISBN 978-3-03911-554-9

Vol. 23 Claudio Canaparo
Geo-epistemology. Latin America and the Location of Knowledge. 284 pages. 2009.
ISBN 978-3-03911-573-0

Vol. 24 Jesús López-Peláez Casellas
"Honourable Murderers". El concepto del honor en *Othello* de Shakespeare y en los "dramas de honor" de Calderón. 321 pages. 2009.
ISBN 978-3-03911-825-0

Vol. 25 Marian Womack and Jennifer Wood (eds)
Beyond the Back Room. New Perspectives on Carmen Martín Gaite. 336 pages. 2011.
ISBN 978-3-03911-827-4

Vol. 26 Manuela Palacios and Laura Lojo (eds)
Writing Bonds. Irish and Galician Contemporary Women Poets. 232 pages. 2009.
ISBN 978-3-03911-834-2

Vol. 27 Myriam Osorio
Agencia femenina, agencia narrativa. Una lectura feminista de la obra en prosa de Albalucía Ángel. 180 pages. 2010.
ISBN 978-3-03911-893-3

Vol. 28 *Forthcoming*

Vol. 29 Soledad Pérez-Abadín Barro
Cortázar y Che Guevara. Lectura de *Reunión*. 182 pages. 2010.
ISBN 978-3-03911-919-6

Vol. 30 Gonzalo Pasamar
Apologia and Criticism. Historians and the History of Spain, 1500–2000. 301 pages. 2010.
ISBN 978-3-03911-920-2

Vol. 31 Victoria Carpenter (ed.)
(Re)Collecting the Past. History and Collective Memory in Latin American Narrative. 315 pages. 2010.
ISBN 978-3-03911-928-8

Vol. 32 Geneviève Fabry, Ilse Logie y Pablo Decock (eds.)
Los imaginarios apocalípticos en la literatura hispanoamericana contemporánea. 472 pages. 2010.
ISBN 978-3-03911-937-0

Vol. 33 Julian Vigo
Performative Bodies, Hybrid Tongues. Race, Gender, Sex and Modernity in Latin America and the Maghreb. 391 pages. 2010.
ISBN 978-3-03911-951-6

Vol. 34 Heike Pintor Pirzkall
La cooperación alemana al desarrollo. Factores condicionantes de su transformación en la década de los noventa y su impacto en América Latina. 374 pages. 2010.
ISBN 978-3-0343-0107-7

Vol. 35 Arturo Casas and Ben Bollig (eds)
Resistance and Emancipation. Cultural and Poetic Practices. 419 pages. 2011.
ISBN 978-3-0343-0160-2

Vol. 36 Pablo Decock
Las figuras paradójicas de César Aira. Un estudio semiótico y axiológico de la estereotipia y la autofiguración. 344 pages. 2014.
ISBN 978-3-0343-0169-5

Vol. 37 Guillermo Olivera
Laboratorios de la mediatización. La experimentación con materiales mediáticos, la teoría y la crítica cultural argentina, 1965–1978.
364 pages. 2011.
ISBN 978-3-0343-0201-2

Vol. 38 Guy Baron
Gender in Cuban Cinema. From the Modern to the Postmodern.
334 pages. 2011.
ISBN 978-3-0343-0229-6

Vol. 39 Claudio Canaparo
El imaginario Patagonia. Ensayo acerca de la evolución conceptual del espacio. 576 pages. 2011.
ISBN 978-3-0343-0287-6

Vol. 40 Inmaculada Murcia Serrano
Agua y destino. Introducción a la estética de Ramón Gaya.
220 pages. 2011.
ISBN 978-3-0343-0251-7

Vol. 41 Bill Richardson
Borges and Space. 266 pages. 2012.
ISBN 978-3-0343-0246-3

Vol. 42 *Forthcoming*

Vol. 43 Ann Frost
The Galician Works of Ramón del Valle-Inclán. Patterns of Repetition and Continuity. 241 pages. 2010.
ISBN 978-3-0343-0242-5

Vol. 44 Milagros López-Peláez Casellas
What About the Girls? Estrategias narrativas de resistencia en la primera literatura chicana. 265 pages. 2012.
ISBN 978-3-0343-0264-7

Vol. 45 Bill Richardson and Lorraine Kelly (eds)
Power, Place and Representation. Contested Sites of Dependence and Independence in Latin America. 268 pages. 2012.
ISBN 978-3-0343-0710-9

Vol. 46 Patricia D'Allemand
José María Samper. Nación y cultura en el siglo XIX colombiano.
177 pages. 2012.
ISBN 978-3-0343-0288-3

Vol. 47 *Forthcoming*

Vol. 48 Emilio Rosales
Baroja. La novela como laberinto. 163 pages. 2012.
ISBN 978-3-0343-0774-1

Vol. 49 Kristine Vanden Berghe
Las novelas de la rebelión zapatista. 171 pages. 2012.
ISBN 978-3-0343-0779-6

Vol. 50 William Rowlandson
Borges, Swedenborg and Mysticism. 267 pages. 2013.
ISBN 978-3-0343-0811-3

Vol. 51 Elena Rodríguez-Guridi
Exégesis del "error". Una reinterpretación de la praxis de escritura en *Libro de la vida*, *Novelas ejemplares* y *Desengaños amorosos.*
175 pages. 2013.
ISBN 978-3-0343-0817-5

Vol. 52 Eva Bru-Domínguez
Beyond Containment. Corporeality in Mercè Rodoreda's Literature.
235 pages. 2013
ISBN 978-3-0343-0888-5

Vol. 53 Gabriele Andreozzi (ed.)
Desaparición. Argentina's Human Rights Trials. 355 pages. 2014.
ISBN 978-3-0343-0857-1

Vol. 54 Mel Boland
Displacement in Isabel Allende's Fiction, 1982–2000.
212 pages. 2013.
ISBN 978-3-0343-0932-5

Vol. 55 Eduardo Tasis Moratinos
El exilio en la poesía de Tomás Segovia y Angelina Muñiz Huberman.
234 pages. 2014.
ISBN 978-3-0343-0941-7

Vol. 56 Santiago Pérez Isasi and Ângela Fernandes (eds)
Looking at Iberia. A Comparative European Perspective.
317 pages. 2013.
ISBN 978-3-0343-0934-9

Vol. 57 Daniel de Zubía Fernández
Señas del esplendor ausente. Itinerarios familiares en *Señas de identidad* y en *O Esplendor de Portugal*
373 pages. 2014.
ISBN 978-3-0343-0963-9

Vol. 58 Helena Usandizaga (ed.)
Palimpsestos de la antigua palabra. Inventario de mitos prehispánicos en la literatura latinoamericana
383 pages. 2013.
ISBN 978-3-0343-0967-7

Vol. 59 *Forthcoming*

Vol. 60 Guillermo Laín Corona
Proyecciones de Gabriel Miró en la narrativa del 27.
250 pages. 2013.
ISBN 978-3-0343-0952-3

Vol. 61 Javier Ordiz (ed.)
Estrategias y figuraciones de lo insólito en la narrativa mexicana (siglos XIX–XXI)
237 pages. 2014.
ISBN 978-3-0343-1729-0

Vol. 62 Anna Vives
Identidad en tiempos de vanguardia: narcisismo, genio y violencia en la obra de Salvador Dalí y Federico García Lorca.
323 pages. 2015.
ISBN 978-3-0343-1792-4

Vol. 63 C.A. Longhurst
Modernismo, noventayochismo y novela: España y Europa. Ensayo de literatura comparada.
262 pages. 2014.
ISBN 978-3-0343-1810-5

Vol. 64 *Forthcoming*

Vol. 65 Ángela Gracia Menéndez
Gaspar de Jovellanos: crítico, reformador y humanista ilustrado.
202 pages. 2015.
ISBN 978-3-0343-1849-5

Vol. 66 Michael W. Stannard
Galdós and Medicine.
240 pages. 2015.
ISBN 978-3-0343-1825-9

Vol. 67 Helena Usandizaga y Beatriz Ferrús (eds.)
Fragmentos de un nuevo pasado: inventario de mitos prehispánicos en la literatura latinoamericana actual.
467 pages. 2015.
ISBN 978-3-0343-1852-5

Vol. 68 Guillermo Laín Corona y Mazal Oaknín (eds.)
Literatura política y política literaria en España. Del Desastre del 98 a Felipe VI.
293 pages. 2015.
ISBN 978-3-0343-1889-1

Vol. 69 Claudio Canaparo
El mundo Ingaramo
176 pages. 2015.
ISBN 978-3-0343-1910-2

Vol. 70 Ana Bravo-Moreno
Desigualdades, diferencias y experiencias de (no) pertenencia en educación: perspectivas transdisciplinares en contextos de diversidad
246 pages. 2015.
ISBN 978-3-0343-1850-1

Vol. 71 Alvaro Quiroga-Cifuentes
The Colombian Political Novel 1951–1987: A Critical Contribution
263 pages. 2015.
ISBN 978-3-0343-1978-2

Vol. 72 Xavier Pla, Maximiliano Fuentes and Francesc Montero (eds)
A Civil War of Words: The Cultural Impact of the Great War in Catalonia, Spain, Europe and a Glance at Latin America
449 pages. 2016.
ISBN 978-3-0343-1950-8

Vol. 73 Pilar Molina Taracena
La poética de la poesía de la Guerra Civil española: diversidad en la unidad
248 pages. 2016.
ISBN 978-3-0343-1933-1

Vol. 74 Santiago Pérez Isasi, Raquel Baltazar, Isabel Araújo Branco, Rita Bueno Maia, Ana Bela Morais, Sara Rodrigues de Sousa (eds)
Los límites del Hispanismo: nuevos métodos, nuevas fronteras, nuevos géneros
236 pages. 2016.
ISBN 978-3-0343-2267-6

Vol. 75 Rogelio Guedea (ed.)
Países en tránsito: estudios de literatura comparada
158 pages. 2016.
ISBN 978-3-0343-1979-9

Vol. 76 Shlomy Mualem
Mazes and Amazements: Borges and Western Philosophy
282 pages. 2017.
ISBN 978-1-78707-197-1

Vol. 77 Anne-Marie Storrs
Loving's the Strange Thing: Jungian Individuation in the Fairy Tales of Carmen Martín Gaite
260 pages. 2018.
ISBN 978-1-78707-844-4